CAMBRIDGE LIBRARY COLLECTION

Books of enduring scholarly value

Maritime Exploration

This series includes accounts, by eye-witnesses and contemporaries, of voyages by Europeans to the Americas, Asia, Australasia and the Pacific during the colonial period. Driven by the military and commercial interests of powers including Britain, France and the Netherlands, particularly the East India Companies, these expeditions brought back a wealth of information on climate, natural resources, topography, and distant civilisations. Their detailed observations provide fascinating historical data for climatologists, ecologists and anthropologists, and the accounts of the mariners' experiences on their long and dangerous voyages are full of human interest.

Narrative and Successful Result of a Voyage in the South Seas

Entrepreneurial, spirited and ambitious, Peter Dillon (1788–1847) spent much of his life as a trader and adventurer in the Pacific region and learnt several Pacific languages. In 1826–7, through contacts in the Santa Cruz Islands, Dillon located the wrecks of La Perouse's Pacific expedition, unaccounted for since 1788. This later earned him a knighthood and annuity from the French government. (La Perouse's despatches, and La Billardière's account of an earlier search for the wrecks are also reissued.) In this two-volume 1829 publication, translated into French and Dutch the following year, Dillon tells the story of his sensational discovery. Volume 1 describes La Perouse's disappearance, Dillon's encounter (now disputed) with Fijian cannibals, and the first items identified from the wreck. It also records his officially backed return to the wreck site, which was punctuated by violent quarrels, attempts at mutiny, and a stay in a Tasmanian jail.

Narrative and Successful Result of a Voyage in the South Seas

Performed by Order of the Government of British India, to Ascertain the Actual Fate of La Pérouse's Expedition

VOLUME 1

PETER DILLON

CAMBRIDGE UNIVERSITY PRESS

CAMBRIDGE
UNIVERSITY PRESS

University Printing House, Cambridge, CB2 8BS, United Kingdom

Cambridge University Press is part of the University of Cambridge.

It furthers the University's mission by disseminating knowledge in the pursuit of
education, learning and research at the highest international levels of excellence.

www.cambridge.org
Information on this title: www.cambridge.org/9781108083331

This edition first published 1829
This digitally printed version 2017

ISBN 978-1-108-08333-1 Paperback

NATIVES OF LA PEROUSE'S ISLAND OR MANNICOLO.

The material originally positioned here is too large for reproduction in this reissue. A PDF can be downloaded from the web address given on page iv of this book, by clicking on 'Resources Available'.

NARRATIVE

AND

SUCCESSFUL RESULT

OF A

VOYAGE IN THE SOUTH SEAS,

PERFORMED BY ORDER OF THE

GOVERNMENT OF BRITISH INDIA,

TO ASCERTAIN

THE ACTUAL FATE

OF

LA PÉROUSE's EXPEDITION,

INTERSPERSED WITH

ACCOUNTS OF THE RELIGION, MANNERS, CUSTOMS, AND CANNIBAL PRACTICES

OF THE

SOUTH SEA ISLANDERS.

———

BY THE

CHEVALIER CAPT. P. DILLON,

Member of the Legion of Honour ; of the Asiatic Society of Bengal, and of the Geographical Society of Paris :
Commander of the Hon. East-India Company's Ship Research.

———

IN TWO VOLUMES.
VOL. I.

═══════

LONDON:

HURST, CHANCE, AND CO., ST. PAUL'S CHURCH-YARD.

———

1829.

LONDON:
PRINTED BY J. L. COX, GREAT QUEEN STREET,
LINCOLN'S-INN FIELDS.

TO

THE CHAIRMAN,

DEPUTY CHAIRMAN,

AND

COURT OF DIRECTORS

OF THE

𝕳onourable 𝕰ast=𝕴ndia 𝕮ompany,

THIS

SIMPLE BUT FAITHFUL NARRATIVE

OF A

VOYAGE OF DISCOVERY,

PERFORMED BY COMMAND OF

THE SUPREME GOVERNMENT OF BRITISH INDIA,

WHICH HAS THEREBY SECURED THE GRATITUDE OF THE FRENCH NATION,

AND OF THE CIVILIZED WORLD,

BY AN ACT EVINCING A NOBLE REGARD

FOR THE CAUSE OF HUMANITY AND SCIENCE,

CALCULATED TO RENDER NATIONS ILLUSTRIOUS,

AND TO CEMENT THE BONDS OF AMITY BETWEEN STATES,

IS RESPECTFULLY DEDICATED,

BY THEIR MOST OBEDIENT,

AND VERY HUMBLE SERVANT,

PETER DILLON.

PREFACE.

———

AMID the numerous books of voyages
and travels continually presented to the
public, it may be thought difficult for a
new work of this kind to obtain attention. But the reader is requested to observe, that this work has many claims to
notice quite peculiar to itself. It is not
an account of nations which resemble
ourselves in manners and civilization, or
of countries which had been a hundred
times before visited and described; on
the contrary, in this voyage the reader
is conducted amid the savage tribes of
the South Seas, through tracts never before fully explored, and made acquainted
with human nature under a new aspect,
described from the personal observation
of a living witness, who has had ample

opportunities of studying their characters both in peace and war, and who had nearly fallen a victim to their cannibal propensities.

This voyage also possesses a peculiar interest, from its having solved a question which divided the opinion of the scientific world for a period of forty years. And the discoverer of the fate of La Pérouse, after having effected this discovery, considered that to lay a narrative of the voyage before the public, was a duty he owed to the French as well as to the British nation, and more especially to the Government of British India, under whose auspices it was performed.

As his professional education, studies, and habits of life, have however been hitherto directed to action rather than to the description of the acts of himself or others, he has entered with diffidence on the task of authorship, only when thus imperatively called on to do so, in order that the world may be put in possession of a correct account of the important transactions and extraordinary scenes in which he has had the honour to take a part. He does not, therefore, attempt to engage attention by an eloquent style or flowery description, but rests his claim to notice on a simple statement of facts, set forth without ostentation in the unadorned language of a plain seaman. He trusts, therefore, that the reader will not expect from him the niceties of diction which may be justly required of a professed author, but will treat the work with indulgence, as the first essay of an unpractised pen.

In conclusion, the author hopes that these pages will meet with a favourable reception from his professional brethren, who are able from their own experience to judge of the difficulties he had to overcome. The successful result of his labours may teach the unfortunate navigator, encountering danger in the cause of science, to bear up *even* amid the greatest calamites : for, on whatever remote island or sequestered shore he may have been thrown, unwearied public sympathy will at last find out the scene of his disasters ; and if, unhappily, too late to restore him to his friends and country, it will erect a trophy to his memory and mourn over his untimely fate.

INTRODUCTION.

THE war which broke out between England and France in June 1778, having been succeeded by the re-establishment of peace in 1783, his most Christian Majesty, the unfortunate Louis the XVIth, took advantage of this happy interval, to follow the example set by England, in undertaking voyages of discovery to extend the bounds of geographical knowledge. His most Christian Majesty and the French nation having determined to contribute their share in enlarging our acquaintance with the surface of the globe, and its inhabitants, they ordered an expedition to be fitted out for that purpose in 1785, consisting of two of the finest frigates in the French service; one named *la Boussole,* the other *l'Astrolabe.* Neither labour nor expense were spared in preparing and completing that expedition, to which were attached some of the most able scientific men in Europe, whose names will be seen in the subjoined list of the ships' companies.

To secure the success of this scientific enterprise, it was deemed necessary to select a man of the highest professional talent to command the expedition, and for this purpose la Pérouse was chosen; his distinguished naval exploits, scientific acquirements, and enterprizing character, having pointed him out to his Sovereign and his country as the fittest person to be honoured with the chief command.

JOHN FRANCIS GALAUP DE LA PÉROUSE was born at the town of Albi, in the South of France, in the year 1741, and received an education at the Marine school; after which he joined the naval service of his country as a midshipman, and highly distinguished himself in the various actions in which he was subsequently engaged. In 1764 he was promoted to the rank of Lieutenant, and made a conspicuous figure in the subsequent wars, in which he attained the rank of Captain.

The French government having determined, in 1782, to destroy the English settlements in Hudson's Bay, the performance of this service was entrusted to la Pérouse, who had a seventy-four and two frigates, with several troops, placed at his disposal for the enterprize. Fort-York and the out-ports appertaining to it were destroyed by the French on the 24th of August; the troops were re-embarked, together with Governor Hearne, the English commander of Fort-York, who had become a prisoner of war. It having come to la Pérouse's knowledge that on his approach several of the English had fled into the woods, to se-cure themselves from falling prisoners into the hands of the invaders, notwithstanding his instructions to destroy the North-west Company's settlements, he did not forget the duty he owed to humanity. For the purpose of alleviating the misfortunes of the fugitives, who had neither food nor shelter left against a severe northern winter, nor arms to defend themselves from the attacks of the savages, this gallant officer generously left them abundant supplies of provisions, arms, and ammunition. This act of benevolence to an enemy's country, even in the heat of war, endeared him to the English mariners, one of whom, in his

account of a voyage to Botany Bay, writes
thus : " That humane and generous man, la
" Pérouse, touched here, and ought to be
" remembered with gratitude, in England
" particularly, for his conduct when ordered
" to destroy our settlements in Hudson's
" Bay."

Governor Hearne, it may be remembered, was an officer in the service of the
Hudson's Bay Company, and in 1772 set
out on a land expedition, accompanied by
Indians, from Fort-Churchill in Hudson's
Bay, to discover the Copper-Mine River.
He failed in his first attempt, but proved
more successful in the second, after an absence of two years' travelling, during which
period he experienced hunger and misery
unparalleled. But on his return, after such
sufferings, little credit was given to his accounts ; the truth of which, however, has
since been clearly established, by his enterprizing, and no less indefatigable successor, Captain Franklin, of the Royal Navy.

Governor Hearne's journals of his travels had been seized as public property by
the French, with various other effects belonging to the Company ; but on his soli-

citing la Pérouse to restore them as his private property, the Count most generously complied with his request, imposing no other condition on him than that, on his arrival in England, he should give his journals publicity. Though this condition does not appear to have been fulfilled for several years after, this second act of generosity towards an enemy deserves to be recorded in honour of the subject of this narrative, and to shew that, though the subject of a foreign state, which political occurrences have too often taught us to regard as a rival and a foe, he was a man of such enlarged philanthropy of mind, as to deserve that the British empire and the world should sympathize in his unhappy fate.

The following are correct lists of the officers and scientific men embarked on board the expedition :

Crew of la Boussole.

De la Pérouse, commodore of the expedition.
De Clouard, acting as captain to the Count.
D'Escures, lieutenant ; drowned at Port François, 13th July 1786.
Boutin, master's mate.

De Pierrevert, master's mate ; drowned at Port
    François, 18th July 1786.
Colinet, ditto, ditto, ditto.
Mel de Saint Céran, midshipman; discharged at
    Manilla, 16th April 1787.
De Montarnal, ditto ; drowned at Port François,
    13th July 1786.
De Roux Darbaud, midshipman.
Frederic Broudon, ditto.
De Monneron, captain in the corps of engi-
    neers, engineer in chief.
Bernizet, engineer and geographer.
Rollin, surgeon major.
Lepaute Dagelet, of the Academy of Sciences,
    professor at the Military School, and astrono-
    mer.
De Lamanon, natural philosopher, mineralogist,
    and meteorologist ; murdered by the natives
    of Maouna, 11th December 1787.
Abbé Monges, regular canon of the Gallican
    church, natural philosopher and chaplain.
Duché de Vancy, draughtsman of landscapes
    and figures.
Prévost, jun., botanical draughtsman.
Collignon, gardener and botanist.
Guery, chronometer-maker.
Ninety warrant and petty officers, seamen, and
    soldiers.
Total number of the crew 110, when the ship
    sailed from France.

Crew of l'Astrolabe.

De Langle, post captain, second in command; murdered by the natives at Maouna, 11th December 1787.

De Monti, lieutenant.

Freton de Vaujuas, master's mate.

Diagremont, ditto.

De la Borde Marchainville; ditto, drowned at Port François, 13th July 1786.

Blondela, master's mate.

De la Borde Boutervilliers, midshipman, drowned at Port François, 13th July 1786.

Law de Lauriston, midshipman.

Raxi de Flassan, ditto, drowned at Port François.

Monge, professor at the Military School, astronomer; left at Teneriffe.

De la Martiniere, doctor of physic, and botanist.

Dufresne, naturalist.

Father Receveur, naturalist, and doing the duty of chaplain. Died at Botany Bay, in February 1788, of wounds received at Maouna, when Captain De Langle was killed, and was buried on shore at the former place.

Prévost, the uncle, botanical draughtsman.

Lavaux, surgeon.

Lesseps, Russian vice-consul, interpreter; put on shore at Kamtschatka with la Pérouse's despatches for Paris. This gentleman is now

living at Paris with the title of viscount, and
has been French consul-general at Lisbon for
several years past.

Ninety-seven warrant and petty officers, seamen, and soldiers.

Total number of the crew 113, when the ship
sailed from France.

Being thus prepared, the expedition
sailed from Brest on the 1st of August
1785, and anchored at the Island of Ma-
deira on the 13th. After taking on board
some refreshments, the frigate sailed again
on the afternoon of the 16th August, and
anchored at Teneriffe on the 19th. The
men of science were employed on shore
in their various pursuits, and the crews
in hoisting and stowing away sixty pipes
of wine on board of each frigate, with
other stores.

On the morning of the 30th August they
set sail from Teneriffe, with a fresh breeze
from the N.N.E., and crossed the equi-
noctial line on the 29th September, in the
18th degree of west longitude from Paris.

On the 6th November the frigates anchored between the island of St. Catherine and the coast of Brazil. The Portu-

guese colony on St. Catherine at that time
was supposed by the French navigator to
consist of three thousand inhabitants, and
four hundred houses. It was found that
vessels might approach St. Catherine without difficulty to within four cable-lengths
of the land, where there is good anchorage in four fathoms water. Provisions
were procured in the greatest abundance.
A large ox was bought for eight dollars, a
hog of 150 lbs. weight for four dollars, and
two turkeys for a single dollar. It was
only necessary to cast the net to haul it up
full of fish. Oranges were brought on
board and sold at the rate of one thousand
for less than a dollar.

Having laid in an abundant supply at
St. Catherine's, the expedition sailed from
thence on the 19th November, and on the
25th January 1786 doubled Cape Horn,
with much greater facility than the Count
had expected. From thence they proceeded to Conception Bay in Chili. After
obtaining refreshments, refitting the ships,
&c., the expedition sailed from Conception on the 17th March, and on the 8th
April sighted Easter Island, situated in

latitude 27° 11' south, and longitude 111°
55' 30" west of Paris. Here the ships remained at anchor one day, and again
sailed on the 10th, having left the islanders
a breed of the most useful animals, such
as sheep, goats, pigs, &c.

On the morning of the 28th of May following they sighted Owhyhee, the most
frequented of the Sandwich Islands, where
the immortal Cook was killed. Here the
ships' crews were employed bartering iron
hoops, nails, fish-hooks, &c. with the
islanders, for hogs, poultry, yams, cocoa-
nuts, bread-fruit, bananas, &c. until the
evening of the 1st June, when they bid
the Sandwich Islands adieu, and shaped
their course for the north-west coast of
America.

On the 23d, Mount St. Elias, of Beh-
rings, on the north-west coast of America,
was visible from the ships' decks. They
spent a few days in exploring this part of
the coast, and discovered a port which the
Count de la Pérouse named Port des Français, and describes as bearing a great re-
semblance to the port of Toulon. Here
the ships anchored on the 4th July, after

narrowly escaping shipwreck at its entrance. This danger arose from the wind
becoming nearly calm, when a strong flood
tide set in with such force as almost to
carry the frigates on the rocks near the
harbour's mouth.

Count de la Pérouse's remarks upon
this accident are: " During the thirty years
" that I have followed the sea, I never
" saw two vessels so near being lost : and
" to have experienced such an event at the
" verge of the world would have enhanced
" our misfortune. But we had now es-
" caped this danger, our long-boats were
" quickly hoisted out, and with our kedge
" anchors we warped off, so that we were
" in six fathoms of water before the tide
" had fallen precipitately. Our keel touch-
" ed the bottom a few times, but so slightly
" as to do the vessel no injury."

From the period of the ships first entering this bay nothing remarkable occurred
until the 13th, on which day a dreadful
disaster befel twenty-one of the ships' company, who composed the crews of two
boats employed in sounding the passage
into the bay. The command of this party

had been given to a very distinguished
officer, who incautiously deviated most
unfortunately from the strict injunctions
laid on him by his very experienced commander. The consequence was, that two
of the boats under his command were upset
in the surf, and the whole of the crews
drowned, consisting of twenty-one persons
The Count, with his usual humanity, erect
ed a monument, bearing an appropriate
inscription commemorative of the disaster
which befel his brave shipmates. On the
30th July the expedition sailed from the
Port des Français, which is situated in
latitude 58° 37′ north, and longitude 139°
50′ west of Paris; and were employed
from that period exploring and surveying
the coast of America to the 15th September, at which period the frigates anchored
at the Spanish settlement of Monterey, in
California. Here they met with a kind reception from the Spanish missionaries :
not such a reception as I and my sick
crew experienced from the pious English
missionaries at New Zealand, as will be
hereafter partly explained.

After refreshing the crews, refitting the

ships, and taking in abundant supplies of provisions, the expedition sailed from Monterey for China on the 24th September, and anchored in Macao roads on the 3d January 1787. In crossing the north Pacific Ocean from California to the port of Macao in China, la Pérouse discovered Necker Island: he also passed a rock during the night, upon which the frigates were in great danger of being lost. They soon after sighted the Island of Assumption, one of the Ladrones, the latitude and longitude of which the Count found to be very erroneously laid down by former navigators. From thence he proceeded to, and determined the latitude and longitude of the Bashee Islands.

After procuring the supplies necessary at Macao, the expedition sailed thence on the 5th February for the Spanish settlement of Manilla, in the island of Luconia, where they anchored on the 28th of the same month. Having been much retarded in their passage by the north-east monsoon in the China seas, they waited at Manilla till the strength of this monsoon was spent, and proceeded from thence on the 9th April, for the express purpose of surveying the eastern coast of Tartary. On the passage they touched at the Island of Formosa, the Pescadore Islands, the islands named Botol, Tobaco, Xima, and run along the Island of Kumi, which is one of the Liqueo Islands (or Loochoo) of Captain Hall. The ships shortly after entered the Japanese sea, and sailed along the coast of China, sighted the Island of Quelpaert, and run along the coast of Corea to the northward. They discovered an island in that quarter, which was named by the Count Dagelet Island. Shortly after they sighted some parts of Japan, *viz.* Cape Noto, and the Island Jootsisima, and fell in with several Japanese and Chinese vessels. After sighting the latter island they proceeded towards the coast of Tartary. They made the land in 42° north latitude, and anchored in the bay Deternai on the 23d June, situated in the latitude of 45° 14′ north, and longitude 135° 9′ east.

After sailing from this port they were employed surveying the eastern coast of Tartary, the western coast of Sagaleen,

and the gulf of that name. They discovered and anchored in several bays on
the shores of the Gulf of Sagaleen, and
had frequent communication with villages
and camps of eastern Tartars. They then
discovered a strait which separates the
northern islands of Japan, called Jesso,
from Oku Jesso. They soon after sighted
the Island of Mareekan, and traversed the
Kuriles; then shaped their course for
Kamtschatka, where they anchored in the
bay of St. Peter and St. Paul, on the 7th
September. They shortly after received
letters from France, which had been forwarded overland by the way of St. Peters-
burgh and Moscow.

During the Count's stay at Kamtschatka
he visited the grave of Captain Clarke, the
companion of the immortal Cook on his
last voyage, and affixed to it an inscription engraved on copper. He also obtained permission from the Russian authorities
to send his interpreter, Viscount Lesseps,
to France with despatches.

Having procured such refreshments as
Kamtschatka could afford, with an abundant supply of wood and water, the expe-

dition sailed from thence on the 29th September, and shaped its course to the southward. It was not until the 14th October that they reached the parallels of $37\frac{1}{2}°$ north latitude. They traversed a space of three hundred leagues in quest of land in that parallel, said to have been discovered by the Spaniards in A.D. 1620. Not being able to discover it, the Count continued his course to the southward, and crossed the line, the third time since leaving France, on the 21st November. The expedition then proceeded towards the Navigator Islands, where a dreadful disaster awaited them, which, for the information of such of my readers as are not acquainted with the account of la Pérouse's voyage, I cannot do better than relate in the Count's own words.

" On the 6th December, at three in the
" afternoon, the most eastern of the Navi-
" gator Islands was visible from the ship's
" deck. Night having come on before the
" ships could reach the islands, they stood
" under easy sail, tacking to windward
" throughout the night, and at daylight of
" the 7th bore away. The 7th and 8th

" were spent in exploring the Easter Is-
" lands of that groupe, and bartering with
" the savages.   Not being able to find
" anchorage, the frigates bore away, and
" anchored on the 9th off the Island of
" Maouna, on a coral bank in the open
" sea, distance from the shore one mile.
" The same evening three boats armed
" landed from the ships, under the com-
" mand of Captain de Langle, of the As-
" trolabe, where they were received in the
" most friendly and hospitable manner by
" the islanders, who brought the people
" birds, hogs, and fruits in abundance.
" After an hour's interview the boats re-
" turned to the ships.   Every person ap-
" peared satisfied with the friendly recep-
" tion they experienced : their only regret
" was, being anchored in such a bad road-
" stead, where the ships rolled as if they
" were in the open sea.

" On the morning of the 10th four boats
" were sent on shore with an armed water-
" ing party, who succeeded in procuring
" abundance of that necessary beverage,
" and returned to the ships without any
" molestation from the islanders.   The

" weather being squally and unsettled,
" with the ships rolling gunwales under in
" this open roadstead, it was deemed pru-
" dent by the commanders to heave up
" the anchors, and keep under weigh dur-
" ing the night off and on from the island.
" The cables were found to be much in-
" jured by the foul ground on which the
" ships had anchored.

" On the morning of the 11th the fri-
" gates were at no great distance from one
" of the places where water could be pro-
" cured. Four boats were accordingly
" despatched for the shore, under the
" command of Captain de Langle, who
" with several others never more rejoined
" the ships, being most inhumanly mas-
" sacred by the islanders. The following
" is a narrative of that unfortunate event
" by one of the officers who was fortunate
" enough to survive the massacre."

Narrative of M. de Vaujuas.

" On Tuesday, the 11th December, at
" eleven in the morning, M. de la Pérouse
" sent his long-boat and barge, laden with
" empty casks, and a party of marines

" armed, to accompany an expedition
" under the command of M. de Langle.
" M. Boutin had already received instruc-
" tions respecting the means of preserving
" order and providing for our security when
" the boats should land. At the same
" time our captain hoisted out his boats,
" and in like manner loaded them with
" casks, and armed them. At half after
" twelve, the ships being within three-
" quarters of a league of the shore, with
" their larboard tacks aboard, the four
" boats set off to take in water in a cove
" that had been reconnoitred by M. de
" Langle. This watering place was to
" leeward of that where we had been be-
" fore, to which M. de Langle thought it
" preferable, because it appeared to him
" less inhabited, and equally commodious.
" The former, however, had the advan-
" tage of a more easy entrance, and suf-
" ficient depth of water for our long-boats
" to be in no danger of grounding.
" M. de Langle asked me, though I was
" a convalescent and weak, to accompany
" him, by way of taking the air on shore.
" He took upon himself the command of

" the barge, and gave that of the long-
" boat to M. Gobien.   M. Boutin com-
" manded the long-boat, and M. Mouton
" the barge of the *Boussole*.   M. Colinet
" and Father Receveur, both invalids, with
" Messrs. de Lemanon, La Martinière, and
" Lavaux, and several persons from both
" ships, were of the party ; making in all,
" with the crews of the two barges, sixty-
" one in number.

" While on our way, we perceived with
" regret that a large part of the canoes
" which were alongside of the ships follow-
" ed us, and came to the same cove : we
" likewise saw several of the natives from
" other villages going to it along the rocks
" which separate it from the adjacent
" bays.   When we came to the reef which
" forms the cove, and which leaves only
" a narrow passage of a little depth for
" boats, we found that it was low water,
" and that the long-boats could not pro-
" ceed into the cove without getting
" aground.   In fact, they touched when
" within half a musket-shot from the shore,
" and we could only get them nearer by
" pushing them on by setting our oars to

" the bottom. This bay had appeared
" much more favourably to the captain,
" because when he visited it the tide was
" not so low.

" At our arrival the savages, who stood
" by the water-side to the number of seven
" or eight hundred, threw into the sea, in
" token of peace, several branches of the
" tree from which the islanders of the
" South Seas obtain their inebriating liquor.
" On landing M. de Langle gave orders that
" an armed marine and a seaman should
" be left to guard each of the boats, while
" the crews of the long-boats were em-
" ployed in getting in the water, under
" the protection of a double line of fusi-
" leers, reaching from the long-boats to
" the watering place. The casks were
" filled and taken into the boats very
" peaceably, the islanders suffering them-
" selves to be kept sufficiently within
" bounds by the armed marines. Among
" them were a certain number of women,
" and very young girls, who offered them-
" selves to us in the most indecent manner,
" and their advances were not universally
" rejected. We saw but few children.

" When our business was nearly ended,
" the number of natives had still increas-
" ed, and they became more troublesome.
" This circumstance induced M. de Lan-
" gle to give up the design he had before
" entertained, of bartering for a little pro-
" vision, and he gave orders to reimbark
" immediately; but previously (and this,
" I believe, was the first cause of our mis-
" fortune) he made presents of a few beads
" to a sort of chiefs, who had assisted in
" keeping the islanders a little at a dis-
" tance. We were certain, however, that
" this kind of police was mere mockery;
" and if these pretended chiefs had any
" authority, it extended to a very small
" number of persons. These presents,
" distributed among five or six individuals,
" excited the discontent of all the rest; a
" general clamour then arose, and we
" were no longer able to check it. They
" suffered us, however, to get into our
" boats; but a party of the islanders fol-
" lowed us into the water, while the rest
" picked up stones on the beach.
    " As the long-boats were aground a lit-
" tle from the shore, we were obliged to

" wade up to the middle in water to reach
" them, and in doing this several of the
" marines wetted their muskets.   In this
" situation began the horrible scene which
" I am about to relate.   We had scarcely
" gotten into the long-boats, when M. de
" Langle gave orders to get in the grapnel
" and push them off.   Several of the most
" robust of the islanders opposed this,
" by holding the grapnel rope.   The cap-
" tain seeing this, and perceiving the tu-
" mult increase, and a few stones reach
" him, endeavoured to intimidate them by
" firing over their heads.   This, far from
" inspiring them with fear, was the sig-
" nal of a general attack. A shower of
" stones, thrown with equal force and
" quickness, poured on us.   The battle
" commenced on both sides, and became
" general.   Those whose muskets were in
" a condition to go off brought down seve-
" ral of these furies; but the rest were no
" way disturbed at it, and seemed to act
" with more vigour.   One party approach-
" ed the boats ; while another, to the
" number of five or six hundred, kept up
" a terrible and fatal discharge of stones.

" On the first act of hostility I had
" leaped into the water to get to the *As-*
" *trolabe's* barge, which was without offi-
" cers. Circumstances gave me strength
" for the short passage I had to make ;
" and notwithstanding my weakness, and
" a few blows I received from stones at
" the time, I got into the barge without
" assistance. I saw with grief that there
" was scarcely a musket in it unwetted,
" and that all I could do was to endeavour
" to get her afloat on the outside of the
" reef as quickly as possible. The battle
" however continued, and the large stones
" thrown by the savages wounded some of
" us. As soon as any one that was struck
" fell into the sea on the side next the
" savages, he was immediately despatched
" with their clubs or paddles.

" M. de Langle was the first victim of
" the ferociousness of these barbarians,
" who had experienced from him nothing
" but benefactions. At the commence-
" ment of the attack he was knocked down
" bleeding from the bow of the long-boat,
" where he had posted himself, and fell
" into the water, with the master at arms

" and the carpenter, who were at his side.
" The rage with which the islanders fell
" upon the captain saved the two latter,
" who contrived to reach the barge. Those
" who remained in the long-boat soon
" shared the fate of their unfortunate
" commander, except a few, who were
" able to escape and gain the reef, whence
" they swam to the barges. In less than
" four minutes the islanders made them-
" selves masters of both the long-boats,
" and I had the affliction to see our un-
" happy companions massacred, without
" being able to assist them. The *Astro-*
" *labe's* barge was still within the reef, and
" I expected every moment to see her
" experience the same fate as the long-
" boats ; but the eagerness of the islanders
" saved her, the greater part fell upon the
" long-boat, the rest contented themselves
" with throwing stones at us. Several,
" however, came to wait for us in the pas-
" sage, and on the reefs.
" Though there was a heavy swell, and
" the wind blew right in, we succeed-
" ed in getting out of this fatal place, in
" spite of their stones, and the dangerous

" wounds which some of us had received ;
" and joined M. Mouton, who was out of
" the cove in the *Boussole's* barge, and who
" had lightened his boat by throwing
" overboard his water, to make room for
" those who could reach him. I had taken
" into the *Astrolabe's* barge Messrs. Boutin
" and Colinet, with several other persons.
" All those who escaped to the barges were
" more or less wounded, so that we were
" in a defenceless state, and it was impos-
" sible to think of re-entering into a bay
" from which we were extremely happy to
" have escaped, to make head against a
" thousand enraged barbarians, as this
" would have been to expose ourselves to
" inevitable death, without the least ad-
" vantage.

" Accordingly we steered our course to
" return on board the two ships, which
" had tacked towards the offing at three
" o'clock, the very moment of the mas-
" sacre, not even suspecting that we were
" in the least danger. There was a fresh
" breeze, and the ships were far to wind-
" ward, which was an unpleasant circum-
" stance for us, and particularly for those

" whose wounds required speedy dressing.
" At four they put about again, and stood
" towards the land.

　" When we had cleared the reefs, I set
" the sails and hauled close to the wind in
" order to get off shore, throwing overboard
" every thing that could impede the pro-
" gress of the boat, which was full of
" people. Happily the islanders, busied
" in plundering the long-boats, thought
" not of pursuing us. We had nothing for
" our defence but four or five cutlasses and
" a charge for two or three muskets, which
" were little to protect us against two or
" three hundred barbarians, armed with
" stones and clubs, and provided with light
" canoes, in which they might keep them-
" selves at what distance they pleased.
" Some of these canoes left the bay soon
" after us, but they sailed along the shore,
" whence one of them departed to inform
" those which had remained alongside the
" ship. The people in this canoe, as they
" passed, had the insolence to make threat-
" ening signs to us ; but my situation ob-
" liged me to suspend my vengeance, and

" reserve our feeble means for our own
" defence.

" When we had gained the offing, we
" pulled away right to windward towards
" the ships, hoisted a red handkerchief at
" the mast-head, and as we drew near fired
" our last three musket-shots. M. Mou-
" ton likewise made a signal for assistance
" with two handkerchiefs; but we were
" not observed till we were almost on
" board. The *Astrolabe*, the nearest of the
" two ships, then bore away for us, and at
" half-past four I put on board her those
" who were most severely wounded. M.
" Mouton did the same; and then we re-
" paired immediately on board the *Bous-
" sole*, where I related to the commodore
" our melancholy tale. His astonishment
" was extreme, after the precautions his
" prudence had induced him to take, and
" the just confidence he reposed in M. de
" Langle, and I can compare his sorrow
" only to my own. This disaster recalled
" to our minds a lively remembrance of that
" of the 13th July 1786, and threw a com-
" plete gloom over our voyage. Still, how-

" ever, we thought ourselves happy, that
" the greater part of those who went on
" shore were saved ; since, if eagerness for
" plunder had not stopped, or for a mo-
" ment called off the rage of the savages,
" not one of us could have escaped.

" It is impossible to express the feelings
" excited by this fatal event on board the
" two ships. The death of M. de Langle,
" who enjoyed the confidence and friend-
" ship of his crew, threw every person be-
" longing to the *Astrolabe* into the utmost
" consternation. Those islanders who were
" alongside when I arrived, and knew no-
" thing of the affair, were on the point of
" being sacrificed to the vengeance of our
" seamen, which we had the utmost diffi-
" culty to restrain. The general affliction
" that prevailed on board was the noblest
" funeral panegyric that could be made
" of the captain. For my part, I lost in
" him a friend, rather than a commanding
" officer ; and the concern he expressed
" for my welfare will lead me to regret
" him as long as I have breath : too happy,
" could I have testified my attachment
" and gratitude by sacrificing my life for

" his ! But this brave officer, more ex-
" posed than the rest, was the first that fell
" a prey to the ferocious beasts by whom
" we were attacked. In the state of weak-
" ness in which I was left by my conva-
" lescence, I had gone ashore without arms,
" and under the protection of others ; and
" when I reached the barge all our ammu-
" nition was expended or wetted, so that
" unhappily I could only give orders of too
" little efficacy.

    " I should not do justice to those, who
" were so fortunate as to save themselves
" like me, did I neglect to add, that
" they behaved with all the coolness and
" bravery possible. Messrs. Boutin and
" Colinet, whose force of mind was un-
" impaired notwithstanding their severe
" wounds, assisted me with their counsel,
" which was of no small advantage ; and
" I was ably seconded by M. Gobien,
" who was the last to quit the long-boat,
" and whose example, words, and intrepi-
" dity, contributed not a little to encourage
" such of the seamen as might have felt
" apprehension. The inferior officers, sea-
" men, and marines, executed the orders

" given them with equal zeal and punc-
" tuality. M. Mouton had equal reason
" to be satisfied with the crew of the *Bous-*
" *sole's* barge.

" Every person who went ashore can
" testify with me, that no violence, no im-
" prudence on our part, preceded the at-
" tack of the savages. Our Captain had
" issued the strictest orders to this effect,
" and no one had infringed them.

" (Signed)   V<small>AUJUAS</small>.

" List of the persons massacred by the
" savages of the Island of Maouna, the
" 11th December 1787.

" The Astrolabe.

" M. de Langle, post-captain, com-
   " mander.
" Yves Humon,
" John Redellec,
" Francis Feret,   } Seamen.
" Laurence Robin,
" A Chinese,
" Lewis David, one of the gunner's crew.
" John Geraud, a servant.

" *The Boussole.*

" M. Lamanou, natural philosopher
" and naturalist.

" Peter Talin, gunner.

" Andrew Roth,⎫
" Joseph Rayes,⎭ of the gunner's crew.

" All the rest of the party were more or
" less wounded."

In consequence of the above dreadful
catastrophe it was necessary the ships
should proceed from this horrid place to a
secure port, for the purpose of building
long-boats to replace those destroyed by
the islanders; the Count therefore determined to proceed to Botany Bay, in New
Holland. He sailed from Maouna on the
14th December, and spent a few days
trafficking at two of the adjacent islands,
named Oyolava and Pola; thence he proceeded on his newly intended voyage, and
communicated with the inhabitants of
Cocoa and Traitor's Islands. A canoe
also visited the ships as they passed Tongataboo.

On their route they sighted Norfolk

Island, and anchored there for a short time in an open roadstead, which enabled them to give a description of that beautiful island ; from whence they proceeded towards Botany Bay, where they anchored on the 26th January 1788. There they found the British squadron under command of Governor Phillip, which had sailed from England the preceding year for the purpose of establishing a British colony at that place. La Pérouse's anchor had not been long let go when the English ships got under sail and steered out of Botany Bay for Port Jackson, which was found to be a much better situation for the new settlement than the former place. An officer from the English frigate *Cyrus* was sent on board the *Boussole* by Captain Hunter, to congratulate the French navigators on their arrival ; which compliment was returned by an officer from la Pérouse waiting on Captain Hunter. Here a clergyman of the expedition died of the wounds received at Mouna. New longboats were built, supplies of wood and water taken on board, and despatches connected with the expedition handed over to Governor Phillip, to be forwarded to France. The expedition sailed thence late in February, and no authentic accounts of it were obtained for a period of thirty-eight years! But after a lapse of this long period of time, I became the discoverer of its fate, in the manner which will be described in the following pages.

As la Pérouse did not return to France, and no accounts of him had been received for three years, the greatest anxiety was felt respecting his fate, especially by scientific and literary men, who considered it due to la Pérouse and his companions to remind the Sovereign of France that measures ought to be adopted to render those great navigators such assistance as the nation could afford. In consequence of their remonstrance the following decrees were passed:

Decree of the National Assembly,
February 9th 1791.

" The National Assembly, after having
" heard the report of its united commit-
" tees of agriculture, commerce, and
" naval affairs, decrees:

" 'That the King be requested to give
" orders to all ambassadors, residents, con-
" suls, and agents of the nation in foreign
" countries, to intreat, in the name of
" humanity and of the arts and sciences,
" the different sovereigns of the nations
" in which they reside, to enjoin all navi-
" gators and agents of every description
" under their command, wherever they
" may be, but particularly in the southern
" parts of the Pacific Ocean, to make all
" possible search after the two French fri-
" gates *la Boussole* and *l'Astrolabe,* com-
" manded by M. de la Pérouse, and after
" their crews; as likewise every inquiry
" that may serve to confirm to us whether
" they be yet in being, or have been lost;
" in order that, if M. de la Pérouse and
" his companions should be found or met
" with, no matter in what place, every
" assistance may be given them, and they
" may be furnished with all possible means
" of returning to their country, and bring-
" ing with them whatever they may have
" in their possession; the National As-
" sembly engaging to indemnify, and even
" to recompense, according to the impor-

" tance of the service, every one that may
" furnish any assistance to these naviga-
" tors, procure intelligence of them, or
" merely be the cause of restoring to
" France any papers or effects that may
" belong or have belonged to their expe-
" tion.

" It farther decrees, that the King be
" requested to equip one or more vessels,
" on board which shall be embarked men
" of science, naturalists, and draughts-
" men ; and to confer on the commanders
" of the expedition the double mission of
" seeking after M. de la Pérouse, in con-
" formity to documents, instructions, and
" orders which shall be given them, and at
" the same time of making researches with
" regard to the sciences and commerce ;
" taking every measure to render the ex-
" pedition, independently of the search
" after M. de la Pérouse, or even after they
" may have found him, or obtained news
" of him, useful and advantageous to
" navigation, geography, commerce, arts,
" and science.

" Collated with the original by us, the
" president and secretaries of the Na-

" tional Assembly. Paris, 24th February
" 1791.

(Signed) " DUPORT, President.
" LIORE, } Secretaries."
" BOUSSION, }

———

*Decree of the National Assembly, the 22d
April* 1791.

" The National Assembly decrees :

" That the accounts and maps sent by
" M. de la Pérouse of part of his voyage
" as far as to Botany Bay, shall be printed
" and engraved at the expense of the
" nation ; and that the expense shall be
" defrayed from the fund of two millions,*
" granted by the fourteenth article of the
" decree of the 3d August 1790.

" That as soon as the edition is finished,
" and such copies as the King may think
" proper to dispose of are taken from it,
" the remainder be sent to Mme. de la
" Pérouse, with a copy of the present de-
" cree, as a testimony of satisfaction at M.
" de la Pérouse's devotion to the common

* £83,333. 6s. 8d.

" weal, and to the promotion of know-
" ledge and useful discoveries.

" That M. de la Pérouse shall still re-
" main on the navy list till the return of
" the vessels sent in search of him, and
" that his pay shall continue to be received
" by his wife, conformably to the direc-
" tions given by him previous to his de-
" parture.

" Collated with the original by us, the
" president and secretaries of the National
" Assembly. Paris, 25th April 1791.

       (Signed)
" REUBELL, President,
" GOUPIL PREFELN,
" MOUGINS-ROQUEFORT, }Secretaries."
" ROGER,

———

Shortly after the passing of the above
decrees, orders were sent to Brest for the
equipment of two frigates to be employed
on a voyage in search of La Pérouse's expedition. The ships received names ana-
logous to the object of the enterprise on
which they were to be engaged ; the Commodore's ship was named " *la Recherche* "
(the Research), and the other received the

name of *l'Esperance* (Hope). The command of the former ship was given to General d'Entrecasteaux, commander-in-chief of the expedition; the command of the other frigate was conferred on Captain Huon Kermadec. Several men of science were attached to the expedition as naturalists, botanists, astronomers, &c.

An account of this voyage was published in France on the return of some of the survivers of that unfortunate expedition to their native country, by M. Labillardière, a very celebrated naturalist who was attached to the *Research*.

After encountering innumerable difficulties on two voyages in the Pacific, both commanders died. The ships put in at the Island of Java, where they were seized by the officers of the Dutch Government, condemned as prizes, and the crews imprisoned in that deleterious island. The narrator of d'Entrecasteaux's voyage obtained permission from the Dutch authorities to proceed to the Isle of France ; and at the period he was thus released from prison there were then living no more than ninety-nine men, out of two hundred and nineteen who had sailed from France with the expedition.

I consider it necessary to give the following brief account of this expedition, for the information of those persons who may not have read Labillardière's book.

Both frigates sailed in company from the port of Brest on the 28th day of September 1791. On the passage towards the Cape of Good Hope they touched at Teneriffe for refreshments, and anchored in Table Bay on the 17th January 1792. The Commodore's instructions prior to leaving France were, that he should follow the route which la Pérouse proposed to pursue from Botany Bay, in his last letter to the Minister of Marine ; but at that place d'Entrecasteaux received some information totally unfounded on truth, which caused him to alter his intended route, which, however, after a fruitless search, he found it necessary to return to and pursue.

A few days after the frigates anchored, the Commodore received a despatch which had been forwarded for him to the Cape, on a French frigate, by the Governor of the Isle of France. The despatch con-

tained the depositions of two French
captains of merchant ships, who deposed
that they were at anchor in Batavia Roads
when Captain Hunter, of the English frigate *Cyrus*, arrived there with his crew,
passengers on a Dutch merchant ship,
after having lost the *Cyrus* at Norfolk
Island. The French commanders further
deposed, that they had seen and conversed
with some of Captain Hunter's officers at
Batavia, who informed them that they
had seen some of the natives of the Admiralty Islands dressed in the uniforms of the
French marine, which could not have been
procured by any other means than from
the wreck of la Pérouse's expedition.

This piece of information determined
d'Entrecasteaux to proceed to the Admiralty Islands as soon as possible. It is to
be regretted that the object of d'Entrecasteaux' mission had not been made known
to Captain Hunter, who with his crew
were passengers on board a transport lying in Table Bay when the French expedition anchored there, from whence he
sailed the next day for England, as Captain Hunter had seen la Pérouse at Bo-

tany Bay in January 1788, and was acquainted with him. Had any such circumstance come to his notice, on passing
the Admiralty Islands, as that alluded to
regarding the savages in uniform, it cannot be doubted for a moment that he
would without delay have made it known
to the commodore of the French expedition.

D'Entrecasteaux sailed from the Cape
for Van Deimen's Land on the 16th February 1792, and anchored in the channel
which bears his name on the 24th of April.
On the passage from Table Bay the
Island of St. Paul's was visited, which
they found in a state of ignition, occasioned by a volcanic eruption.

While the ships lay at anchor in d'Entrecasteaux's channel, abundance of fire-
wood, water, and fish of various descriptions, were procured, and a very friendly
intercourse was maintained with the natives. Having accomplished the object
for which the frigates put in here, the
commodore sailed on his newly planned
route. He coasted the south-west and
west parts of New Caledonia, discovered

a small cluster of islands to the northward of it, and had a distant view of the islan- ders on shore, but did not land. Then steering away to the north-west, he got a distant view of the Arsacides and of the Treasury Islands ; coasted the western part of Bougainville's Island and the Isle of Bouka ; communicated with the islan- ders in their canoes, and nearly got on the reefs off Bougainville's Island.

The expedition proceeded from the lat- ter island and anchored in Carteret Har- bour, a port in New Ireland, on the 17th July. Here the necessary supply of wood and water was procured. Recent traces of the islanders having visited that port were discovered, but none of them were seen by the navigators. A human skele- ton was found in a state of decomposition among the rocks. During the time the ships lay in this port there was an incessant fall of rain, such as had never been expe- rienced by the oldest navigators on board.

On the 24th July the expedition sail- ed from Carteret Harbour through St. George's Channel, had a view of the Port- land Islands, and shortly after visited the

Admiralty Islands, where they were not so successful as to find anchorage; but had several interviews with the islanders, amongst whom they could not perceive the smallest fragment or raiment of French uniform, or discover any other circumstance which could induce them to believe that la Pérouse's expedition had either visited or been shipwrecked at those islands, as supposed to have been stated by some of Captain Hunter's officers at Batavia.

The commodore having now reason to believe that he had been misled, made the best of his way from the Admiralty Islands to Amboyna, a Dutch settlement of the Moluccas. On the passage to that place they had a view of the Hermit and Exchequer Islands, passed in sight of New Guinea, sailed through Pitt's Straights, and anchored at Amboyna on the 6th of September 1792.

Prior to the ships' arrival at Amboyna the crew were very sickly, occasioned by that dreadful scourge to sea voyages the scurvy. Some opposition was made by the Dutch to the general's anchoring at

Amboyna, which he managed to avoid.
Subsequently he met with very hospitable
treatment from the agents of the Dutch
East-India Company there. By the 15th
October the crews were completely recovered, on which day the expedition sailed
for the purpose of re-entering the Pacific,
and of pursuing the route proposed by
la Pérouse in his last letter from New
South Wales.

On the passage towards Van Diemen's
Land, where it was proposed they should
refresh a second time, a large extent of
coast was surveyed, from the south-west
cape of New Holland towards the eastward, and several islands discovered, lying at the distance of from one to fifteen
and twenty leagues from the coast. The
search was then abandoned, in consequence of the expedition becoming short
of fresh water, and they anchored at Van
Diemen's Land the second time on the
22d January 1793. Here they procured
such supplies as the country then afforded,
and resumed their voyage on the 1st
March.

On the passage toward the Friendly

Islands they passed near to the north cape
of New Zealand, and were visited by some
of the natives in a canoe. On the passage
from New Zealand they discovered a few
uninhabited islands, one of which they
named Research's Island, after the ship;
it is situated in latitude 29° 20' south, and
longitude 179° 55' east. They sighted
Curtis's Islands, and then bore away for
Tongataboo, the capital of the Friendly
Islands, where the expedition anchored
on the 25th March.

Here they met with a most hospitable
and friendly reception from some of the
old friends and acquaintance of Captain
Cook. This was the second vessel which
had anchored at Tonga subsequent to the
Dutch navigator Tasman, who discovered
it. Their good understanding with the
natives was, however, of short duration,
from the islanders being greatly addicted
to theft. One of the sentinels on shore,
while on his post doing duty over the
tents, was most treacherously knocked
down by a blow given from behind his
back. The perpetrator of this took advantage of his prostrated victim, and ran

away with his musket. The armourer of the *Research* was also knocked down with clubs by the natives, who afterwards stript him in open day, within sight of the ships. Those frequent outrages on the part of the islanders led to consequences which proved fatal to one of their chiefs, who was shot dead in a scuffle with one of the boats' crews. Notwithstanding those frequent quarrels, a good understanding was kept up between the general and the highest order of chiefs. The ships were abundantly supplied with provisions, in yams, bananoes, cocoa-nuts, poultry, and pigs. Several of the latter were slaughtered and salted for sea stock.

Inquiries were made by means of " Cook's Vocabulary of the Tonga Language," to ascertain if la Pérouse had visited the island. Either the natives could not understand these inquiries, or the interrogators were unable to comprehend the replies ; otherwise the islanders must have answered in the affirmative; as it is now certain that he visited Namoca, one of the islands to the northward ; and he was known there by the name of Lowagey,

and two of their countrymen had left their
homes and gone with him. This information I procured from old and intelligent
natives of Tonga. However, I had advantages which the General did not possess,
for I had a tolerable knowledge of the
Tonga language myself, and was supplied
with interpreters perfectly conversant with
the native dialect, as will be seen by the
accounts which I received from the natives
of that island, while at anchor there in
August 1827, on the subject.

Being abundantly supplied with provisions and every description of refreshment
the island could afford, the expedition
sailed on the 10th April for New Caledonia,
and sighted the following islands: Turtle
Island of Captain Cook, Eerronan, and
Annatom, Tanna, of the same, which are
a part of the New Hebrides. They discovered an island which they named
Beaupré Island, situated in latitude 20° 14′
south, longitude 163° 47′ east of Paris.

On the 19th the ships anchored at New
Caledonia, in the same port where Cook
had anchored in 1774, and whilst at anchor
there, the navigators endeavoured by all

the signs and gestures they could devise,
but without success, to learn from the
natives if their unfortunate countrymen
had visited their shores. During the sojourn
of the expedition, the men of science frequently landed on professional duty, and
had several interviews with the islanders,
who appeared by no means hostile towards
their newly arrived visitors. Yet they made
several attempts to seize on the ships'
boats, from which however no fatal consequences arose. They gave Labillardière
more proofs than one of their being cannibals, as he found a young man one day
regaling himself by picking the thigh-bone
of a youth aged about fourteen.

Prior to the ship's departure from New
Caledonia, Captain Huon, of the *Espérance*,
died from general debility of constitution,
which had been of long standing.

Early on the morning of the 10th May,
the expedition set sail, and was employed
for four days ranging along the eastern
side of the extensive reefs which run out
some degrees to the northward of the island. On the morning of the 20th the
island off Santa Cruz, alias Egmont Island

of Captain Carteret, was visible from the
deck, to the north-west, at seven leagues
distance.

It appears by all modern charts of this
part of the Pacific, that this expedition
passed at no greater distance than nine or
ten leagues from Mannicolo, or la Pérouse's
Island. This must have happened at night,
at which time it might easily have been
passed without being seen, as Labillardière,
in his account of the voyage, does not
mention having seen the island. This was
rather unfortunate, for had the island been
visited at so early a period, it is probable
some of the survivors from the wreck might
have been recovered, and restored to their
country, to relate the melancholy disaster
which proved fatal to the most important scientific expedition that ever sailed
from Europe. At all events, large portions
of the wreck might then have been procured, which prior to my arrival at Mannicolo were destroyed, or dispersed by the
destructive hand of time and by the bois-
terous elements.

It appears from the account of the
voyage, that the commodore stood close in

for the entrance of Beautiful Bay, in the Island of Santa Cruz, so named by the Spaniards, where he had some intercourse with the islanders in their canoes, but did not anchor.

While one of the boats was employed searching for anchorage near to the south-east point of the island, a native shot an arrow which slightly grazed or scratched the forehead of a sailor. The wound was so slight that the honest tar thought light of the matter, and on returning to his ship would not allow it to be dressed. But though the wound healed up, in seventeen days after the man died from its effect: which left no doubt on the minds of the medical men of the expedition as to the arrow being poisoned. The native who so wantonly shot the arrow, was fired at from the boat and killed.

Finding no traces of la Pérouse or his companions at this island, the expedition bore away before a brisk trade wind, and sailed along the south shore of the Solo-mon Islands, at more than a proper distance to be of any service to such unfortunate mariners as might have been ship-

wrecked there. A few interviews were
obtained with the islanders in their canoes,
who behaved in the most treacherous
manner to their visitors.

The expedition from this part proceeded
to reconnoitre the northern shores of Louisiade, then passed through Dampier's
Straits, which separates New Britain from
New Guinea, and explored the northern
coast of the former island. While employed on this service, General d'Entrecasteaux fell a victim to the scurvy, also some
part of the crew. From the coast of New
Britain the expedition proceeded towards
the Portland Islands ; and on the afternoon
of the 12th July the most easterly of the
Admiralty Islands was in sight from the
decks.

The expedition proceeded westward, and
on the 18th passed the Anchorite's Islands.
On the 2d August the Traitors' Islands
were in sight; on the 11th they passed the
Cape of Good Hope of New Guinea,
and on the 16th cast anchor at the large
island of Waygion, near New Guinea. The
crew were at this period reduced to the most
deplorable state of wretchedness by the

scurvy, and the want of proper food.
Their biscuits were so much injured and
destroyed by insects, such as cockroaches
and wevils, and the salt provisions had become so very offensive, that several of the
crew, although starving, could not make
use of them. Those evils were remedied
by the supplies procured at this island,
chiefly consisting of turtle, weighing from
200 to 240 pounds each, dried turtles'-
eggs, broiled turtle-flesh, fowls, and hogs,
of which there was the greatest abundance, oranges, cocoa-nuts, papaya, gourds
of different kinds, rice, sago-bread, sugar-
cane, pimento, Turkey corn roasted, and
fresh sprouts of the papaya-tree. Aided by
such refreshments, the crews of the frigates
soon recovered. On the 28th the expedition sailed from Waygion, and on the 4th
September cast anchor in the roadstead of
Bourou, a Dutch settlement, which is
guarded by a few European and Malay
soldiers.

After the death of General d'Entrecasteaux the command of the expedition devolved upon M. Daoribeau. On the 16th
the expedition proceeded towards Java.

A few days after the new commander became dangerously ill, and was confined to
his bed ; on which M. Rossel, the next
senior officer, took charge. This gentleman is still living, and resides at Paris, after
having attained the honourable rank of
Admiral in his country's service   He is
now a member of the National Institute,
and of several other scientific and literary
societies in Paris.

The expedition experienced some difficulties, occasioned by light winds and
calms in the straits of Bouton, and near to
the coast of Celebes, and anchored at Sou-
rabaya on the 28th October.   Prior to the
ship's arrival at the last port a dysentery
broke out amongst the crew, which occasioned the death of six men.   After passing the straits of Bouton, the anchor had
not been long gone before the officers of
the expedition were made acquainted by
letters that a war had broke out between
France and Holland, and that they must
consequently consider themselves prisoners
of war.   The ships were accordingly made
prizes ; and it appears by Labillardière's
account, that himself and shipmates re-

ceived during their captivity very cruel treatment from the Hollanders. After several months' detention they were allowed to depart for the Isle of France, from whence Labillardière and Admiral Rossel returned to Europe in March 1796, to relate to their countrymen the disastrous termination of the expedition. France being at that period in a dreadful state of convulsion occasioned by the revolution, and the generality of men's minds being wholly occupied about their own personal safety, no further steps were taken to ascertain the fate of the far-famed and ill-fated Count de la Pérouse.

Some months subsequent to the departure of General d'Entrecasteaux's expedition from France, an English merchant-ship was captured and brought into the port of Morlaix, where the commander's deposition was taken before the mayor, regarding the fate of la Pérouse's expedition. It certainly is rather an extraordinary statement ; but I will give it a place, and leave such seamen as may read this account to judge for themselves as to the credit it deserves.

Extract from the Minutes of the Justice of Peace of the City and Commune of Morlaix.

" George Bowen, captain of the ship
" *Albemarle*, on her voyage from Bombay
" to London, brought into Morlaix, being
" interrogated respecting what he knew of
" la Pérouse, who sailed from France on
" a voyage round the world, made answer,
" that in December 1791, being on his re-
" turn from Port Jackson to Bombay, he
" himself saw on the coast of New
" Georgia, in the eastern ocean, part of the
" wreck of M. de la Pérouse's ship float-
" ing on the water,* and that he imagines
" it to have belonged to a French-built
" ship. That he did not go ashore, but
" that the natives of the country came
" aboard his vessel. That he could not
" understand their language, but that he
" conceived from their signs some ships
" had visited those parts. That these

---

* La Pérouse must have been wrecked in 1788. I leave it to those who are acquainted with the effects of the waves on a shipwrecked vessel, to judge whether these remains could still exist floating on the water at the end of December 1791.

" poeple were acquainted with the use of
" several implements of iron, of which
" they were very desirous. That he, the
" deponent, had bartered several iron arti-
" cles with these Indians for beads and
" bows. That, with regard to the charac-
" ter of these Indians, they appeared to
" him to be peaceable and better inform-
" ed than the inhabitants of Otaheite,
" since they had a perfect knowledge of
" the implements of iron. That their ca-
" noes were made in a superior manner.
" That when the natives were on board his
" ship he did not yet know any thing of
" the wreck; but sailing along the coast,
" he perceived it about midnight, on the
" 30th of December 1791, by the light of
" a large fire which was burning on the
" land.* That had it not been for this
" fire he should probably have run on the
" rocks of Cape Deception. The depo-
" nent further declares, that all along this

* It is surprising, that the wreck seen by George Bowen,
and asserted to be that of la Pérouse's ship, and of French
construction, whence we must suppose it to have been considerable in size, and examined with attention by a person very
near, should have been merely perceived at midnight by the
light of a fire on the land.

" part of the coast of New Georgia he
" observed a great number of cabins or
" huts.   That these Indians were of a stout
" make and gentle disposition ; whence
" he presumes that if M. de la Pérouse,
" or any of his crew, were on the land,
" they are still living; and that he knows,
" of all the vessels which have navigated
" these seas, none but M. de Bougainville,
" the *Alexander*, the *Friendship* of Lon-
" don, M. de la Pérouse, and the depo-
" ponent, ever were at this place ; conse-
" quently, he presumes, the wreck must
" have belonged to the ship of M. de la
" Pérouse, since the *Alexander* was sunk
" in the strait of Macassar, and the *Friend-*
" *ship* arrived safe in England.

    " ·Being interrogated, whether he had
" seen any garments upon the natives of
" the country, denoting them to have had
" communication with Europeans, he an-
" swered that these Indians were naked,
" that the climate is very hot, and that he
" understood by their signs that they had
" seen ships before.   That he saw in the
" possession of these Indians, fishing-nets,
" the threads of which were made of flax,

" and the meshes were of European work-
" manship. That he took a piece of one
" out of curiosity, from which it would be
" easy to judge that the materials and
" workmanship were European."

These were the only accounts of the fate
of the unfortunate Count's expedition
which came to my knowledge up to 1826,
the time I touched at Tucopia, except some
unfounded reports respecting a cross of
St. Louis having been found on a nameless
island, without either latitude, longitude,
or date of discovery affixed to it, but said
to be situated in the Pacific between New
Caledonia and New Guinea.

CONTENTS

lxxii CONTENTS.

Page

lics from those ships, which turn out to have belonged to la
Pérouse's expedition. Prevails on Martin Bushart to leave the
island. Proceeds from Tucopia to Bengal.

CHAPTER II.

Negociation with the Government of British India
which led to the fitting-out of the expedition . . 37

Arrival at Bengal. Informs the government of British India
of the accounts received at Tucopia. Addresses a letter to the
government on the subject of la Pérouse's shipwreck. The
Asiatic Society solicit from government assistance to the supposed survivors of the French expedition. Government takes
up the affair. Expedition ordered under Capt. Dillon's command. The surgeon appointed to the expedition pretends to be
naturalist and botanist. He decyphers four stamps found on a
silver sword-guard brought from Tucopia by Capt. Dillon.
Supreme Council orders the ship *Research* to be equipped to
proceed in search of the survivors of the French expedition.
Treachery of the surgeon. His attempt to oust the commander
of the expedition, and place himself at the head of it. His
turbulent conduct on joining the ship.

CHAPTER III.

Occurrences from Calcutta to Van Diemen's Land   79

Sail from Bengal. Progress of the vessel on her voyage.
Renewed attempt of the surgeon to be placed at the head of
the expedition. He attempts to excite mutiny on board, and
writes to the first officer. New Zealanders on board threaten to
kill and eat the surgeon, when he lands in their country. The
surgeon and second officer quarrel. Officers quarrel among
themselves. Commander being informed of the surgeon's design,
he is arrested. Van Diemen's Land sighted. Ship encounters
a dreadful gale, and arrives in the river Derwent.

CHAPTER IV.

Occurrences at Van Diemen's Land 123

Intepriew with the Lieutenant-Governor, who promises to fa-
cilitate the necessary supplies to enable the expedition to proceed. At the instigation of Dr. Tytler withholds the assistance
promised. Dr. Tytler prosecutes his commander for arresting
him. The trial. New South Wales jury and judge. Extraordinary statements of the prosecutor. Commander found
guilty of assaulting his surgeon. Sentence passed on him by
the judge, which detained the expedition two months, at a
considerable expense to the East-India Company. Respectable
inhabitants petition the Lieutenant-Governor. Consequent

CONTENTS

VOL. II.

---- - - - -

CHAPTER I.

CHAPTER II.

APPENDIX.

Public Opinion in the East on the subject of Captain Dillon's voyage, and the opposition and ill-treatment he experienced at Van Diemen's Land, consisting of:

Testimonies of Approbation as to the successful result of Captain Dillon's voyage.

P. line.
4   5 *for* 1828 *read* 1808.
36   19 *for* or Malay *read* and Malay.
47   2 *for* 25th of November *read* 25th of October.
70   9 *for* Louiscarde *read* Louisiade.
90   5 *for* Fresher *read* Fraser.
135 11 *for* six *read* seven.
191   3 *for* ekes out *read* makes out.
197   7 *for* Wangeroa *read* Wangaroa.

P. line.
215 25 *for* Mr. Blackhall *read* Blacksell.
222 23 *for* Marley *read* Moly.
258 12 *for* Eawa *read* Eoaa.
288 21 *for* Vavow *read* Vavaoo.
295 12 *for* Juckafinawa *read* Fuckafinawa.
298 27 *for* Otata *read* Atata.
299 26 *for* schnappers *read* snappers.
300 29 *for* Hanga Tonga *read* Honga Tonga.
301   1 *for* Hanga Hapai *read* Honga Hapai.

P. line.
2   19 and 25, *for* Eavaoo *read* Vavaoo.
13   15 *for* Kamoa *read* Hamoa.
20   4 *for* Hamón *read* Hamoa.
20   9 *for* Toonga *read* Tonga.
28   25 *for* Tooleo *read* Tooho.
32   14 *for* Lefroga *read* Lefooga.
126 14 *for* Barilla *read* Morilla.
147 14 *for* Mancolans *read* Mannicolans.
164 12 *for* there *read* therefore.
168   9 *for* Thamaca *read* Thowmaco.
206   6 *for* grape shot *read* shot.
218   2 *for* skills *read* skulls.
230 29 *for* Hapley *read* Hopley.
253 19 *after* respect *read* for the secretary of the Marine Board of Calcutta.
265   3 *for* preternatural *read* supernatural.
272   6 *for* Mayhanger *read* Moyhanger.
284 19 *for* New Lark *read* New Sark.
285 21 *for* Tucopian who resides *read* Tucopians who resided.

P. line.
289 16 *for* takee, takee *read* tokee, tokee.
306 17 *after* inexpedient *read* to which I gave my consent solely on account of the unhealthy state of my crew.
316   7 *for* holy *read* booby or balony.
320 16 *for* Huvalley *read* Cavalley.
320 *last line, for* Carroraricka *read* Corroraruka.
324   6 *for* a man *read* the man before-mentioned.
328 14 *for* Hakihanga *read* Hokeiangha.
330   4 *after* benighted ministers *read* as they are called by their opponents at New Zealand.
346 24 and 26 *for* Erronam *read* Erronan.
350 11, 15, and 17, *for* Ethaey *read* Ethoey.
368 23, *read* March 22.
Plate—for canoe of Indenny or Santa Cruz *read* La Pérouse's Island, or Mannicolo.

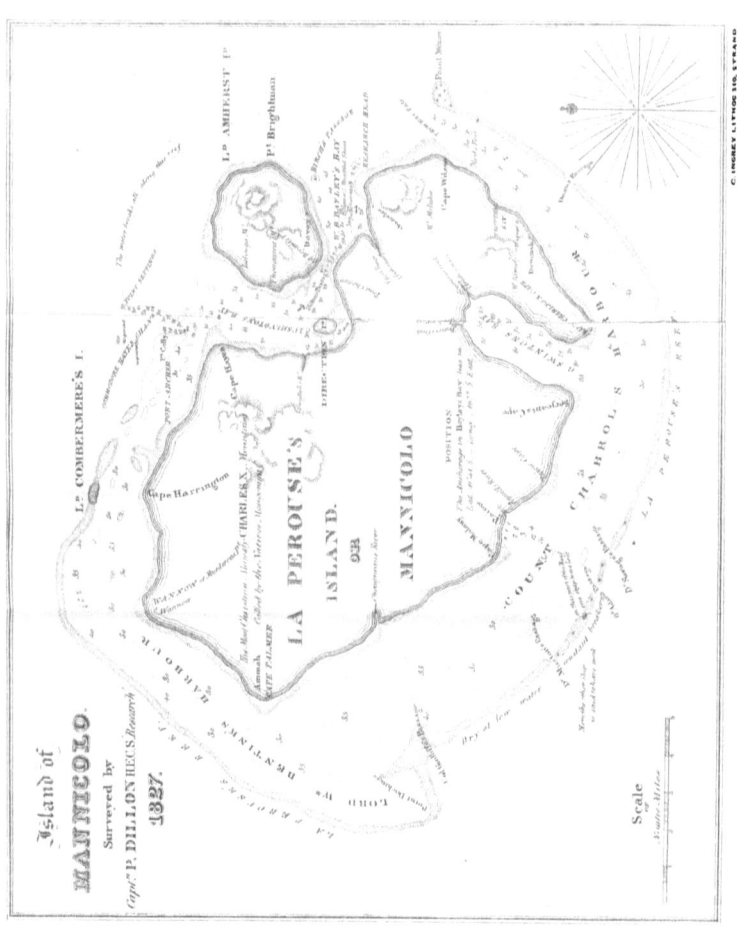

The material originally positioned here is too large for reproduction in this reissue. A PDF can be downloaded from the web address given on page iv of this book, by clicking on 'Resources Available'.

NARRATIVE,

&c. &c.

CHAPTER I.

VOYAGE IN THE SOUTH SEAS, DREADFUL MASSACRE AT
THE FEJEE ISLANDS, AND OCCURRENCES WHICH LED TO
THE DISCOVERY OF THE FATE OF LA PÉROUSE.

In 1812 and 1813 I sailed as an officer in
the Calcutta ship *Hunter*, Captain Robson, on
a voyage from Bengal to New South Wales, the
Beetee Islands (commonly called the *Fejee* Islands), and Canton. I had before visited these
islands in 1809, and remained among them for
four months, during which time, being in the
habit of associating very much with the natives,
I made a considerable progress in learning their
language. On joining the *Hunter* I found Captain Robson had been at these islands twice
before, and had obtained considerable influence
over the natives of a part of the Sandal-wood
coast, by joining them in their wars, and as-
sisting them to destroy their enemies, who were
cut up, baked, and eaten in his presence. The

chief with whom he was most intimate was
Bonasar, of the town of Vilear and its depen-
dencies in the interior.

On the afternoon of the 19th February 1813
the ship *Hunter* anchored in Vilear Bay, at a
distance of a quarter of a mile from the entrance
of a small river that led to the town. The
town of Vilear is about a mile, or perhaps one
and a half, from the anchorage, situated on the
verdant banks of a beautiful stream. The sides
of the river are covered with thick forests of
mangrove bushes to within a short distance of
the town, where the land is somewhat elevated
and clear of wood.

Before the anchor was let go, the chief's
brother came on board to congratulate the captain on his return; and shortly after, the chief,
with several other chiefs and priests, with a
Lascar or East-Indian sailor, who had deserted
from the *Hunter* at this place about twenty
months before. The chief informed the captain,
that shortly after his departure for Canton last
voyage, the towns which he had conquered on
the coast and interior by the captain's assistance, revolted, and being joined by the powerful tribes who reside on the banks of a large
river, called Nanpacab, they had waged a
furious war against him.

The chief then hinted at the impossibility

there was of obtaining sandal-wood until this
powerful alliance was put down by force of
musketry, and requested the commander to
join him in a new campaign. To this request
he did not then accede. The chief urged the
danger to which his subjects would be exposed
while they were in straggling parties cutting
the sandal-wood for us, as the enemy would
lay wait for them, and cut them off when they
least expected it. I went on shore with the
captain and chief to the town, where we were
exceedingly well received, and got presents of
a hog, yams, and cocoa-nuts. We were visited
next day by Terrence Dun and John Riley,
British subjects : the former was discharged
from the *Hunter* last voyage, and the latter
from an American brig at the same time.

They informed me that they had resided during their time on shore at various parts of the
islands, and were exceedingly well treated by
the inhabitants ; but that their countrymen
who resided on the neighbouring island of Bow
had become very troublesome to the islanders.
Such was their bad and overbearing conduct,
that the natives rose on them one day and
killed three of them, before the king of Bow
had time to suppress the wrath of his people,
who wished to destroy all the Europeans on
the island. Dun was therefore of opinion, that

the surviving Europeans would be prevented from visiting the ship.

It is here necessary to explain how so many sailors of different countries got on shore to reside at these islands. In 1828 an American brig from the river Plate was lost on one of the islands with 40,000 Spanish dollars on board. The crew were saved in the vessel's boats, and part of them joined an American ship then lying at Myanboor Bay, on the Sandal-wood coast; others escaped to the neighbouring island of Bow, with as many of the dollars as they could conveniently carry off. Shortly after the above shipwreck several vessels, English, Indian, American, and New South Wales men, came to the coast for the purpose of procuring sandal-wood. The seamen on board these vessels became allured by the report of so many dollars being on shore at the neighbouring islands. With a view of enriching themselves, some deserted, and others were regularly discharged by their commanders and proceeded to the field of wealth. Some of those men, with the few dollars then procured, bought fire-arms and gunpowder, with which they rendered important assistance to the king of the neighbouring island of Bow, and were on that account thought highly of by the islanders, from among whom they procured wives and lived very com-

fortably, until their insolence and cruelty induced the natives to destroy a part of them;
and it will shortly be seen what a dreadful fate
awaited the others in consequence of Captain
Robson's proceedings.

From the time of our arrival up to the end
of March following, the sandal-wood came in
but very slowly. The natives in our neighbourhood begged several times of the captain
to assist them in their wars, and promised, as a
reward for such service, to load the ship with
the desired article in two months after their
enemy was conquered. Captain Robson consented; and we accordingly set out for the
island of Nanpacab, situated about six miles up
the river of the same name, and distant from
the ship forty or fifty miles. The armament
consisted of three armed boats carrying twenty
musketeers, and in one of the boats there was
a two-pound cannon mounted. We were accompanied by forty-six large canoes, carrying I
suppose near a thousand armed savages, besides three thousand more that marched by
land to the scene of action. The weather being
wet and stormy, we were obliged to rendezvous
at an island near the entrance of the Nanpacab
until the morning of the 4th, at which time we
entered the river, and were saluted by showers
of arrows and stones from slings by the enemy

who were standing on its banks. On getting near the island of Nanpacab we found it fortified. After a few discharges of the two-pounder, the defenders abandoned the fortress and escaped to the main land, from whence they were soon driven by the fire of the musketry. There were eleven of the Nanpacab people killed on this occasion, whose bodies were placed in the canoes of our party, excepting one, which was immediately despatched in a fast-sailing canoe to Vilear, to be there devoured. After this short skirmish we proceeded fifteen miles up the river, and destroyed the towns and plantations on its banks. In the evening we returned to a landing-place, where the islanders began to cook their yams in a kind of oven which will be hereafter described. The dead bodies were placed on the grass and dissected by one of the priests. The feet were cut off at the ankles, and the legs from the knees; afterwards the private parts; then the thighs at the hip joints; the hands at the wrists, the arms at the elbows, the shoulders at the sockets; and lastly, the head and neck were separated from the body. Each of these divisions of the human frame formed one joint, which was carefully tied up in green plantain leaves, and placed in the ovens to be baked with the *tara* root.

On the morning of the 5th we proceeded along the coast to the eastward, but found the towns, forts, and plantations abandoned. On the night of the 8th we returned to the ship.

Early in May we were joined by our tender, the *Elizabeth* cutter, Mr. Ballard master, which had sailed from Port Jackson before us for the Sandwich Islands, and in a few days after we were visited by the Europeans who resided at Bow. The captain employed them to work in the ship's boats, for which they were to be paid at the rate of £4 per month, in cutlery, glass-beads, ironmongery, &c. at a fixed price, and to return to Bow when the ship was prepared to proceed on her voyage.

May, June, July, and August passed over, and we had only procured one hundred and fifty tons of sandal-wood from the islanders, which was not more than one-third of a cargo. They then declared their inability to procure more wood, as the forests were exhausted by the great number of ships which had frequented the coast for some years past.

The chiefs and men of consequence kept away from the ship, being apprehensive they might be detained as hostages until their engagements of loading the vessel were fulfilled. Captain Robson was very much displeased at this trick played on him by a savage and cunning people, and vowed vengeance against his old and faithful allies, whose stomachs he had so often helped to glut with the flesh of their enemies.

Early in September two large canoes from Bow, carrying about two hundred and twenty or two hundred and thirty men, visited the ship, for the purpose of taking home the Europeans and their wives that joined us in May. Captain Robson, about that time being sixty miles distant from the ship in the tender, attacked a fleet of Vilear canoes, and took fourteen of them; on which occasion a native of the latter place was shot dead by a small cannon-shot. On the ship and cutter rejoining company, the captain proposed to heave the cutter down, to repair some damage she had sustained in her bottom. However, he deemed it prudent, before doing so, to endeavour to possess himself of the remainder of the Vilear canoes, to prevent, as he said, their attacking the people while employed about the cutter, as it would be necessary to haul her on shore at high water.

On the morning of the 6th of September the Europeans belonging to the ship were all armed with muskets, also those Europeans from Bow, and placed under the direction of Mr. Norman, the first officer. We landed at a place

called the Black Rock, a little way to the
eastward of the river : the two canoes shortly
after landed at the same place. We were
joined by the Bow chiefs and a hundred of
their men. The canoes and boats then put
off into deep water, which precaution was used
to prevent their getting aground by the tide
ebbing.

On landing, the Europeans began to dis-
perse into straggling parties of two, three, and
four in a group. I begged of Mr. Norman, our
commander, to cause them to keep close together in case of a sudden attack from the islanders; but no attention was paid to my remonstrance. We proceeded by a narrow path
over a small level plain without interruption
until we arrived at the foot of a hill, which we
ascended, and soon gained the level or table-
land on its top. There a few natives shewed
themselves, and by shouts and gestures tried
to irritate us.

Mr. Norman turned to the right along a
narrow path, which led through a thicket to
some native houses : I followed him with seven
other Europeans and the two Bow chiefs, with
one of their men. Here a few natives tried
to dispute our passage : they were fired at,
one shot dead, and the others retreated. Mr.
Norman then directed the chief's house with

some others to be set on fire. The order was immediately complied with, and all were in flames in a few seconds. A few minutes after we heard dreadful yells and shoutings of the savages proceeding from the road by which we had ascended to the table-land. The Bow chiefs understood from the yells that some of their men as well as Europeans were killed by the Vilear people, who lay concealed in ambush until they got us on the table-land, where they attacked our straggling parties, who having discharged their muskets, were killed before they had time to reload. Others, I afterwards understood, on seeing themselves nearly surrounded by the savages, threw down their muskets and ran towards the boat: only two of whom escaped. In Mr. Norman's party there were ten musket-men, with the two Bow chiefs and one of their followers. We determined to keep close together and fight our way to the boats.

We immediately got out of the thicket on to the table-land, where there were not more than three of the islanders, who shouted and called out to us that several of our men were killed, as also a number of the Bow men, and that we should immediately share a similar fate. On reaching the brink of the path by which we were to descend to the plain, we found Terrence Dun lying dead with his brains beaten

out by a native club, and the whole plain between us and the boats covered with thousands
of infuriated savages, all armed.   Before des-
cending to the plain, a young man named John
Graham separated from us, and ran into a
thicket of bushes on the left-hand side of the
road, where he was quickly pursued by the
three savages above-mentioned, who despatched
him.   This young man was the son of a publican at Port Jackson, and had served his time
to the sea , he had joined an American brig
about two years before, as interpreter for these
islands, and after procuring a cargo for her,
was paid off and discharged at his own request.
The remainder of us proceeded down the precipice.   On getting to the bottom the savages
prepared to receive us ; they stood in thousands on each side of the path, brandishing
their weapons, with their faces and bodies be-
smeared over with the blood of our slaughtered
companions.

At this moment a native who came down
the precipice after us, threw a lance at Mr.
Norman, which entered his back and passed
out of his breast: he ran a few yards and
fell down apparently dead.   I fired at this native and reloaded my musket as soon as possible, when on turning round I found my companions had all run off by different routes.

Taking advantage of the absence of the natives, who had all quitted the path and pursued our unfortunate flying men, I dashed along with all the speed that was possible, but had not proceeded more than a few yards when I came on the dead body of William Parker, who was prostrated across the path with his musket by him, which I took up and retreated with.

About this time the natives observed me and gave chase. One of them came up so close to me that I was obliged to throw Parker's musket away, as also a pistol which I had in my belt. In a moment after this I reached the foot of a small steep rock that stood on the plain. Finding it impossible to get to the boat through the crowds of natives that intercepted the pathway, I called out to my companions (some of whom were on my right), " take the hill ! take the hill !" We then got to the top of it, where I joined the following persons : Charles Savage, Luis a Chinaman, and Martin Bushart, with Thomas Dafny and William Wilson. The three former men resided at Bow, and joined us at this island for the purpose before mentioned ; the two latter were seamen belonging to the ship. Mic Macabe, with Joseph Atkinson and the two Bow chiefs, were killed : those men had joined us also here. Dafny fired his musket on the plain and then broke it off at the butt in

defending himself. He was wounded in several
parts of the body, and he had four arrows stuck
in his back : the point of a spear had pierced
his shoulder, having entered from behind and
came out in the fore part under the collar bone.

It fortunately happened that the rock or hill
to which we escaped was so steep that few persons could ascend it at a time ; and it was too
much elevated for the natives to annoy us much
with their spears or slings.   They however shot
several arrows at us, which were impeded by
a strong gale of wind that blew them off their
intended course.   Our chief officer having
fallen, I now, as next in rank, took command
of the party, and stationed them in the best way
I could to defend our post.   I did not allow
more than one or two muskets to be fired at
a time, and kept the wounded man loading
for us.   Several of the natives ascended the
hill to within a few yards, and were shot by us
in self-defence as fast as they approached.
After some of them had been killed in this
manner the rest kept off.   Having but little
ammunition left, we were as sparing of it as
possible ; besides which we did not wish to irritate the natives more than they already were
by firing, except when driven to it by necessity.   From our elevated situation we had a
clear view of the landing-place, the boats at

anchor waiting our return, the two Bow canoes, and the ship. This we had but little prospect of ever again rejoining, though I had some hopes that Captain Robson would make an effort to rescue us, by arming himself, six Indian soldiers that were on board, two or three Europeans, and the Bow people in the canoes. These hopes soon vanished, when I saw the Bow canoes set sail and steer towards their island without passing alongside the ship.

The plain which surrounded the rock was covered with the armed savages assembled from all parts of the coast, amounting to several thousands, who had been in ambush waiting for us to land. This assemblage now exhibited a scene revolting to human nature. Fires were prepared and ovens heated for the reception of the bodies of our ill-fated companions, who, as well as the Bow chiefs and their slaughtered men, were brought to the fires in the following manner. Two of the Vilear party placed a stick or limb of a tree on to their shoulders, over which were thrown the bodies of their victims, with their legs hanging downwards on one side, and their heads at the other. They were thus carried in triumph to the ovens prepared to receive them. Here they were placed in a sitting posture, while the savages sung and danced with joy over their prizes, and fired several

MASSACRE AT THE FEJEE ISLANDS IN SEPT.^r 1813.

Dreadful Situation of Capt Dillon, and the two other Survivors.

The material originally positioned here is too large for reproduction in this reissue. A PDF can be downloaded from the web address given on page iv of this book, by clicking on 'Resources Available'.

musket-balls through each of the corpses, all
the muskets of the slain having fallen into their
hands. No sooner was this ceremony over,
than the priests began to cut up and dissect
these unfortunate men in our presence. Their
flesh was immediately placed in the ovens to be
baked and prepared as a repast for the victors,
after the manner already described ; meanwhile
we were closely guarded on all sides but one,
which fronted the thick mangrove forest on
the banks of the river. Savage proposed to
Martin Bushart to run for that, and endeavour to escape to the water's side and swim
for the ship. This I opposed, threatening to
shoot the first man dead that left the hill, and
my threat for the present had the desired effect.
By this time the fury of the savages was somewhat abated, and they began to listen attentively to our harangues and offers of reconci-
liation. I reminded them that on the day the
fourteen canoes were seized and taken, eight
of their men had been made prisoners on board
the ship, where they were now confined. One
of them was the Nambeatey (or high priest) of
Vilear's brother. I represented to the multitude, that if we were killed the eight prisoners
would be put to death on board; but that if I
with my five companions were not sacrificed,
we would cause the eight prisoners to be re-

leased immediately. The head priest, who is
regarded as a deity by these savages, immediately asked if I was speaking truth, and if
his brother and the other seven men were alive?
I assured him they were, and that I would send
a man on board to the captain to order them to
be released, if he would convey the man safe
down to the boat from among the multitude;
this the priest promised to do immediately. As
Thomas Dafny was wounded and had no arms
to defend himself, I prevailed on him to venture
down the rock with the priest, and thence to
the boat. He was then to inform Captain Robson of our horrid situation, which may be more
easily imagined than described. I also directed
him to tell the captain that it was my particular
request that he should release one-half of the
prisoners, and show them a large chest of ironmongery, whales' teeth, &c. which he might
promise to deliver to the remaining four prisoners with their liberty, the moment we returned to the ship.

This man proceeded as directed, and I did
not lose sight of him from the time he left us
until he got on the ship's deck. A cessation of
arms took place in the mean time, which might
have continued unbroken had it not been for
the imprudence of Charles Savage, who put a
greater temptation in the way of the natives

than they could withstand. During this interval several native chiefs ascended the hill, and came within a few paces of us, with prostrations of friendship, and proffered us security if we would go down among them. To these promises I would not accede, nor allow any of my men to do so; till Charles Savage, who had resided on the islands for more than five years, and spoke the native dialect fluently, begged of me to permit him to go down among the natives with the chiefs to whom we were speaking, as he had no doubt their promises would be kept, and that if I allowed him to go he would certainly procure a peace, and enable us all to return safe to the ship. Overcome by his importunities, I at last gave my consent, but reminded him that I did not wish him to do so, and that he must leave his musket and ammunition with me. This he did, and proceeded about two hundred yards from the foot of the rock to where Bonasar was seated, surrounded by chiefs, who were happy to receive him, their secret determination being to kill and eat him. They conversed with him, however, for some time, and then called out to me in the native dialect, " Come down, Peter, we will not hurt you : you see we do not hurt Charley !" I replied that I would not go down until the prisoners landed. During this discussion the Chi-

naman, Luis, stole down the opposite side of
the hill unknown to me, with his arms, for the
purpose of placing himself under the protection
of a chief with whom he was intimately acquainted, and to whom he had rendered important service in former wars. The islanders,
finding they could not prevail on me to place
myself in their power, set up a screetch that
rent the air: at that moment Charles Savage was
seized by the legs, and held in that state by six
men, with his head placed in a well of fresh
water until he was suffocated; whilst at the
same instant a powerful savage got behind the
Chinaman, and with his huge club knocked the
upper part of his skull to pieces. These wretched men were scarcely lifeless, when they were
cut up and put into ovens ready prepared for
the purpose.

We, the three defenders of the hill, were then
furiously attacked on all sides by the cannibals,
whom our muskets however kept in great dread,
though the chiefs stimulated their men to ascend and bring us down, promising to confer
the greatest honours on the man who should
kill me, and frequently inquired of their people
if they were afraid of three white men, when
they had killed several that day. Thus encou-
raged, they pressed close on us. Having four
muskets between three of us, two always re-

mained loaded : for Wilson being a bad shot, we kept him loading the muskets, while Martin Bushart and I fired them off. Bushart had been a rifleman in his own country, and was an excellent marksman. He shot twenty-seven of the cannibals with twenty-eight discharges, only missing once : I also killed and wounded a few of them in self-defence. Finding they could not conquer us without a great sacrifice on their part, they kept off and vowed vengeance.

The human bodies being now prepared, they were withdrawn from the ovens, and shared out to the different tribes, who devoured them greedily. They frequently invited me to come down and be killed before it was dark, that they might have no trouble in dissecting and baking me in the night. I was bespoken joint by joint by the different chiefs, who exultingly brandished their weapons in the air, and boasted of the number of white men each had killed that day.

In reply to all this I informed them, that if I was killed, their countrymen confined on board our vessel would be killed also, but that if I was saved they would be saved. The ruthless savages replied, "Captain Robson may kill and eat our countrymen if he please ; we will kill and eat you. When it is dark you cannot see to shoot at us, and you have no more powder."

Myself and companions, seeing no hope of mercy on earth, turned our eyes towards heaven, and implored the Almighty Ruler of all things to have compassion on our wretched souls. We had now not the most distant hope of ever escaping from the savages, and expected to be devoured as our companions were but a few minutes before. The only thing which prevented our surrendering quietly was, the dread of being taken alive and put to the torture.

These people sometimes, but not very often, torture their prisoners in the following manner. They skin the soles of the feet and then torment their victims with firebrands, so as to make them jump about in that wretched state. At other times they cut off the prisoner's eye-lids and turn his face to the sun, at which he is obliged to look with his bare eyes: this is said to be a dreadful punishment. From the fingers of others they pull off the nails. By all accounts, however, these punishments are very rare, and only inflicted on persons who have given the greatest provocation ; such as we had done this day, by shooting so many men in our own defence.

Having no more than sixteen or seventeen cartridges left, we determined, as soon as it was dark, to place the muzzles of our muskets to our hearts with the butts on the ground and discharge them into our breasts, thus to avoid the danger of falling alive into the hands of these cannibal monsters.

At this moment the boat put off from the ship and soon got close to the landing-place, where we counted the eight prisoners landing from her. I could not imagine how the captain could have acted in this strange way, as the only hope presented of our lives being spared was by allowing a part of the prisoners to land, who would, of course, intercede with their friends on shore to save us, that we might in return protect their countrymen when we returned to the ship. But this precaution not having been attended to, all hope seemed now fled, and the only means of relief left consisted in the dreadful determination of destroying our own lives in the mode already mentioned.

Shortly after the eight prisoners landed, they were conveyed unarmed up the rock to me, preceded by the priest, who informed me that Captain Robson had released the eight men, and sent a chest of cutlery, ironmongery, &c. on shore for the chiefs, with orders that we were to deliver our muskets to them, and that he would see us safe to the boat. I replied, that as long as I lived I would not part with my musket, which was my own property, as I was certain they would slaughter me and my

companions, as they had done Charles Savage
and Luis.

The priest then turned to Martin Bushart,
and harangued him on the policy of our complying. At this moment the thought entered
my head of making the priest a prisoner, and
either to destroy him or regain my liberty. I
tied Charles Savage's musket with my neck-
handkerchief to the belt of my cartridge-box,
and presenting my own musket to the priest's
head, told him that I would shoot him dead if
he attempted to run away, or if any of his countrymen offered to molest me or my companions.
I then directed him to proceed before me to
the boat, threatening him with instant death in
case of non-compliance. The priest proceeded
as directed, and as we passed along through the
multitude, he exhorted them to sit down, and
upon no account to molest Peter or his countrymen, because if they attempted to hurt us he
would be. shot, and they of course must be
aware they would consequently incur the wrath
of the gods in the clouds, who would be angry
at their disobedience of the divine orders, and
cause the sea to rise and swallow up the island
with all its inhabitants.

The multitude treated their priest's injunctions with profound respect, and sat down on the
grass. The Nambety (which is the term for priest)

proceeded as directed towards the boats, with
the muzzles of Martin Bushart's and Wilson's
muskets at each of his ears, while the muzzle
of mine was placed between his shoulders.
Finding that night was approaching, and anxious
to prolong life, I had recourse to this dreadful
expedient, being aware of the influence and
sway which the priests in all barbarous nations
have over their votaries.

On getting to the boats, Nambety made a
sudden stop. I ordered him to proceed. This
he refused doing in the most positive manner,
declaring that he would go no further, and that
I might shoot him if I liked. I threatened to
do so, and asked him why he would not go to
the water's edge? He replied, " you want to
take me on board alive, and put me to the torture." There being no time to spare, I told
him to stand still, and turned my face to him
with my musket presented, threatening to shoot
him if he attempted to move until I got into
the boat. We then walked backwards to the
water-side, and up to our breasts in water, where
we joined the boat, and had no sooner got
into her than the islanders came down, and
saluted us with a shower of arrows, and stones
from slings.

Being thus once more out of danger, we
returned thanks to Divine Providence for our

escape, and proceeded towards the ship, which we reached just as the sun was setting. I expostulated with Captain Robson on his extraordinary conduct, in causing so many human beings to be unnecessarily sacrificed. He made use of some absurd apologies, and inquired if we were the only persons who had escaped: I replied, yes; but that if the natives could have made proper use of the muskets which fell into their hands on that occasion, we must all have been killed.

On inquiry, I found that only two of our musketeers had escaped: George, a New Zealander, and Oreyow, a native of Otaheite, both ordinary sailors belonging to the ship. The following is a list of the killed, who fell into the hands of the natives. The first six were a part of the ship and cutter's crew, *viz.*

1. Mr. Norman, first officer.
2. Mr. C. Cox, third ditto, son to Mr. Cox, paymaster of the New South Wales Corps. or 102d Regiment.
3. Jonow (a lascar), boatswain's mate.
4. Hassen (ditto)   seaman.
5. Mosdean (ditto)   ditto.
6. Louis Evans   ditto. This young man was said to be the son of Governor Phillip, the first governor of New South Wales.

The undermentioned persons, who joined us at the island on the terms before-mentioned, were also killed.

7. Charles Savage, a Swede, who had been shipwrecked in the *Eliza*.

8. John Graham, of New South Wales, discharged from an American.

9. Terrence Dunn, an Irishman, discharged from the *Hunter* last voyage.

10. Michael Maccabe, ditto, ditto from the English ship *City of Edinburgh*.

11. Joseph Atkins, ditto, ditto.

12. William Parker, of London, deserted from an American.

13. Luis, a Chinese, shipwrecked in the *Eliza*.

14. Pemi, of Otaheite, discharged from an American.

Mr. Ballard (the master of the tender) saved his life by being under arrest on board, and of course not one of the party.

The following persons were left on board the ship from the Bow canoes: Saoo, a Chinese, formerly one of the shipwrecked *Eliza's* crew; one lascar named Joe, formerly belonging to the brig *Hibernia;* three native females and one man from Bow, with one Friendly Island carpenter. One of the females was related to the royal family at Bow, and was the wife of Joseph Atkins: the second was the

wife of Martin Bushart; the third the wife of
William Sibley, one of the cutter's crew, who
is now alive at New South Wales. These
people begged of us not to land them at Vilear,
where they would most undoubtedly be destroyed by the enemy, who had killed their
chiefs and relations that morning. Captain
Robson promised them to stand as near to the
island of Bow as the wind would permit, and
then embark the party into one of the canoes
we had on deck, so as to enable them to return
to their homes and friends. Our party landed
from three boats, in each of which two armed
boat-keepers were left in charge. William
Sibley, who had charge of my boat, informed
me that about forty of the Bow people had
escaped to the canoes with their arms broken;
some of them were desperately wounded. He
endeavoured, by signs and gestures, to prevail
on them to proceed with their canoes to the
ship; but to this proposal they paid no attention.

I was immediately appointed to the command of the cutter, and all the strangers were
ordered to embark in her. Captain Robson proposed to sail with both the ship and cutter next
morning for China. I requested of him, as I
was anxious to recover the bones of Mr. Cox,
a young man for whom I had a great regard,

to permit me to pull close in-shore next morning with two boats, and offer a ransom for them
to the savages.   To this he assented.

Next morning, the 7th of September, I pulled
close in-shore, and got the native of Bow, who
I had in the boat with me, to hail the Vilear
people in their own tongue.   On their answer-
ing and inquiring what we wanted, he informed
them of our object.   They replied that they
had neither the flesh nor bones to spare, as
they had all been devoured the night before.
One of the savages held up the two thigh-bones
of Mr. Norman (as he informed us), and inquired
what I would give for them.   I offered an axe.
He exultingly laughed, and flourished the bones
about, saying he would not sell them ; that they
would make excellent sail-needles to repair his
canoe sails.   The natives saluted us with a
shower of stones and arrows, which we answered by a discharge of musketry, and then returned to the ship.   The anchor was soon after
weighed and we made sail.

On account of calms and light winds, we
were not able to get out clear of the islands
and innumerable reefs for six days. On passing
the place where Captain Robson intended to
send the Bow people into the canoe, it blew
too hard for a canoe to exist, we were therefore
obliged to proceed on our voyage.

As Martin Bushart's wife was pregnant, and
not far from her confinement, he, and also the
Lascar, begged to be landed on the first coast
we met with. On the morning of the 20th of
September we came in sight of a small island,
which we supposed to be uninhabited : here
the captain was determined to land the whole
party excepting the Bow man. This intention
was made known to Martin Bushart, who approved of the measure. Pumpkin and other
seeds were prepared for him, with a few fowls
to breed from.

On approaching the island we found out our
mistake, as it was thickly inhabited. Several of
the islanders came off in canoes, who, we all
conjectured, had never before seen Europeans.
They were unarmed, but very wild. They came
on deck without reserve, seized upon bars of
iron from the forge, and jumped overboard
with that metal, as also a frying-pan, the cook's
axe, knife, saucepans, &c. The firing of a
musket in the air had not the least effect upon
them   I became alarmed on account of the
smallness of the cutter in which I was, as they
had only to make one step out of their canoes
on board of it. On flourishing a light-horse-
man's sword, however, and cutting a piece out
of the rail, it alarmed them. Those on deck
jumped overboard, excepting one, who was

carrying off our compass, when one of the Beetee girls on board became alarmed at our danger, and therefore seizing him by the throat with one hand and by the privates with the other, in this way got him under her, where she certainly would have strangled him, had I not interfered. Order was soon after restored, when an elderly chief came on board, to whom we made several presents of iron-hoops, glass beads, &c. &c. The boat being got out, I embarked in her with Martin Bushart, the lascar, and chief. On reaching the shore the chief landed, and conducted Martin to the king, who was sitting under the shade of some cocoa-nut trees chewing the betel-nut. He made his majesty a few presents, and by signs, words, and gestures, informed him that himself, the Lascar, his wife, and others, were coming to reside on the island. The chief appeared much pleased with this arrangement, and they returned to the boat.

On rejoining the ship, Martin and the Lascar put their things into the boat, with Martin's wife. The other two women objected to go, and entreated me to beg of Captain Robson to take them to a country where there were ships, so as they might, by means of them, return home on a future day. They also represented to me, that if they landed here, they would, in the first place, run the risk of being ill-treated, if not killed, by the islanders; in the second place, they would never again have an opportunity of returning from this place to their own country.

I mentioned this conversation to Captain Robson. His reply was, " they must go on shore, as he had not the means of providing a passage back for them." I observed, that as I had been on shore at Bow for four months on the ship's duty, I felt interested for the king's subjects, and that I would undertake to provide for one of the females until a fit opportunity offered for her return. To these terms he consented. I then set out for the shore a second time, with the persons destined to reside there. On coming near the beach I found it crowded with the islanders, who appeared very clamarous. They invited me to land, which I declined, and gave them to understand I wanted one of their canoes to land the people out of the boat. The canoe having come off accordingly, Martin Bushart with his wife, and Joe the lascar, stepped into her and landed. The other Beetee girl would not land from the boat; neither did I compel her to do so, as I considered it the height of injustice to land against her will, the subject of a prince from whom we received so much attention, and whose brother, nephew, and sixty of his best men, were killed in our cause. I found in the course of the day that the islanders called their island by the name of Tucopia. They appeared to be exceed· ingly rejoiced on getting the three persons already mentioned on shore among them, and they invited me to land and sleep on shore that night. I made them understand that I must sleep on board the ship, and would call in the morning to see them.

I set out for the vessel and reached her at dusk. The captain was much displeased at my not having forced the poor woman on shore. He returned to the ship, at which time we set sail and steered to the westward. The next morn· ing we were distant from a large high island about eight leagues.* Here the ship and cutter parted company : the former for Canton in China, and the latter for Port Jackson in New South Wales.

It is here necessary to observe, that I am now preparing a complete history of the Beetee Islands, from its first discovery to A. D. 1825, which will describe the manners, customs, &c. of these people, and also account for the persons taken off in the *Hunter*.

From the year 1813 to May 1826 I heard no-thing of Martin Bushart. On my way then from Valparaiso and New Zealand towards Bengal,

* This afterwards proved to be la Pérouse's island.

I came in sight of Tucopia on the morning of
the 13th May, and shortly after several canoes
put off from the shore and pulled towards the
ship. In the foremost of them I recognized
the lascar Joe, and invited him on board. He
had not the most distant recollection of me
until I made myself known to him, by saying I
was the captain of the cutter which brought
him from the Beetee Islands and landed him on
Tucopia with Martin Bushart. He appeared
to have forgot the East-Indian dialects, and
could not reply to me or my servants, three
of whom were his countrymen. His conversation was composed of a mixture of Bengalee,
English, the Beetee, and Tucopia dialects.

The next canoe that reached the ship had
Martin Bushart on board. Having invited him
on deck, I found that he also had lost all recollection of me : until I reminded him of our old
acquaintance, and providential escape from Vilear. He then informed me that no ship had
visited the island for the first eleven years after
he landed there; but that about twenty months
back a whaler came off the island, and whaled
for one month, during which time he went on
board and remained with her until she sailed
for England. He also mentioned that a second
whaler had passed the island about ten months
back, he went on board in a canoe, and remain-

about twenty minutes, when she set sail and stood to the westward.

One of my officers informed me that the lascar Joe had sold my armourer the silver guard of a sword. I sent for it, and on inspection observed five cyphers on it, not one of which however I could make out. On inquiry of Martin Bushart how he came by it, he informed me that on his first arrival at Tucopia he saw in the possession of the natives several ship's iron bolts, chain-plates, axes, knives, china and glass beads, with the handle of a silver fork, and many other things. He at first supposed that a ship must have been cast away here, and that the islanders procured those things from her wreck, but upon learning the language about two years after he had landed on the island, he found out his mistake.

The natives then informed him, that those things which he had seen, with the sword-guard, had been brought in their canoes from a distant island, which they called Malicolo,* and that two large ships, such as the *Hunter* was, had been wrecked there, when the old men now in Tucopia were boys, and that there yet remained at Mannicolo large quantities of the wrecks. The lascar confirmed this report, and

---

* Since ascertained to be more correctly called Mannicolo or Vannicolo.

said he had been there about six years back, and that he had seen and conversed with two old men who belonged to the ships. A native of Tucopia was then called in, who had returned from thence not more than six or seven months : he said that he had resided at the island where the ships were wrecked for two years, on his last visit, and that there were several parts of the wreck to be yet found. From all these statements being delivered in the undesigning manner in which they were, I immediately came to the conclusion that the two ships wrecked must be those under the command of the far-famed and lamented Count de la Pérouse, as no other two European ships were lost or missing at so remote a period.

I inquired of the islanders if any ship had been at Mannicolo since the two in question had been lost there. They replied, no : that ships had been seen passing the island at a great distance, but never had any communication with the shore.

I was very short of provisions, but notwithstanding this I determined to proceed to Mannicolo, and with such means as were in my power, to rescue from the hands of the savages the two survivors, who I had not the least doubt were Frenchmen.

I begged of Martin Bushart and the lascar

to accompany me. Martin assented to my request, on condition of being returned to Tucopia ; but the lascar positively refused compli-
ance. Martin, however, succeeded in prevailing on one of the Tucopians to accompany us.
That evening I shaped my course and steered
for the westward, as it was in that direction the
island of Mannicolo was said to lie. I had
light winds and calms all night and the next
day, and did not reach Mannicolo before the
second day after leaving Tucopia. Here the
ship was becalmed for about seven days, at the
distance of eight leagues from the shore, and
set to and fro by the currents. The ship was
exceedingly leaky ; added to which misfortune,
we were short of provisions, occasioned by the
length of our voyage : I therefore determined,
with reluctance, to abandon the search for the
present. I bore away before a light fair wind
that sprung up, for the island of Indenny, commonly called Santa Cruz, on passing which
the day following, several canoes came off, into
one of which the native of Tucopia embarked
and proceeded for the shore. During the night
we were becalmed within a few leagues of the
Volcano Island of Captain Carteret. We afterwards touched at the following islands before
getting to Bengal, *viz.* New Ireland, Duke of
York's Island near New Britain, in St. George's

Channel, Pulosiang, the Dutch settlement of
Bouro, one of the Moluccas, Savu, Christmas
Island, and reached Bengal on the 30th of
August. We laid at anchor in Gore's Harbour
in New Ireland for four days, where we completed our water, and were visited by the islanders, who were completely ignorant of the
several dialects spoken to them by the following persons, who were part of my crew and
passengers :—*viz.* Brian Boroo, a prince of New
Zealand ; Morgan Mackmurragh, a nobleman
of the same place ; four natives of Otaheite,
two of the Marquis Islands, and one of the
Sandwich Islands.

I attempted to converse with them in the
Beetee language, but without success; and
Martin Bushart was not more successful with
the Tucopian dialect. I then tried the Bengalee or Malay, but with the same result.

Convinced in my own mind that la Pérouse's
expedition had perished at the island of Mannicolo, and entertaining a sanguine hope that,
if means were immediately adopted, some of the
survivors might still be rescued, I determined,
on my arrival in Bengal, to use every endeavour to accomplish that object.

CHAPTER II.

NEGOCIATIONS WITH THE GOVERNMENT OF BRITISH IN-
DIA, WHICH LED TO THE FITTING OUT OF THIS EXPE-
DITION.

On the 19th September 1826 I commenced
my correspondence with the Bengal Government by addressing the following letter:

To C. LUSHINGTON, Esq., Chief Secretary to the Government in Bengal.

SIR :—Convinced as I am that you partake of the spirit of
philanthropy which has always marked the measures of the
British Government, I shall require no apology for bringing
to your notice the following circumstances, relative to the
unfortunate French navigator Count de la Pérouse, whose
fate has been involved in uncertainty for nearly half a century.
Any intelligence relative to one who so zealously promoted
the cause of science, and who fell a sacrifice to the pursuit,
cannot but be welcome to the world, more especially to the
nation which gave him birth.

I am further induced to this step by the decree of the
National Assembly, made in 1791 (of which I have the honour to enclose a copy), which enjoins, "that all ambassadors,
" consuls, &c. at the courts of foreign powers, do, in the
" name of humanity and of the arts and sciences, engage
" their respective sovereigns to charge all navigators and
" agents whatsoever, to make every inquiry in their power
" relative to the fate of the French frigates *Boussole* and
" *Astrolabe*, under the command of M. de la Pérouse,
" &c. &c." In conformity to this injunction, and the impulse of my own feelings, I shall now have the honour to lay

before you, for the information and consideration of the Right Hon. the Vice President in Council, such intelligence as I possess on the subject, with the hope that the statement may be laid before the French authorities in this country, in order that steps may be taken to set a question at rest which has so long been agitated, and restore to their native country some of the crew of the French frigates, whom, I have every reason to believe, are still in existence on one of the islands in the South Pacific. I beg to premise, that I shall advance nothing but what I am fully able to substantiate by the most conclusive evidence, oral and collateral.

It will be necessary, to make my narrative clearly understood, to go back to the year 1813; and I beg, Sir, for your attention, as I fear I may be somewhat tedious.

In September 1813 I was an officer in the Bengal ship *Hunter*, Captain Robson, on a voyage from Calcutta to New South Wales, the Fejee (or more correctly the Beetee) Islands, and Canton.

While laying at the Fejees, we discovered that several Europeans were living on the islands: some had been ship-wrecked, some deserters, and some discharged from various vessels which had touched at the islands prior to our arrival. We employed those men in the ship's boats, in collecting beche de mer, sandal-wood, and the other productions of the island. Unfortunately a misunderstanding arose between the natives of a town called Vilear, on the Sandal-wood coast, and an affray occurred on the 7th of September, in which all the Europeans were killed except myself, a man named Martin Bushart (a native of Stettin in Prussia, who had been on the island), and one of the ship's company, William Wilson. I beg to refer you for the particulars of the fight, and the means by which we escaped, to the Calcutta Government Gazette for the 6th of February 1817. Martin Bushart and a lascar, Achowlia, whom we also found on the island, took refuge on board the *Hunter*; and as they certainly would have been sacrificed if they landed again, they begged Captain Robson to give them a passage to the first land he fell in with in the prosecution of his voyage to Canton. This he agreed to.

We sailed from the Fejees on the 12th of September, and on the 20th made land, which proved to be the island of Tucopia, in lat. 12° 15′ S., and east lon. 169°. This island is called Barwell Island in the charts, but Tucopia by the natives. The ship *Barwell* passed it in 1798. The Prussian and his wife, a Fejee woman, with the lascar whom he brought with him, requested to be landed on this island; they were left accordingly, and we proceeded on our voyage.

On the 13th of May 1826, in command of my own ship, the *St. Patrick*, bound from Valparaiso to Pondicherry, I came in sight of the island of Tucopia. Prompted by curiosity as well as regard for an old companion in danger, I hove my ship to off Tucopia, with the hope of ascertaining whether the persons left there in 1813 were still alive. Shortly a canoe put off from the land and came along-side : in it was the lascar. Immediately after another canoe came off with Martin Bushart, the Prussian. They were both in sound health, and were exceedingly rejoiced to see me. They informed me that the natives had treated them kindly; that they lived very comfortably among them ; that no ship had touched there from the time they were first landed until about a twelvemonth previous to my arrival, when an English whaler visited the island for a short time, and a little after another whaler touched there. The lascar had an old silver sword-guard, which he sold for a few fishing-hooks to one of my people. I inquired of the Prussian where it had come from : he told me, that on his first arrival on the island, he saw in the possession of the natives the sword-guard, several chain-plates belonging to a ship, also a number of iron bolts, five axes, the handle of a silver fork, a few knives, tea-cups, glass beads and bottles, one silver spoon with a crest and cypher, and a sword, all of French manufacture. He further stated, that as soon as he became sufficiently acquainted with the language, he asked the natives how they obtained those articles, as they said that the *Hunter* was the first ship they ever had any communication with. They replied, that about two days' sail in their canoes to leeward there was a large group of islands, under the general name of Malicolo, to which they were frequently in the habit of making voyages, and that they obtained these articles from the inhabitants of the Malicolo Islands, who had a number of similar articles in their possession.

Upon examining the sword-guard minutely, I discovered, or thought I discovered, the initials of Pérouse stamped on it, which excited my suspicion, and made me more exact in my inquiries. I then, by means of Bushart and the lascar, questioned some of the islanders respecting the way in which their neighbours procured the silver and iron articles. They told me that the natives of Malicolo stated, that many years ago two large ships arrived at their islands; one anchored at the island of Whanoo, and the other at the island of Paiou, a little distance from each other. Some time after they anchored, and before they had any communication with the natives, a heavy gale arose, and both vessels were driven ashore. The ship that was anchored off Whanoo grounded upon the rocks. The natives came in crowds to the sea-side, armed with clubs, spears, and bows and arrows, and shot some arrows into the ship, and the crew in return fired the guns and some musketry on them, and killed several. The vessel continuing to beat violently against the rocks, shortly went to pieces. Some of the crew took to their boats, and were driven on shore, where they were to a man murdered, on landing, by the infuriated natives: others threw themselves into the sea; but if they reached the shore, it was only to share the fate of their wretched comrades, so that not a single soul escaped out of this vessel.

The ship which grounded on Paiou was driven on a sandy beach, and the natives came down and also shot their arrows into her; but the crew prudently did not resent the aggression, but held up axes, beads, and other toys as peace offerings; upon which the assailants desisted from hostilities. As soon as the wind moderated, an aged chief put off in a canoe to the ship. He was received with caresses, and presents offered him, which he accepted. He went on shore, pacified his countrymen, and assured them that the people on board were good and friendly men; upon which several of the natives came on board, and were all presented with toys. They soon supplied the crew with yams, fowls, bananas, cocoanuts, hogs, &c., and confidence was established between them.

The crew of the vessel were obliged to abandon her, and went on shore, bringing with them a great part of their stores. They remained for some time, and built a small vessel from the wreck of the large one. As soon as the small craft was ready to sail, as many as could conveniently get room embarked, being plentifully supplied with fresh provisions by the islanders. Several of their shipmates were left behind, and the commander promised to return speedily with presents for the natives, and to bring off the remainder of his crew: but she was never heard of afterwards by the islanders. Those who remained of the crew, distributed themselves among various chiefs, with whom they resided until their death. They had been left several muskets and some gunpowder by their comrades, and by means of these were of great service to their friends in battle with the neighbouring islanders.

The Tucopians asserted, that a great number of the articles are on the islands, in a state of preservation, which originally were taken from the vessels. About seven months before I touched at Tucopia, a canoe had returned from Whanoo and brought with them two large chain-plates, and an iron bolt about four feet in length. I myself spoke with some of the crew of the canoe which had last made the voyage to Malicolo. They said that there were abundance of iron materials still remaining on the islands belonging to the wrecks. Those which Martin Bushart saw were much oxydized and worn. The only silver spoon, as far as I could learn, that was brought to Tucopia, I regret extremely, was beat out into a wire by Bushart, for the purpose of making rings and other ornaments for the female islanders.

I have now in my possession the sword-guard and one of the rings made from the spoon, and some glass beads, all of which came from the wrecks.

The Prussian had never himself ventured to make a trip to Malicolo with the Tucopians, but the lascar had gone once or twice. He positively affirmed, that he had seen and conversed with two Europeans at Paiou, who spoke the language of the islanders. They were old men, he said, and told him that they had been wrecked several years ago in one of the ships, the remnants of which they shewed him. They told him, also, that no ship had touched at the islands since they had been on them; that most of their comrades were dead; but they had been so much scattered among the various islands, that they could not tell precisely how many of them were alive at the time. I have several other particulars of the conversations I held with the lascar and islanders, strongly corroborative of their statements; but I forbear mentioning them, as I fear I have already wearied your patience.

On hearing so many circumstances, all tending to confirm the suspicions which I conceived from the moment I saw the silver sword-guard with the cypher, I determined to proceed as quickly as possible to the Malicolo Island, examine the wrecks myself, and if practicable, bring off the two men of whom the lascar spoke, who said they were French. For this purpose I asked him to accompany me; but from the first I dreaded a refusal, and my fears were verified. He said he was married on the island, and comfortably settled; that it was his intention to remain there for life; and neither threats, intreaties, nor promises, could induce him to deviate from his resolve. I even promised to bring him back to Tucopia, but he would not listen to me. The Prussian, on the contrary, was tired of the savage life he had led for the last fourteen years, and was anxious to stay with me. I gladly acceded to his wishes, and also prevailed on a Tucopian to come with me, one of whom are at present on board my ship; and he shall be at any time forthcoming, to bear me out in the statement I have the honour to submit.

We sailed from Tucopia on the ... of May, and made the Malicolos in ...... days. Unfortunately as we made the land it fell a perfect calm, and continued so for seven days. At this time my stock of dry provisions was nearly exhausted, and there was no animal food to be procured on Tucopia. We lived principally on New Zealand potatoes and bananas. My vessel, too, was very leaky, from a long continuance at sea, and a person on board interested in the cargo had been, during my stay at the islands, particularly discontented, and had frequently and warmly remonstrated at what he considered my unnecessary and useless delay. For all these reasons, therefore, I determined, though with the greatest reluctance and regret, to take advantage of a breeze which sprung up, and continue my voyage; and, through the Almighty's assistance, I arrived at this port with much difficulty, on account of the leaky state of my ship.

I have thus, Sir, laid before you a plain and unadorned statement of the facts as they came into my possession, and trust that you, Sir, will excuse any informalities or inaccuracies which it may contain. I have from my boyhood been a son of the sea; it is needless to say, therefore, that "little can I grace my tale." It has truth, at least, for its ornament; and I trust the information it contains will not be unacceptable to the scientific men of Europe generally, and particularly to the French nation.

I now, Sir, offer my services for the rescuing of the individuals on the Malicolos, whom, I firmly believe, belonged to the crew of one of the frigates under the command of the Count de la Pérouse, and I think my information respecting the South Sea Islands may be rendered available for the purpose. I have been for eighteen years engaged in the South Sea trade, and speak with fluency the language of most of the islands: besides, having the Prussian with me, he may be eminently useful. If, therefore, the French authorities in this country should think fit to employ me, I shall most willingly undertake the service. But, at the same time, I beg distinctly and solemnly to declare, that I am actuated by no hopes of emolument to myself in making this statement; and, let what may occur, I shall, if possible, revisit the islands, and bring off the Europeans if alive, and ascertain more accurate details relative to the wrecked vessels.

I now, Sir, conclude, gratefully thanking you for following me through the lengthy details I have thought it necessary to go into, and beg to assure you, that

I am, &c.

(Signed)   PETER DILLON,

Master and Owner of the

Calcutta,

19th Sept. 1826.

ship St. Patrick.

In reply to the above letter I was invited to hold a verbal conversation with Mr. Lushington. This worthy gentleman, I am happy to say, coincided in all my views relative to the propriety of an attempt being made to rescue the unfortunate French survivors from the Mannicolos.

At this time I was about to proceed to Spanish America, in my own ship the *St. Patrick*, and it was first proposed that, on my return towards India I should touch at the Mannicolos, and bring off any person I found there belonging to the French frigates ; but some days after, finding I could not sail for some time to come, I wrote the following letter :—

To CHARLES LUSHINGTON, Esq., Chief Secretary to the Government in Bengal.

SIR :—In consequence of the conversation I had with you a few days ago, relative to the unfortunate Count de la Pérouse, I beg leave to say, that there is no probability of my returning to South America for a considerable time to come, and I cannot, of course, render any assistance to the unfortunate survivors of the French nobleman's crew.   However, for the sake of humanity and science, I hope some steps may be taken for their relief.   Such an opportunity will never again offer.   Here is Martin Bushart, the Prussian, mentioned in my former letter, who speaks the Tucopian language fluently, and could prevail on some of his friends to accompany any one who might be sent to Mannicolo, and through the means of those people all the necessary information relative to the shipwreck could be ascertained, in case the two Frenchmen seen by the lascar were dead.

I shall now submit the following proposal to your consideration :—In the first place, my ship, the *St. Patrick*, before she can go to sea requires to be docked and repaired. Should the authorities here deem it prudent to defray the expenses of the ship's repair and outfit, I would proceed immediately to the Mannicolos, and render the necessary assistance to the survivors, and, through the means of the Prussian and Tucopians, ascertain all the facts and particulars relative to the shipwrecks.

To secure the government here for what advances they might make, I would give a bottomry on the vessel, and make the insurance in their name to the amount of the sums advanced, with interest thereon. Independent of performing my duty towards the crew of the French ships, I would procure a cargo of spars, tortoise-shell, curiosities, &c. &c., which would enable me on my return to liquidate the sum so advanced on bottomry, and depend on the honour of the French government to remunerate me for my services. Should the Government here disapprove of the above plan, I beg leave to submit the following one :—namely, to supply me with one of the Bengal pilot vessels, manned and armed in such way as I may point out; and I will perform the voyage under their directions, still depending on the honour of the French government, and the faith of the French National Decree passed on the 9th of February 1791, for such remuneration as they may think proper to award for my services.

I have, &c.

Calcutta,   (Signed) PETER DILLON.
10th Oct. 1826.

In reply to this letter I received a note from Mr. S. Fraser, acting secretary to government, Mr. Lushington having gone to sea for the benefit of his health. This caused me much uneasiness, as he was a kind and cordial supporter of my propositions. However, I was happy to find in his successor, Mr. George Swinton, secretary to the government in the secret and political department, and Mr. E. Molony, the acting secretary to government, two able friends and supporters, who rendered me every assistance in their power.—The note was as follows :—

To Captain P. Dillon.

Sir :—I am directed to acknowledge the receipt of your letter of the 10th instant, and in reply to inform you, that the Right Honourable the Vice President in Council is fully disposed to assist in the furtherance of your liberal and humane views for the relief of the survivors of Count de la Pérouse's crew ; but before deciding on the steps to be taken, has referred your letter to the Marine Board, with a view to obtain a report from them as to the probable expense of repairing your vessel, and how far the bottomry and insurance offered by you may be considered as affording sufficient security for the reimbursement of any sum which the government may advance as requested by you.

I am, &c.

Council Chamber,   (Signed)   S. Fraser,
12th Oct. 1826.   Acting Secretary to Government.

After receiving this reply I heard nothing more on the subject till the 25th of November, when Mr. Sargent, one of the members of the Marine Board, informed me that Mr. Sepping, the Hon. Company's marine surveyor, had examined my ship, and reported that the probable amount of her repair and outfit would be about 40,000 rupees, and that she would then be totally unfit for the Hon. Company's service, on account of her large size and draft of water. I was astonished at his report, knowing the vessel to be a beautiful model, perfectly sound, and built of the almost everlasting wood of Paraguay in South America. Knowing there was no appeal from the sentence

of Mr. Sepping, I did not urge any farther the
proposal of employing my ship ; though I was
well aware that the expense attending the out-
fitting and sending of one of the Hon. Company's ships would amount to at least a lac and
a half of rupees.   Mr. Sargent asked me if I
would have any objection to proceed to the
Mannicolo Islands on the Hon. Company's ship
of war *Ternate*, then lying at Rangoon, intimating that her commander would be placed
under my directions : to which I replied, I
had no objections whatever. He then informed
me, that it was the wish of the Right Hon.
the Vice-President in Council, Lord Combermere, that I should be despatched as soon as
possible, and that a government steam-vessel
was to proceed for Rangoon in a few days,
when it would be necessary for me to hold
myself in readiness, with my interpreters, Indians, &c., to embark in her, and proceed there
to join the *Ternate* and sail for the Mannicolos.

On the evening of the first Wednesday in
November I was invited by Mr. Horace Hay-
man Wilson, secretary to the Asiatic Society,
to accompany him to a meeting of that distinguished body at their rooms in Chowringhee.
I accordingly accepted the invitation, and on
entering was introduced to several of the members. Before the meeting broke up, Colonel

Bryant, one of its members, who sat next to me, entered into conversation respecting my voyages to and from the islands in the South Seas, and informed me that he attached great importance to my statement relative to the loss of the *Boussole* and *Astrolabe*, and that as a member of the Asiatic Society, which had been embodied for the purpose of disseminating knowledge, he considered it a duty incumbent on him to make a proposal to the meeting, to cause a deputation from their members to wait upon the Vice-President in Council, to recommend that some step should be taken to rescue the survivors of the Count de la Pérouse's expedition from the islands where they were supposed to have been shipwrecked. He further observed, that as the Count had been engaged in the pursuit of knowledge for the benefit of mankind in general, he or the survivors had a strong claim on the consideration of the Asiatic Society.

A motion was accordingly made to that effect, and unanimously approved by the meeting. The Hon. J. H. Harington, president of the society, and one of the members of the supreme council, mentioned, in an address from the chair, that he understood arrangements were making by order of the Vice-President in Council, issued to the Marine Board, for sending me, in the

way proposed by Mr. Sargent, to Mannicolo; however, Colonel Bryant's motion should
meet with his cordial support. One of the
members then present, a medical gentleman on
the Bengal establishment, said it would afford
him great pleasure to accompany me on my
expedition to Mannicolo, as he entertained· a
great love of scientific research. On inquiring
who this person was, I learnt from Colonel
Bryant that it was Doctor Robert Tytler, who
had written so much on the cholera morbus,
Ouse rice, the Queen of Sheba, Mount Ophir,
and other such subjects. About half-past nine
or ten o'clock the meeting broke up.

The next day Doctor Tytler met me at one
of the auction-rooms, when we talked over
the matter relative to la Pérouse, and he then
expressed himself in the following terms: That
he had a great wish to acquire a knowledge of
the islands in the South Seas, and their productions; that he was particularly desirous of
quitting Calcutta for ten or twelve months,
being much persecuted by the public authorities, on account of his independent spirit in
having brought to the notice of the public,
through the medium of the gazettes, the "vil-
lanous conduct" (as he termed it) of the commissariat department in the late war with Rangoon, where thousands of his Majesty's subjects

perished, as he alleged, through the measures
adopted by the above department. He also
stated, that he was placed in a similar predica-
ment with respect to the officers of the Marine
Board, having brought to the notice of the
public their "inhuman" conduct in sending a
ship to Arracan for the sick and wounded, which
with the greatest difficulty could be prevented
from sinking, owing to her leaky state. His elo-
quence, and the melancholy account he gave of
his situation and sufferings, made such an impression on me, that I really fancied him a most
patriotic and persecuted man ; I therefore promised to use my interest to get him attached
to the expedition as surgeon, and recommended
him to write to the Government on the subject,
expressing his wish to accompany me, that I
and my friends might use our influence in his
behalf. The return he made me for this act of
kindness will hereafter appear.

On mentioning to a friend, a gentleman high
in the civil service, my intention of taking Doc
tor Tytler with me, he remarked, " You will be
much better without him ; he never has been
placed under the command of any individual
as yet, whom he has not tried to scandalize and
ruin : his general disposition is mischievous,
and you will feel the effects of it before you

return." This warning I was sorry to find so
very soon verified.

I heard nothing more on the subject of the
expedition until Saturday the 11th of November, when I was sent for by Mr. Sargent,
who informed me that the steam-vessel would
not be ready to sail for a considerable time,
and that it would be a difficult matter to
victual the *Ternate* at Rangoon for so long a
voyage. That besides this, the European crew
on board of her were engaged to serve in
the country, and might object to go on so
long a voyage : he would therefore recommend
my taking the command of the Hon. Company's
ship *Research*, which vessel had just arrived in
the river from Rangoon, and proceed with her
to Mannicolo. To this proposal I agreed. He
then requested me to make out a statement
of such a crew as would be required, and we
immediately arranged that part of the business.

I then recommended that a surgeon, naturalist, draughtsman, and botanist, should be attached to the expedition, for the purpose of obtaining all the knowledge possible relative to the
character of these unfrequented islands and
their inhabitants ; and observed, that if an individual could be procured (such as Doctor Wal-
lich, of the Hon. Company's botanic garden)

who understood the science of surgery as well as natural history and botany, it would be a great saving in the outfit of the expedition. I therefore ventured to propose my new friend and acquaintance, Doctor Tytler, to fill the above situation, as he had given me to understand that he was perfectly well acquainted with all the above sciences.*

On the 16th November I received the annexed letter, with the three documents which follow it, from Mr. E. Malony, acting secretary to the Government.

To Captain P. Dillon.

Sir:—In continuation of the letter addressed to you by Mr. Acting Secretary Fraser on the 12th ultimo, I am directed to inform you, that the Right Hon. the Vice-President in Council has this day been pleased to resolve, that the Hon. Company's surveying vessel, the *Research*, shall be placed under your command, for the purpose of enabling you to proceed to the Mannicolo Islands, with a view to obtain full and accurate information in regard to the shipwreck of the two vessels enumerated in your narrative of the 19th September last, which you consider, apparently upon very probable grounds, to have been the French frigates under the command of the Count la Pérouse, of whose fate no certain accounts have hitherto been ascertained.

I am likewise directed to forward to you, for your information and guidance, a copy of a resolution this day passed by

---

* He indeed pretended to every kind of knowledge, human and divine, with about as much justice as to the above sciences, as I soon after discovered.

Government, in which you will find more particularly detailed
the objects which this Government have in view, in fitting out
the expedition now placed under your command. You will
likewise receive herewith, copies of letters which have this
day been addressed, by order of Government, to the Marine
Board and to Doctor Tytler, respectively.

You will be pleased to place yourself in communication
with the Marine Board, from which authority you will receive
such further instructions as may be necessary for your guidance in the performance of the duty now entrusted to you ;
and it only remains to intimate to you, the reliance which
Government places in your zealous exertions, to leave nothing
undone to accomplish the object of this enterprize, and their
most anxious hope that those exertions may be crowned with
complete success.

I am, &c.

Council Chamber,   (Signed)   E. MOLONY,
16th Nov. 1826.   Acting Secretary to the Government.

EXTRACT *from the* PROCEEDINGS *of the Right Hon. the
Vice-President in Council, in the General Department,
under date the* 16th *November* 1826.

Read and recorded a letter from the Secretary to the
Asiatic Society, dated 4th instant ; a letter from Doctor
R. Tytler, dated 6th instant ; and a letter from the Marine
Board, dated 13th instant.

Read again the proceedings of the 12th and 24th ultimo,
on the subject of Captain Dillon's proposal to Government to
proceed to the Mannicolo Isles in search of the survivors of
the Count de la Pérouse.

Resolution 1. Upon a mature consideration of all the circumstances set forth in the correspondence above recorded,
the Vice-President in Council is satisfied that the facts which
have been laid before Government by Captain Dillon are

sufficient to justify the hope, that if proper measures are adopted, some certain information may be obtained in regard to the loss of the French frigates *Boussole* and *Astrolabe*, commanded by the celebrated Count de la Pérouse, whose fate, notwithstanding the most anxious inquiries during a period of nearly forty years, has never yet been ascertained.

2. The facts which are detailed in the narrative submitted by Captain Dillon, appear to have been accurately ascertained. They afford in themselves a reasonable ground for the conclusion that the French frigates were actually lost at the Mannicolo Islands, inasmuch as there is nothing connected with them, either as to date or geographical situation, which is inconsistent with the latest ascertained information on record, in regard to the course pursued by la Pérouse; and it is understood, in particular, that the sword-guard in the possession of Captain Dillon has been inspected by the officers of the French service, and is considered by them clearly to be of the form and description worn by naval officers of that nation at the period when the Count de la Pérouse is supposed to have been shipwrecked. They conclude, also, from an examination of the cypher on it, which appears to correspond with the initials of that unfortunate commander, that it probably belonged to him.

3. There appears, too, from the rest of the evidence adduced by Captain Dillon, to be at least a probability that some of the crews of the ships wrecked at the Mannicolo Isles (whether they shall really prove to have been those commanded by la Pérouse or others) are still in existence.

4. Adverting, therefore, to the above circumstances, to the anxiety which has been expressed by the French authorities at Chandernagore that the inquiry should be prosecuted, and to the deep interest which the fate of la Pérouse has ever excited in Europe, his Lordship in Council cannot doubt that the Hon. Court of Directors will fully approve any measures, founded on information holding out a reasonable

hope of success, which this Government may adopt, for endeavouring to ascertain the fate of the French frigates, and
of discovering and restoring to their country any of the survivors of their crews who may be found.

5. His Lordship in Council accordingly resolves, in pur-
suance of the recommendation of the Marine Board, that the
Hon. Company's surveying vessel the *Research* shall be
immediately fitted out in the manner proposed by the Board,
and placed under the command of Captain Dillon, for the
purpose of proceeding to the Mannicolo Islands, by such route
and under such instructions as shall be furnished, and of
endeavouring, by all practicable means, to ascertain fully
every circumstance connected with the loss of the two ships
alluded to in his narrative, as well as to discover any individuals of the crews of those vessels who may still be in
existence.

6. The Marine Board will be requested to prepare and
submit, for the approval of Government, a draft of any instructions with which they deem it necessary that Captain Dillon
shall be furnished. From the long experience which Captain
Dillon has had of the manners and customs of the natives of
the South Sea Islands, it is obvious that much must be left
to his discretion; and his Lordship in Council does not
doubt that his proceedings, in furtherance of the important
duty now entrusted to him, will be conducted with all the
prudence required, without in any manner diminishing the
zeal and energy which the occasion is calculated to call into
action.

7. The Vice-President in Council fully concurs in opinion
with the Marine Board, that an officer should be attached to
the expedition in the capacity of naturalist and mineralogist,
as likewise to afford medical aid to those engaged in it; and.
accordingly his Lordship in Council is pleased to resolve that
Dr. R. Tytler, a surgeon on this establishment, who has, with
a spirit of enterprize highly creditable to himself, volunteered

his services on the occasion, shall be attached to the expedition in the above capacity.*

8. Captain Dillon, as commander of the expedition, will of course direct all the proceedings which are to be adopted when the *Research* shall arrive at her destination. As the commander of the vessel, and the chief director of all the communications which are made with the natives on the islands, there is no doubt that Captain Dillon's time will be fully occupied, and therefore, in addition to keeping an accurate and full journal of all matters connected with natural history, mineralogy, and generally of a scientific nature, his Lordship in Council is pleased to assign to Dr. Tytler the additional duty of keeping a separate and complete journal of all occurrences, and of every information connected with the main object of the expedition; and his Lordship in Council is satisfied that this duty will be cheerfully undertaken and zealously performed by Dr. Tytler.

9. The Marine Board will be requested to select and nominate, for the approbation of Government, a fit person to be attached to the expedition in the capacity of draughtsman, reporting at the same time the scale of allowance to be assigned to the individual selected for that duty.

10. Adverting, likewise, to the anxiety which the officers of the French Government must feel in regard to the objects of the present expedition, his Lordship in Council is further pleased to resolve, that a communication shall be made to

---

* From the eagerness with which the Government embraced the offer of Doctor Tytler, it is clear they were very glad of so good an opportunity to get rid of him, at least for a while. He had some years before been sent off to Bencoolen, a remote convict station, with a similar view. Knowing his propensity to use his pen to the great annoyance of every one, they were well pleased at a prospect of finding employment where, it was to be hoped, his literary talents might be exercised in such a way as to do good instead of doing mischief.

the chief of the French establishments in Bengal, with a view to ascertain whether he is desirous that a gentleman of that nation shall accompany the expedition. Should he nominate an individual for the above purpose, his Lordship in Council will direct that he be suitably accommodated on board the *Research.*

11. The Marine Board are authorized to communicate fully with Captain Dillon, and to take immediate measures for completely manning and equipping the *Research,* in such manner, both as regards stores and arms, as may be deemed by them necessary. His Lordship in Council likewise, adverting to the period (probably eight or ten months) during which he will be engaged on this duty, authorizes the payment of 6,000 rupees, as proposed by the Board, to Captain Dillon, as a compensation for his services ; one-half of which they are hereby empowered to advance to him immediately. The Board are also authorized to attach to the expedition the several individuals enumerated in the last paragraph of their letter of the 13th instant, at the rate of pay therein specified.

12. His Lordship in Council further directs, that the Marine Board will call upon Captain Dillon to furnish them with a detailed statement of such articles as he may deem it advisable to take with him, for the purpose of making presents to the natives of the Mannicolo Islands, or of being exchanged for provisions, or to be otherwise used in facilitating the objects of the expedition. The articles to be shipped for the above purposes will, of course, be selected by Captain Dillon, and the Board are authorized to expend in the purchase of them a sum not exceeding 2,000 sicca rupees.

13. His Lordship in Council is pleased to assign to Dr. Tytler a salary of 800 rupees per mensem, in lieu of all pay and allowances which he would draw as a military surgeon : to take effect from the 1st proximo.

To G. Chester, Esq. and the Members of the Marine Board.

Gentlemen :—I am directed by the Right Hon. the Vice-President in Council to acknowledge the receipt of your letter dated the 13th instant, and, in reply, to forward to you the accompanying copy of a resolution this day passed by Government, on the subject of the expedition to be commanded by Captain Dillon.

You are requested to take measures for carrying the orders contained in that resolution into effect with as little delay as possible ; and you will be pleased to submit at an early date, the draft of the instructions alluded to in the sixth paragraph : in preparing which, you will clearly keep in mind that the entire command of the expedition is to be entrusted to Captain Dillon, and that every person who is attached to it, is distinctly placed under his orders. The instructions should likewise contain distinct orders to Captain Dillon, to avoid all delay which can, consistently with the object in view, be obviated, and that he is to return to this port, after he has accomplished the duty entrusted to him at the Mannicolo Islands, with all practical despatch.

In nominating for the approval of Government an individual to accompany the expedition as draughtsman, you are requested particularly to specify the nature of the duties on which you conceive such an officer may be usefully employed, and to prepare such instructions for his guidance as you may deem proper.

With reference to the eleventh paragraph of the resolution, by which you have been authorized, in communication with Captain Dillon, to provide such articles for presents and barter with the natives of the Mannicolo Islands as he may consider necessary, to the value of 2,000 rupees, I am directed to intimate to you, that if Captain Dillon shall consider it advisable to take with him any number of muskets, or other small arms and ammunition, the number required can probably be conveniently furnished from the arsenal, on your making an application for that purpose to the Military Department.

With reference to the appointment of Dr. Tytler for the duties specified in the resolution, you will be pleased to assign to him suitable accommodation on board the *Research*. Doctor Tytler will, of course, be accommodated at Captain Dillon's table, for which you are requested to make suitable provision in directing the equipment of the expedition.

I have, &c.

Council Chamber,   (Signed)   E. MOLONY,
16th Nov. 1826.   Acting Secretary to Government.

EXTRACT of a Letter to R. TYTLER, Esq., M.D.

SIR :—I am directed by the Right Hon. the Vice-President in Council to acknowledge the receipt of your letter dated 6th instant, and, in reply, to transmit for your information a copy of a resolution this day passed by Government, in regard to the expedition to be commanded by Captain Dillon.

That document will put you in full possession of the duties which the Government expect you to perform, and the Marine Board have been directed to assign to you suitable accommodations on board the *Research*, in your capacity of naturalist and medical officer attached to the expedition.

In performance of the duties thus assigned to you, it is the wish of Government that you shall clearly understand that you are, in common with every other officer attached to the expedition, placed under the general command of Captain Dillon; and his Lordship in Council does not doubt that your cordial and most zealous endeavours will be exerted, to aid that officer in the final and successful accomplishment of the important object which has led to the undertaking.

I am, &c.

Fort-William,   (Signed)   E. MOLONY,
16th Nov. 1826.   Acting Secretary to Government.

On receiving the letter from Mr. Molony,
with a copy of the proceedings in council, I
was highly pleased to find Doctor Tytler had
been appointed to the expedition according to
my suggestions. My time of rejoicing, however, was short ; for many days had not elapsed
when I had occasion to regret that I had en-
cumbered myself with so dangerous an assistant,
as I discovered that he had already begun
secretly backbiting and misrepresenting me, so
soon as the object for which he had courted my
friendship seemed to be secured.

In consequence of letters received from the
Government and Marine Board, I entered into
arrangements with Captain Clapperton, one of
the assistants to the Master-attendant, to meet
him and Mr. Seppings, the Hon. Company's
marine surveyor, on board the *Research*, on the
22d of November, at 7 o'clock in the morning,
when I took charge of her, and in conjunction
with the surveyors made the necessary arrangements for fitting out the ship.

On returning to town from Kidderpore, where
the ship lay at anchor, I called on my agent
in Calcutta, and informed him of the engagement I had entered into with the Government, and requested him to take charge of my
own ship, the *Saint Patrick*, with her cargo,
and to dispose of both to the best advantage on

my account. In a few days after the *Research* was hauled into dock for examination, and nothing being found necessary in the way of repairs, she was again hauled out. The crew then began to fit her out ; but the want of gun-carriages, which had to be supplied, detained us a considerable time.

On Thursday, 14th of December, I was taken ill with a severe cold, and sent for Doctor Tytler ; who came in, felt my pulse, ordered my head to be shaved, took thirty-two ounces of blood from my arm, and immediately after called in two other medical gentlemen. This attention I naturally supposed, arose from the purest motives of humanity. On this and the two following days I was up and walking about the room, not being in the least danger, as was evident from my ability to take such exercise, of which Dr. Tytler was well aware. On Sunday, the 17th, however, a friend called at my house, and seeing me out of bed and dressed ready to go to church, expressed great surprise. He informed me that within the last three days Doctor Tytler had made two communications to the Marine Board, in which he had represented me to be in such a state of health that it would be impossible for me to proceed on the voyage, and that it was therefore necessary, without loss of time, to appoint another com-

mander to the expedition.   He also alleged,
that I was subject to apoplectic fits, that a return of them was to be expected, that I should
be carried off by the first attack with which I
was visited, and that I was now labouring under
insanity.* I asked my friend how the man could
be so void of good faith as to make such false
representations ; that through the whole course
of my life I had enjoyed most excellent health,
and safely could make oath that I never had a
fit of any kind from the day of my birth.   My
friend replied, " You do not know Tytler : he
is one of the most cowardly fellows on earth :
he has been frequently horsewhipped and otherwise chastised for his insolence.   He has been
informed that you are not in the habit of allowing people to insult you with impunity, and
therefore wishes to get you out of the way, that
a creature of his own may be put into the command of the expedition."

My friend took his leave after staying with
me about half an hour.   Immediately after, the
celebrated Doctor Savage, who wrote the account of New Zealand, one of the medical gentlemen called in by Tytler on the 14th ultimo,
paid me a visit.   He informed me that the day

* It is proper to notice here, that the person who invented this
calumny, has long since been placed under restraint for the very
malady which he wickedly imputed to me : so awful and speedy,
sometimes, are the dispensations of retributive justice !

before he had received a letter on service,
requiring his opinion as to the state of my
health, and whether I could with safety take
charge of the expedition; to which he had replied, that he certainly saw nothing to prevent
me. Doctor Adam, secretary to the Medical
Board, the other gentleman called in by Tytler
to see me, was of the same opinion as Doctor
Savage. I could hardly bring myself to believe
that any man in his senses could have acted in
the treacherous manner that Tytler had done.
On Monday, the 18th, I called on Doctor Fle-
ming, who had been in the habit of acting as
my medical adviser for the last ten years, and
obtained from him a certificate that he had attended me for that long period, had always
considered me to possess a very strong constitution, and never knew me to be subject to fits
of any kind. I immediately after went to the
police-office and had an affidavit drawn out, to
which I made oath, to the effect that I was not
subject to apoplectic fits or constitutional disease of any kind.

With these two documents I proceeded to
the Marine Board, the gentlemen composing
which were surprised to see me, after having
been represented only two days before as so
dangerously ill, that I should not be able to take
charge of the expedition. I immediately after

waited on the acting chief secretary of Government, who received me with his usual cordiality,
and expressed himself quite at a loss to account
for the motives that induced Doctor Tytler to
make the statements which he did regarding
my health.   However, I soon unriddled the
mystery, by plainly shewing him what Tytler's
plans were.

While industriously circulating these reports
of my utter incapacity to command the expedition, Doctor Tytler had intimated that with any
marine officer to take charge of the ship, he
was perfectly competent to conduct the expedition himself, and carry it through to the satisfaction of the Government, with the assistance
of Martin Bushart and the South-Sea islanders.

Let me here observe, that I had been for
many years collecting the intelligence and
forming the connections that enabled me to
undertake this expedition.   That in my last
voyage from Valparaiso, I had brought with me
from different islands eleven natives of the
South Seas, one of the rank of a prince, with
another of noble birth sent as his companion,
who were to serve me as guides and interpreters, besides Martin Bushart the Prussian ;
that I had maintained them for a long period
by sea and land at my sole expense ; and had
also relinquished my own mercantile pursuits

for the sake of this voyage of discovery, on which my whole mind was bent. What were my thoughts and feelings, then, to find myself nearly tricked out of it by a man brought forward and patronized by myself, who had never incurred one farthing of expense on account of the object in view, and who knew no more of the language or manners and customs of the South Sea islanders than the great Mogul !

I mentioned the above conduct of the Doctor's to some of my friends, who requested me to take no notice of what had passed. I complied with the advice of those who had so kindly interested themselves in getting my plans carried into execution.

About this time a paragraph appeared in the *John Bull*, a Calcutta newspaper, stating that the brig *Margaret*, belonging to Messrs. Montgomery and Co., and commanded by Captain Corbin, had sailed for the Mannicolo islands, to render assistance to the unfortunate survivors of la Pérouse's crew. The Doctor on reading over this paragraph became outrageous, and vehemently asserted that Messrs. Montgomery and Co. were interfering with the arrangements of Government, and ought to be sent out of the country ; that it was shameful to attempt in this manner to deprive the person who made the discovery at the Mannicolo Islands of the reward to which he was justly entitled; though that such occurrences were not without a precedent, the great Columbus himself, the discoverer of America, was an instance. The Doctor then hurried from one end of Calcutta to the other, as if quite bereft of his senses, making inquiries about the mysterious voyage of the *Margaret* (which however all vanished in smoke). He concluded in his summary way by declaring that Montgomery and Co. ought to be transported for seven years to Botany Bay: so keenly was the Doctor alive to his own interest when the honour of the enterprize was threatened to be carried off by another party.

Finding all his artifices about my state of health were ineffectual, and that in spite of his predictions I had come to life again, the Doctor devised a new plan for upsetting the expedition. His attack was now on the vessel, and he gave out that the *Research* was completely unfit for the voyage; that she would not steer, sailed badly, and would certainly be lost. He applied to me to join him in a protest against the officers of the Marine Board for putting the Government to a useless expense, by selecting a vessel which they were aware was totally unfit for the voyage and must go down. I replied, that I considered myself as good a judge of a ship as he was; and that I and my crew were

perfectly satisfied with the *Research*'s capabili-
ties, and considered her a very fit vessel for the
voyage ; that if she proved otherwise, however,
I would get another at Van Diemen's Land to
assist me as a tender; and that he might protest if he thought proper, but not to attempt to
mention my name in his protest. Thus ended
for the present his attack on the character of
the good ship *Research*. On the 23d of December I received the following letter of instructions from the Marine Board :—

SIR :—Government having been pleased to appoint you to
the command of the Hon. Company's ship *Research*, for the
purpose of ascertaining, if possible, whether the French frigates *la Boussole* and *l'Astrolabe*, under the command of the
late Count de la Pérouse, were wrecked among the islands
composing the archipelago to the northward of New Caledonia, which there is great reason to believe was the case
from the information furnished by you, and, in the event of
this conjecture proving true, to institute strict inquiry
whether any of the officers and crew of those ships still survive ; I am directed by the Marine Board to desire, immediately the *Research* is ready, that you will proceed to sea,
and make the best of your way either to Port Dalrymple or
the Derwent, for the purpose of procuring refreshments,
replenishing your stores, and making such refit as may be
required. Your course will be to the south-east, outside the
islands lying off Sumatra, by which you will have the benefit
of the north-west monsoons, and on getting the south-east
trade, you will proceed to the southward, until you reach the
westerly winds, when you will shape your way to Van Diemen's Land, to fill up your supplies at one of the places

above-mentioned. This you will be careful to carry into execution with all possible despatch, and not suffer delay by any intermediate researches not connected with the object of the expedition.

2. On quitting Van Diemen's Land you will proceed to the north-east, keeping to the southward of Norfolk Island and to the eastward of New Caledonia and the New Hebrides, and being careful to give the two last a good offing, as well to avoid calm and variable winds in the neighbourhood of the land, as to give you sufficient easting to enable you to make the island of Tucopia without difficulty.

3. On arriving at Tucopia, you will, through Martin Bushart and the lascar, if still there, from each of whom you have already received much information, make any inquiry calculated to produce a further confirmation of the present impression, and endeavour by all means to induce the latter, or other inhabitants of the island who may be able to speak to the point, to proceed with you to the Mannicolo islands. It is not unlikely that on your arrival at Tucopia, you may find some of the inhabitants of the Mannicolos about to return from their periodical visits during the north-west monsoon.

4. The measures to be adopted in the immediate search of the Mannicolos must necessarily be left much to your own discretion. Should you be fortunate enough to discover the wreck of the frigates, you will endeavour to ascertain as correctly as possible all particulars of their loss, and be careful to obtain the most complete and satisfactory proofs obtainable of the identity of the vessels, as well as to recover any property which might be capable of being proved to belong to any of the unfortunate sufferers.

5. You will of course, in case of discovering the wreck, make the most minute inquiries as to the existence of any of the crews, and it is in prosecuting these inquiries that the Board consider your prudence, vigilance, and discretion, to be more immediately required, since they will necessarily lead to

communications with the natives on shore much more minute than your inquiries after the wreck may require. Should any survivors be found, it is needless to say that you are to offer them the opportunity of returning to their native land, and to afford them every comfort in your power.

6. Should you, however, not discover the wreck in the islands situated to the westward of Tucopia, it will remain for you to be guided in any further research among the other islands, whether from the east towards the Louiscarde, or to the southward, by such information as you may have received. But before you proceed to act on any information which may tend to delay your return to this port after an unsuccessful search of the Mannicolos, you will call a meeting,* composed of Dr. Tytler, M. Chaigneau, the French officer who accompanies the expedition, and your chief officer, at which the probability of success is to be discussed, and the whole subject maturely considered, and you will consider yourself bound to abide by the decision of the meeting; which decision, with the reasons on which it is grounded, is to be recorded in writing at full length, and communicated to the Board for the information of Government. Should the voices be equal, you will of course have the casting vote, leaving the dissentient members the option of recording the reasons of their dissent. When the resolution is taken to return, whether successful or not, you are positively enjoined to make the best of your way to this port, and on no account to be led away by any desire for researches, however laudable in themselves, much less to admit of an hour's delay by motives of personal benefit to any individual on the expedition.

7. You will of course keep, for transmission to Govern-

---

* The proposed consultation was to be confined, it will be observed, to this point only, the course to be pursued in such a case as that supposed: in all other matters and emergencies, the commander of the expedition was to follow his own discretion.

ment on your return, a duplicate of your journal, which is to
be as full as possible on all subjects of nautical interest
calculated to be useful to other navigators; and to lose no
opportunity of observing, especially among the islands, whose
bearings and distances are to be carefully noted at the same
time, together with the depth and nature of the soundings.
The observations themselves are to be noted in the journal,
for the purpose of being worked at leisure. It is of importance that every island which you visit should be accurately
described; its approach noted, whether dangerous or not;
the anchoring places particularly marked, and their character described, as well as the best landing-places —whether
water and refreshments are procurable—their quality—the
description of articles best adapted for bartering with the natives—their character—all matters connected with the tides
—the general state of the winds and weather—particularly
when the monsoon changes. You are moreover particularly
requested to ascertain, as far as possible, the extent to
which the north-west monsoon prevails.

8. Although you are not to suffer yourself to be drawn
away from the main object of the expedition, yet you are to
allow every advantage to be taken of circumstances to enable
Doctor Tytler to make observations in natural history.
Dr. Tytler having been directed by Government to keep an
accurate and full journal of all matters connected with natural history, mineralogy, and generally of a scientific nature,
you will consider it one of your first duties to afford him all
the assistance in your power, consistently with the more immediate purposes of the expedition: consequently you will
afford every facility for the conveyance on board of all specimens of the animal, mineral, and vegetable kingdoms, which
Doctor Tytler may be successful in collecting, and you can
conveniently stow on board, causing the utmost care to be
taken for their preservation. To secure accuracy in respect
to the local position of the ship in the journal of Dr. Tytler,

you are to furnish him in writing under your signature, at
noon each day, with the latitude and longitude of the ship,
noting whether by lunar observation, dead reckoning, or
chronometer; and at intermediate times, when required by
Doctor Tytler, you will in like manner make known to him
the change which may have taken place.

9. Government having also authorized a draughtsman to be
employed on the expedition, Mr. Russell has been appointed
to that situation; and you are to allow Doctor Tytler to
have the full benefit of his talents, in making such drawings
as he may desire. Mr. Russell will, of course, take views of
all islands, bays, harbours, headlands, &c., and construct such
charts as may be necessary to shew the relative positions of
the different islands.

10. At no period of the voyage are you to take on board
any passengers, except such as may be required for the purpose of information relative to the object of the expedition.

11. It is scarcely necessary to urge on your mind the
great advantages which must arise from conciliating the natives of the different islands which you may visit in your
search; it will be one of your most essential duties to impress
on all persons composing the expedition the absolute necessity of abstaining from every thing having a tendency to irritate the natives of any island, especially those belonging to
the islands situated in the immediate vicinity of your search.
The strictest injunctions are to be given as to the use of
fire-arms, which are not to be resorted to but in cases of
extreme danger, which however, from your intimate acquaintance with the general character of the South Sea
islanders, and the opportunities you have for conciliating
them, the Board trust will not occur.

12. Every precaution is to be taken to prevent collusion,
by restraining the intercourse of the natives with the crew
as much as possible; confining the bartering for commodities
within moderate limits, and not allowing too many natives

to be on board at the same time. This latter you can effect by means of your boarding nettings, which are at all times, when among the islands, to be spread.

13. The above precautions will reduce the opportunities for those petty acts of pilfering on the part of the natives, which have on so many occasions produced fatal results. It will nevertheless be incumbent on you to use every other precaution against surprise, never on any account suffering the deck to be an instant without an officer in charge of it, and on the alert.

14. The Board deem it also proper to warn you against placing too much confidence in the natives who accompany you from this port; by a judicious use of the articles intrusted to you as presents for the natives ; a mild and conciliating tone in every intercourse with them ; and, what is of as great importance as either, a mutual good-will and cordiality among yourselves, you will afford the best hopes of ultimate success.

15. You are not, during any period of your voyage, to allow an opportunity to pass without communicating to the Board, for the information of Government, the fullest detail possible of your proceedings.

16. The route which it may be most expedient for you to take on your return home, must be left to your own judgment and discretion, with a view to the most expeditious passage, which you will consider your sole object, after the search shall have terminated. On your arrival at Calcutta you are to wait on the Board, with your journal and all other papers or documents connected with the voyage.

17. The entire command of the expedition being intrusted to you under the sanction of Government, every person attached to it will be informed that he is distinctly placed under your orders. The Board have the fullest reliance that the confidence placed in your prudence, judgment, and discretion, will be met by a demeanour calculated

to ensure perfect civility among all parties composing the expedition; who will be given to understand, that good conduct will not fail to secure to them the favourable consideration of the Government, while those who conduct themselves in a manner tending either to defeat or throw discredit on a project calculated of itself to keep alive the best feelings, will not fail to meet its severe displeasure.*

18. Since writing the above, the Board have been furnished by Government with a communication from Captain Cordier, the chief of the French establishments in Bengal, from which there is reason to believe that the French corvette *l'Astrolabe* was despatched in April last from Toulon, for the purpose of exploring the coast of New Guinea and those of New Zealand, with a view to discover the spot where the Count de la Pérouse perished.

19. You will very likely fall in with this vessel at sea, or at some of the ports or places at which you may touch, in which case you are desired to make the commander acquainted with the object and destination of the *Research*, and with the grounds for your supposing that the French frigates under the command of the Count de la Pérouse were wrecked on or in the vicinity of the Mannicolo islands.

20. The Board also desire it to be observed as an additional instruction, that all journals, papers, or documents of whatsoever description which may be in the possession of any individuals, including Monsieur Chaigneau (whose papers will ultimately, of course, be forwarded unopened to the French authorities) be sealed up by the person to whom they belong, and be delivered to you on your return to this port, for the purpose of being transmitted by you to this office; and there is another point, which is, that no individual on board the ship is to be allowed to take on shore with him any

---

* This caution was evidently thrown in as a warning to Dr. Tytler, whose late suspicious conduct had come to the knowledge of the Government.

journal or documents of the above description, in the event
of the *Research* touching at any intermediate port on her
return from the Mannicolo islands.

I have, &c.

Marine Board,   (Signed)   J. TROTTER,
22d Dec. 1826.   Secretary.

Before these instructions were given, framed
on the information I had furnished, some persons, pretending to superior knowledge, had
recommended that the *Research*, on sailing at
the appointed time (the 15th December), should
proceed through the Malacca Straits, across the
China Sea, and out into the North Pacific
through the Strait of St. Barnardino, which
separates Luconia on the south from the other
islands. I informed them, that to make a passage in the way proposed at this season of the
year was impracticable, and I believed had
never been attempted or thought of in the
north-east monsoon, which blew directly from
the point of the compass on which the ship's
course lay, though I admitted that such a passage could be accomplished in the south-west
monsoons with the greatest ease. I at the same
time remarked, that if a passage in the north-
east monsoon could be made across the China
Seas out through the Straits of St. Barnardino,
why did the English, American, Bombay, Madras, Calcutta, Penang, and Batavia ships, take

the benefit of the north-west monsoon, and proceed to China by the eastern passage along the
south coast of Java to Timore, and pass out
thence through Bouro and Dampier's Straits,
along the north coast of New Guinea, until
they made sufficient easting so as to be enabled
to run to the north-westward for Canton with
the north-east monsoon? To these suggestions
my opponents were unable to reply. I then
inquired, if the passage they proposed was so
easily performed, why had not the various ships
bound to the east coast of New South Wales
and South America adopted it in preference to
going round Van Diemen's Land; and I begged
of them to inform me whether there was a
single precedent on record, naval or mercantile,
of a vessel having passed out into the South
Pacific, either by the Straits of St. Barnardino
or by the north coast of New Guinea, through
the channel which separates New Guinea from
New Britain, Saint George's Channel, or round
New Hanover? To all these questions I obtained no reply.

I then observed, that I was clearly of opinion
that a passage into the Pacific was practicable
during the north-west monsoon along the north
coast of New Guinea, through St. George's
Channel, or round New Hanover, but that it
had never yet been adopted, except in the in-

stance of the celebrated Dampier, in the *Roe-buck* discovery ship, in A.D. 1704, having gone as far east as New Ireland, and having sailed along the east coast of that country to its south point (Cape St. George), and of his having there, in the month of March 1704, bent his course to the westward back to Timore. I also stated, that it came within my knowledge that an expedition was fitted out from India by order of the East-India Company in 1793 in the ships *Duke* and *Duchess of Clarence*, under the command of Commodore John Hayes (now master-attendant at Calcutta), for the purpose of exploring the east coast of New Guinea and adjacent islands, and that after losing several weeks in trying to pass to the eastward, they were obliged to bear up, and proceed round Van Diemen's Land, where they anchored in the Adventure Bay of Captain Cook. On this voyage the Derwent river was discovered by the commodore, and named by him. His discovery led to the colonizing (a few years after) of that part of Van Diemen's Land. It is now a flourishing colony, and *owes its existence to that gallant officer.*

A few days after this I was called on to attend at the Marine Board, where I was applied to, to state what route I meant to pursue towards the Mannicolos. I replied that it was my intention to adopt the same route Commodore Hayes had pursued on his voyage in the *Duke* and *Duchess of Clarence* to New Guinea, and assigned my reasons as above mentioned for so doing. My plans being approved of, instructions were made out accordingly, directing me to proceed by the way of Van Diemen's Land.

Shortly after this conference I was furnished with the following letter, directing me to refresh the ship's crew at Van Diemen's Land.

To Captain P. DILLON, commander of the Hon. Company's ship *Research*.

SIR :—In continuation of my letter under date the 22d ultimo, and with advertence to that part which refers to your calling at Port Dalrymple, or the Derwent, in progress to the Mannicolo Islands, I am directed by the Marine Board to convey to you their authority for the purchase of such fresh provisions, &c., as you may find it absolutely necessary to provide for the crew of the Hon. Company's ship *Research*, under your command; and also in the event of your finding it requisite, to draw on the authorities there, on account of this Government, for such small sums as the circumstances of the case may call for, giving the Board the earliest information of your proceedings on this and all other points connected therewith.

I have, &c.

Marine Board,   (Signed)   J. TROTTER,
9th Jan. 1827.   Secretary.

CHAPTER III.

OCCURRENCES FROM CALCUTTA TO VAN DIEMEN'S LAND.

THE subsequent occurrences of the voyage I shall give in the form of a diary, as they actually took place and were put on record in the journal of the *Research;* that being the shape in which the information conveyed will be most useful and acceptable to the mariner, the geographer, and the man of science.

6th Jan. 1827.—The carpenter's work being nearly completed, I determined to send a pilot on board in the morning to take the vessel down the river; but having some business to settle in Calcutta, I obtained permission from the Marine Board to remain in town until the ship got as far down the river as Diamond Harbour.

7th.—At 10 A.M. an assistant harbour-master came on board and hauled the ship from her moorings into the middle of the stream. Shortly after the sea pilot took charge and dropped her down the river with the ebb tide to Garden Reach, where she anchored for the night.

8th.—Shortly after day-light Mr. Lushington and Mr. Swinton, chief secretaries to Government, sent on board five garden boxes, containing young coco-nut trees, to be planted on such islands in the Pacific as should be found to possess none of those most useful of all fruits.

11*th.*—From Monday to this day I was engaged in making the necessary preparations for the voyage and in taking leave of my friends; while the ship was gradually proceeding down the river with light and variable winds, which retarded her progress.

Having been late up at a farewell party last night, on arriving at my lodgings this morning I directed my faithful Prussian servant to desire my sircar when he came, to have my boat ready for embarking, and intimated that during the interval I would repose on the couch. Shortly after I was awoke by the servant and sircar, who informed me that during my sleep Doctor Tytler had slipped into my room, and commenced reading some of my letters and papers; but on perceiving me move in the bed, he withdrew in a precipitate manner, and inquired of the Prussian if I was very ill. The man replied that I was not *ill;* but that having at an early hour returned from a party, I had lain down to take a nap previous to embarking for the ship. The Doctor then inquired of my servant if I always slept with arms by the bedside? who answered in the affirmative. He then asked if I was in the habit of drinking spirituous liquors at sea. The Prussian informed him that I never drank liquors from the beginning of my voyages until the end of them; that on shore I was very abstemious, never taking any liquors in my own house, and only doing so abroad out of courtesy to my entertainers. The Doctor then begged of the servant to prevail on me not to go to the ship that day, as I was, he said, exceedingly ill, and that he would call again.

On being informed of the Doctor's strange proceedings, I began to suspect that he again intended to misrepresent the state of my health to the Marine Board: and it shortly appeared I was not mistaken, for having gone to the tavern to breakfast, on returning to my lodgings I found the Doctor with another medical gentleman at the door. He inquired in the most kind and affectionate manner how I found myself after *these violent attacks*, and if I thought the *state of my health* would allow me to go to sea. I replied, that I never was in better health in my life than at the present time, and that I intended to leave town for the vessel that morning. This declaration appeared completely to disconcert him, as he had brought the other medical gentleman (as I afterwards learnt) for the purpose of holding a *survey* on me, and reporting in conjunction with him, had his friend

been base enough to do so, that I would not
be able to proceed on the expedition.

The remainder of the day was spent in getting my baggage embarked in the boat, and
waiting for the tide. During this interval, I
was informed that the Doctor, ever plotting and
restless, was busily engaged, endeavouring to
obtain from Commodore Hayes and others,
documents to prove that the *Research* was not
seaworthy, to enable him to present a protest
against the ship to the Government, so as to
put a stop to the expedition as now planned.

At about half past six this evening I left
Calcutta for the ship, and anchored abreast of
the Budge Budge Hotel. At day-light next
morning we moved forward, and arrived on
board the *Research* at eight o'clock. The pilot
got the anchor up twice that day, but let it go
again, being prevented from proceeding by a
thick fog coming on.

15th.—Nothing remarkable having occurred
since the 12th, I shall pass over those days.
The anchor was got up several times; but we
were obliged to let it go again, the winds blowing up the river, counteracting the strength of
the ebb tide.

This morning we reached Diamond Harbour,
where we anchored. I received instructions
from the Marine Board to proceed no further

without orders, some difficulty having arisen in procuring a register for the ship. I also received private letters from town cautioning me to be on my guard when Doctor Tytler joined the ship, as it was his intention to get rid of the voyage by some artifice, and that if his other schemes failed in accomplishing his point, he would most likely endeavour to provoke me into a quarrel, which would afford him an excuse for carrying his design of leaving the ship into execution.

16th.—Not being allowed to proceed down the river till further orders were received, I employed the crew as necessary about the rigging, and getting the water-casks refilled which had been emptied on the passage from Calcutta to this place.

At eight o'clock we sat down to breakfast. At this moment the Doctor joined the ship, accompanied by his natural son, a youth of about fourteen years of age, and Captain Speck, a passenger.

As had been foreseen, the Doctor this same day raised a dispute on board, by insisting that I should victual from my own table a person named Helmick, employed as his dresser, or what on board ship is usually called a loblolly boy. I politely informed him, that according to the orders of the Marine Board, that person should be victualled, not from my table, but in the same manner as the petty officers and European part of the crew. The Doctor said in an imperious tone of voice, " I wish to see those orders." Though the demand was an impeachment of my veracity, I informed him he had already seen them; but, as a matter of courtesy, not as a matter of right, I would allow him to see them again. He started up in a violent rage, and said, he could not sit there and hear me make use of such ungentlemanly language, in presence of the second officer, as to tell him he had no right to see my letters; and that he would immediately protest against my conduct, and not proceed an inch with the ship until the business was settled. After this ebullition of violence he began to write a long despatch to the Marine Board, which when ended he read to me :—As nearly as I recollect, it stated that, notwithstanding the orders of the Board regarding the keeping up of a good understanding between all parties on the expedition, I had refused to victual his dresser Helmick from the cabin table. I tried, in the most gentle manner, to dissuade him from troubling the Board on a subject they had already settled; and at the same time asked (knowing him to have been an enthusiastic admirer of masonry) whether this was proper

conduct for a freemason to use towards a brother? In a loud voice he exclaimed, " what is
freemasonry, sir? you are a public servant, and I
am another: if you have any thing to communicate, write to me officially." Finding that any
further attempt at conciliation or concession on
my part was useless, and that he was determined
to raise a quarrel, as had been intimated to me
by letter, I resolved to preserve my coolness,
and disregard his insolence as long as possible.
I found it necessary, however, to write a letter
to the Board detailing the true state of the
case, that they might see what the Doctor's
conduct had been when he was only seven
hours on board the ship. I also requested
the second officer to commit to paper what he
recollected of the Doctor's conversation with
me, and as it corroborated my statement, I
sent a copy of it to the Marine Board with my
own letter.

What rendered the Doctor's demand, with
the insolence which accompanied it, more ag-
gravating and unreasonable, was, that I had
already out of kindness to him voluntarily undertaken to victual his son (before mentioned, p.
83) at my own table throughout the voyage, at
my sole charge, free of any expense to his
father: who now tried to thrust upon me
another of his dependents; while there were

many others in the vessel who had a much
stronger claim on my consideration, as the New
Zealand prince, and my faithful follower Martin
Bushart, who looked up to me as a parent and
protector.

17*th*.—Not being able to depart to-day from
Diamond Harbour, on account of the register
not being yet sent, I employed the crew as
necessary about the rigging, artillery, small-
arms, &c.

18*th*.—Received orders to proceed to Kedgeree. At nine weighed and made sail, and
stood down the river. At eleven, the flood
coming in, anchored a little above Culpee. The
carpenter was employed fitting cleats and
making a cabin for the dresser Helmick. At
half past three weighed. At sun-set came-to
off the Silver Tree in seven fathoms : wore to
thirty-five fathoms : furled sails.

In reply to my letter of the 16th instant, addressed to the secretary to the Marine Board
respecting the surgeon's assistant, I received the
following :

To Captain P. DILLON, commander of the Hon. Company's
ship *Research*.

SIR :—I am directed by the Marine Board to acknowledge
the receipt of your letter dated yesterday, and in reply to
acquaint you, with regard to the dieting of Leonard Helmick,
dresser to Doctor Tytler, that he should, the Board think,

in addition to the rations already allowed him, be furnished with fresh victuals from your table to the extent of a
plate-full at each meal, and for which an allowance will be
made you, to be adjusted on your return, of two sicca rupees
per diem.

I have, &c.

Marine Board,   (Signed) J. TROTTER,
17th Jan. 1827.   Secretary.

This letter shews at once the laudable disposition of the Marine Board to conciliate the
outrageous person who was unfortunately to
accompany us; and proves the utter ground-
lessness of his first *public* attack on my conduct,
commencing as it did, 1st. with a charge against
me of defrauding his dependent of the provisions due to him; 2d. with an imputation
on my veracity, in demanding *written* proof that
I was not defrauding him of any thing; and
3dly. with an attack on my public character, in
accusing me to the Board of violating my instructions. The assignment of a new ration for
the loblolly boy, with an allowance for the same,
proved clearly that no such allowance or ration
had previously been intended.

19th.—At day-light weighed, made sail, and
run a little below the Silver Tree, where we
anchored. At eleven again weighed and made
all sail, but in consequence of a strong tide
made little progress. At two P.M. Mr. Seppings,
the Hon. Company's Marine Surveyor, came on

board with the ship's register, and orders to
proceed on the voyage.

20th.—At daylight weighed and made sail,
and at nine passed Kedgeree : carpenter employed caulking in the ports. Noon, light north-
east winds, making but little progress over the
flood tide. At half past four P.M. anchored in
eleven and a half fathoms in Saugor Roads, and
sent on board an Indiaman to get some caulkers
to assist in caulking in our ports. Furled sails.
Wore to forty fathoms. Midnight, pleasant
breezes and thick weather.

21st.—Commenced with moderate breezes
and thick weather. Employed getting ready for
sea. Carpenter and two caulkers from the ship
Rose employed caulking in the ports. Noon,
northerly winds and gloomy weather. At four
finished the caulking, weighed, and made sail.
At sun-set came to an anchor off Saugor Point in
nine and a half fathoms, wore to thirty fathoms,
furled sails, and hoisted the top-sail yards to the
mast head, ready for a start in the morning.

22d.—At day-light weighed and made sail.
At eight P.M. came too in the eastern channel in
five and a half fathoms, with the starboard
bower ; wore to thirty fathoms, and furled sails.

23d.—About six A.M. we got the anchor up,
set all sail, and stood down channel towards the
floating-light. At half past eight we passed the

Reef buoy, and shortly after one of the pilot brigs sent a boat to the *Research* to take out the pilot. We immediately set all sail and passed the *Torch* floating-light vessel at eleven o'clock. The *Torch* is moored in the eastern channel of the Tail of the Saugor Sand, for the purpose of guiding ships into the proper channel in both monsoons.

At noon the latitude observed was 21° 3′ north, and longitude 88° 27′ east. The carpenter of the ship appearing to be a very indifferent one, and totally unfit to perform the duty for which he shipped, I disrated him.

24th.—This day commenced with increasing breezes and fine weather ; the latitude at noon was 19° 57′ N., the longitude by chronometer 88° 0′ 30″. Run about seventy-one miles from noon yesterday on a S.½E. course.

Shortly after noon I received a letter and book from Doctor Tytler, ruled to contain the ship's latitude and longitude each day at noon. This book being made out in a different way to that in which I was directed to supply him with the ship's situation each day, I declined making any entry in it. The letter contained a request, or rather a demand, that I would allow my private servant, Martin Bushart, to undergo a private examination in the Doctor's cabin. This I considered an extraordinary demand, as he was not on the sick list, and wrote the Doctor a letter to that effect.

This day at dinner the first officer and myself had some conversation respecting a Mr. Fresher, a botanist and naturalist at New South Wales. I said it was my intention to get him to proceed with us on this voyage to aid us in our scientific researches. Doctor Tytler immediately remarked that he would be very glad of it. The cause of my making the observation was, that Doctor Tytler had frequently asked me if he could not get a few stones and fragments of rock at Van Diemen's Land, to fill up the chest sent by the Bengal Government for specimens of natural history. I replied, that specimens of botany, mineralogy, &c. the produce of Van Diemen's Land had already been well ascertained by naturalists of the first-rate ability, and that it would be exceedingly wrong to impose on the Government such trash as he mentioned, while there were many valuable specimens of botany and natural history to be procured at the islands to which we were bound. The Doctor replied, that it was immaterial whether it were clods of dried mud or stones of any sort: so that he brought a *large* cargo it would answer the purpose, as there was no person, he said, in the Asiatic Society capable of judging as to their qualities. He further stated, that on the expedition being first fitted out, Mr. Swinton had informed him that the Court of Directors were very much displeased at large sums being paid to some naturalists, botanists, &c. (whose names I forget), who had been employed by the Bengal Government in the Burmese territory, and who had sent very few specimens of their researches to the Asiatic Society ; that as he was determined not to be censured on that score, he would bring them a plentiful supply of earth, clods of mud, stones, logs of wood, &c. &c. I, of course, considered it my duty to prevent the Government from being imposed on in the way he proposed ; and determined to engage Mr. Fresher, or some other man of science, the first opportunity, in order to promote the enlightened views of the Asiatic Society and my honourable employers, to render the expedition as useful as possible to the cause of science.

25th.—This day the wind appeared inclined to settle in the proper quarter for the northeast monsoon weather. The latitude observed at noon was 18° 27′ N. and longitude 88° 14′ E. We ran ninety-five miles upon a S.$\frac{1}{2}$E. course to-day. The weather began to increase in heat, the thermometer in the shade standing at 78°.

The Doctor favoured me with another long letter to-day on the subject of holding examinations in his cabin, to which I had not time to reply; but I mentioned to my New Zealand friends that the Doctor wished to converse with them. They replied, " We have seen the Doctor abuse you very much at Diamond Harbour. You are our friend, and protector; you have brought us from our native country over a sea three months long (referring to the length of the voyage from New Zealand), and you have victualled and clothed us : you have also loaded us with presents to take to our country; you are the relation of our fathers and friends in New Zealand : we are therefore directed by our god to fight for you. Those men that are not your friends cannot be our's. We will not speak to the Doctor. We will kill and eat him if he land in our country."

On hearing this plain statement, I did not wish to force them to converse with the Doctor, knowing it to be useless. I however recommended them, for the sake of their New Zealand god, and all my friends and relations in their country, on no account to molest the Doctor; saying that if they did, Lord Combermere, who had behaved so kind to them, and appointed this ship to carry them home, would be angry. The prince paid some attention to this remonstrance; but "his excellency" Morgan M'Murragh was inflexible in his resolution, and openly declared that it was positively his intention to have the poor Doctor grilled as an entertainment for his numerous wives and friends, the first opportunity that offered after his arrival in the river Thames in New Zealand.

I should not have mentioned this conversation, were it not that I wish to shew those in civilized life what the poor, ignorant, and uncultivated savages of New Zealand are capable of doing, and how susceptible they are of the sentiment of gratitude.

26th.—Throughout these twenty-four hours the winds were settled and steady in the northeast quarter. Our latitude observed at noon was 16° 28′ S.; the longitude by chronometer was 88° 53′. We run S.½E. per log one hundred and twenty miles this day. The thermometer in the shade stood at 80°. I had occasion this morning to enter the second officer's cabin, to open a clothes-chest of mine kept there, not having room for it in my own. On the top of the chest lay an open book, in which I observed my name mentioned, and curiosity inducing me to read it over, I found it contained words to the following purport: "That on the 24th instant, Doctor Tytler had said to the second officer that I (the captain) was mad, and had all the actions of a madman; that he had observed me eating the carpenter's chips, which he said was a symptom of madness, and that I ought therefore to be confined to my cabin, and lose a large quantity of blood," &c. I was much alarmed at these remarks, and immediately perceived that the Doctor was still plotting how to upset the expedition, and place himself at the head of it. That, all other means of effecting this having failed, he was now attempting to deprive me of the command, and make me a prisoner on board, under pretence that I was insane.* I immediately loaded my pistols, and mentioned what I had observed to my faithful Prussian servant Martin Bushart; at the same time directing him to be on the watch as to what passed between the Doctor and officers, to acquaint me with it immediately, and be ready to come to my assistance. I then wrote a letter to the Doctor, in which I stated to him, that after what had happened, I deemed it an imperative duty to adopt every precaution to prevent mutiny and insub-

---

* Having once got me into his hands, and ruined my character with the ship's company, he could easily foresee that it would be impossible for me to resume the command, after the course of medicine and Bedlam-discipline which he had prepared for me, and which would have been enough, under such circumstances, to disturb, if not destroy, the intellects of the most sane and temperate person in the world.

ordination in the ship, and that as to permitting him to hold private consultations in his cabin, it was out of the question.

January 27.—Fine weather throughout these twenty-four hours; winds from N.E. to N.N.E. The ship was at noon in latitude 14° 10′ N.; longitude 88° 14′ E. We ran by the log 143 miles, S. by E. the last twenty-four hours, and experienced a current setting to the westward.

Having occasion to be much displeased with Doctor Tytler's conduct, both at Calcutta and on board the ship, I wrote him a letter which I hoped would make a favourable impression on his mind, and deter him from prosecuting his mutinous schemes any farther. I informed him that I was perfectly aware of his treacherous conduct towards me at Calcutta, in attempting to prevent my going with the expedition, into which I had brought him, by insidiously endeavouring to obtain proof that I was in such a state of health and of mind as to disqualify me; that I had not forgotten his outrageous proceedings immediately on joining the ship, when he insolently impugned my conduct as a public officer, my character as a commander, and my honour as a gentleman, by alleging that I was defrauding his dependent,—and misrepresenting my orders, to justify it; that I bore in mind his proposal of imposing on the Government

chests of worthless rubbish as specimens of natural history; and had yet no evidence that his
proceedings towards myself were more honest
and sincere. That, after such occurrences, he
could not expect me to rest entirely satisfied
of his sense of duty to me as his superior officer;
especially when it was well known that he had
not scrupled to violate one of the first and most
sacred of human laws, in possessing himself of
the wife of a person in whose house he resided;
thus at once outraging the feelings of a husband,
and profaning the sacred roof of hospitality;
and, for the last fourteen years, he had been in-
dulging in the fruits of this achievement with
the wife of the person whose peace of mind he
had destroyed for ever. Could I reasonably
hope that he would be more restrained by a
sense of duty or of gratitude to me, or have
more respect for the rights of his superior officer,
when it was notorious that for many years he
had been engaged in quarrelling with and libel-
ling his superiors in authority, as well as others,
particularly the Commissariat, and the late lamented Sir David Ochterlony, on whom after
his death he heaped the foulest aspersions. I
concluded by warning him, that if he proceeded
in such a course with me, he would find he had
to deal with a person of some firmness and decision.

27th.—This day at dinner the Doctor's conversation, as usual, was employed in ridiculing
the ship to the lowest pitch, in the hearing of
the officers, servants, and seamen at the wheel,
and predicting her loss, apparently with the
view of getting the crew to rise on me and force
me to return. I knew that, with proper encou-
ragement, they would not hesitate a moment
in doing this, being all nearly four months'
pay in advance; and that they might use, as a
plea of justification, the apprehensions under
which they were placed by Dr. Tytler's representations, regarding him as one of the leaders
of the expedition, which he took care to repre-
sent himself to be; on this account I determined, the first time that he should make use
of similar language again, to inquire what he
meant by it.

28th.—At 10 A.M. divine service was performed on the quarter-deck for those who chose
to attend; for I did not consider it proper to
force all hands to prayers, there being several
Roman Catholics, Presbyterians, and Mahome-
tans on board. We were favoured with fine
monsoon weather throughout these twenty-four
hours. Our latitude observed at noon was 12°
7' N.; longitude by chronometer, 88° 28' E.

We sat down to dinner at the usual hour, and
Doctor Tytler introduced his favourite topic of

ridiculing the ship, talking in a vociferous tone, so that all the people on board might hear him. He commenced by saying that the *Research* would not steer, and must certainly go to the bottom in a high sea; that she was fit for nothing but a rice hulk; and, though she might get so far on her passage as Van Diemen's Land, that if she proceeded farther, she would certainly be knocked to pieces on the rocks of Tucopia, and, to give more force to what he said, he professed that such was the opinion of the head of the Marine Board at Calcutta. On these remarks being made, I observed, by the altered counte-nance of some of the individuals within his hear-ing, that his harangue and gloomy predictions had made a strong impression on their minds.

It would now appear that the Doctor himself left Calcutta under great apprehension of being lost in the ship ; and, being of a weak and super-stitious turn of mind, he used all means in his power to get clear of her. His language to-day might be used for the purpose of intimidating the young officers and crew from proceeding, in hopes that they would take the ship from me or compel me to return. If either of these events took place, he would have an excellent oppor-tunity of escaping from his engagement with the Government, and from the dangers which his visionary imagination pictured as ready to swallow him up on the voyage. His ridiculing the ship was besides intended as an insult to me, because I agreed in opinion with the officers of the Marine Board as to the *Research*'s capability to perform the voyage to the Mannicolos and back. He was much displeased with me because I would not be so accommodating as to join him in a protest against the officers of Government charged with the management of the marine affairs.

I consequently rose from the table, much disgusted at his conversation, and was immediately followed by the first officer, who remarked to me that the Doctor had began his old discourse again. I replied, " I will shortly put a stop to it."

But from the circumstance which I saw recorded in the second officer's log-book, of the 24th instant, with the Doctor's subsequent conduct of to-day, I suspected that a mutiny had long been hatching, and would probably break out on my adopting any measures to check its ringleader. Not knowing who might be concerned in it or not, I deemed it prudent first to take the precaution of arming myself and followers, and I resolved to lose my life rather than the ship should return, or my person be arrested, as the Doctor had proposed. I then called for the gunner, asked him where my blun-

derbuss was, and told him that there was a person on board trying to bring about a mutiny,
and that it was time to arm and prevent it.
Upon hearing this, the Doctor interrupted me,
saying, "Captain Dillon, there is not the least
occasion for this trouble; I will do whatever
you wish me."

I then asked what he meant by ridiculing the
ship in the way he had done, if it was not his
intention to deter the young and inexperienced
officers and others on board from proceeding on
the voyage, or to breed a mutiny in the ship, so
as to cause her return to Calcutta.

He replied, that he heard those opinions expressed by Captain Crawford and other gentlemen in Calcutta.   I replied, that this allegation
(which indeed was a libel on those gentlemen,
who had fitted out the expedition) could be no
excuse for his mutinous conduct; and that, if he
persisted in acting thus, I would, if necessity
compelled me for the general safety, bring him
to the capstan and have him flogged with five
dozen, or put him in double irons.

This plain unvarnished declaration of mine,
uttered under the impulse of that indignation
his perfidy could not but inspire, had a much
better effect than if I had converted a ream of
paper into letters. The Doctor, now alarmed
about the consequences of his misconduct, pro-

mised to behave better in future; on which I withdrew from the cuddy.

29th.—The day commenced with fresh breezes and cloudy weather; as such it continued to eight P.M., when it had a very squally and unsettled appearance. In expectation of meeting with bad weather, took in all the small sails. Being still under some apprehension on account of Doctor Tytler's mutinous conduct, I sent him a letter on service, which is hereafter inserted, pointing out the impropriety of his proceedings. I also had an indirect hint to-day of his secret endeavours to have me confined. Considering him upon the whole a very dangerous man, I determined not to furnish him with the ship's situation at noon in future.

To R. Tytler, Esq., surgeon to H. C. S. *Research.*

Sir :—Your conduct yesterday, and on various occasions since having left the Pilot, has been such, as to cause me to be much alarmed for the safety of the ship and welfare of the expedition entrusted to my care ; I therefore take this opportunity of informing you, that should you in future pursue a similar line of conduct, I shall be put to the disagreeable necessity of close confining you, till an opportunity offers of handing you over to a military tribunal for trial.

Your aspersions on the ship, and predictions of the dreadful disasters which are to befal her, in the presence of the crew, cannot, for a moment, be misunderstood. You are discontented and disappointed; you therefore wish to breed a disaffection between the officers of the ship and myself, and to deter every individual on board from proceeding on the intended voyage.

It is to be hoped you will consider and see the impropriety of your proceedings, and adopt a more honourable and honest line of conduct; if not, I shall be necessitated to have recourse to more rigorous measures than that of confining you.

H. C. S. *Research* at sea,　　　　I have, &c.
　　29th Jan. 1827.　　　　(Signed)　P. DILLON.

During my late residence in Calcutta, four of the eleven South Sea Islanders whom I brought with me died of consumption; two of them were from the island of Otaheite, one from Owhyhee, and one from Whylootackey. The latter, with another now on board dangerously ill, were the two first who ever left their native country. The poor man, who could not survive many days, was inconsolable for the loss of his countryman and fellow-traveller, who had died at Calcutta.

I was also sorry to find that a very good man, named Wahoey, a native of the Marquis Islands, who had sailed with me for nearly two years and a half, was dangerously ill, and not likely to recover.

Latitude at noon this day 9° 54′ N. Longitude by mean of two chronometers, 88° 30′ 30″ E. Longitude by account, 90°.

30th.—Nothing remarkable occurred during these twenty-four hours. The weather somewhat inclined to be squally with dark clouds,

flashes of lightning, and drizzling rain at intervals. This is rather unusual for the north-east
monsoon.

31st.—We had fine weather throughout this
day, and made a rapid progress on our passage.
The latitude at noon was 5° 50′ N., and longitude 88° 21′ E. About seven A.M. there were
four tropic birds flying about the ship, of the
white tail species : they were the first aquatic
birds I observed since we sailed. The current
I found setting as yet to the westward ; and
although we steered south and by east the last
twenty-four hours, with the wind free, we did
not make better than a south course. Nothing
remarkable having occurred, or likely to occur
at sea, out of sight of land, it cannot be expected that the journal for this part of the
voyage should contain any matter interesting
to the curious reader.

The two Indians as yet remain dangerously
ill ; their loss to us would be serious, as they
could be of great use on the present expedition.

At half past nine P.M. the weather became
very squally, with rain. Took in the small sails,
and reefed the top-sails. Towards midnight
the wind shifted to south-east and south, where
it is likely to continue for some time.

1st Feb. 1827.—The early part of this day,

the weather was squally, with rain and dark clouds all round. At half past four in the morning I wasawakened by a sudden crash upon deck; and on going out, found that the whale boat on the larboard quarter of the ship had fallen into the sea, from the slings having given way. I immediately shortened sail, and after much trouble got the boat hoisted up, but she was so much staved as to be useless. Towards noon the weather became somewhat steady, and the wind appeared to settle in the north-west quarter, which disappointed me much, as I expected the north-east monsoon to take me to 3° north latitude, where I should meet with variable winds and calms until I entered the north-west monsoon in 3° south.

The sun being clouded at noon I could not get the latitude : the ship's situation at noon, by account, was 4° 39′ N., and the longitude brought forward from chronometer No. 1 was 88° 27′. Being apprehensive of bad and squally weather, got the guns housed, and the ports lashed in.

About half-past twelve at noon I was much surprised to find Doctor Tytler in close conversation with the man at the wheel, and taking his attention from his duty. I mentioned to both of them the impropriety of such conduct, and directed the officer of the watch not to

permit any person in future to converse with
the man at the helm.

2*d.*—Throughout the first half of this day
the winds were light from the north-westward,
with cloudy weather. At noon the breezes in-
creased a little, but the weather continued so
cloudy till sunset as to prevent my getting
sights for the chronometer. The sun having
shewed out a little before twelve o'clock, I got
the latitude correct, which was 3° 30′ N. The
longitude brought forward from chronometer
No. 1, 88° 41′; by dead reckoning it was
90° 57′.

This forenoon we got the whale boat hoisted
in upon deck and broke her up, she being rendered totally useless by the accident of the 1st
instant.

3*d.*—The first eight hours of these twenty-
four were rather squally with light rain, the
wind variable from west by south to north. At
noon the sun was clear: observed the latitude
2° 3′ N., longitude 88° 46′ E. The thermometer
in the shade on deck stood at 82°.

At two P.M. the heaviest squall we had yet
met with passed the ship; but we did not feel
it much, having taken in our sails in time.
About eight P.M. we had another smart squall;
when the wind shifted to the south-west, and
backed again to the westward.

4*th*.—This day was ushered in with strong
squalls and light rain, and so continuing, we
made and shortened sail as necessary. The
weather being unsettled, the officiating chaplain was prevented performing divine service
on deck as usual. The latitude by a bad observation shewed our situation to be 17′ N. of the
equator; longitude 89° 7′ E. At half past three
this afternoon, supposed the ship to be on the
line. I was extremely sorry to find my young
friend Bryan Boroo, the New Zealand prince, ill
of the measles, which I fear he caught from a
boy, the servant of M. Chaigneau, the French
gentleman on board, who sickened of that complaint two days after we sailed.

5*th*.—The first and latter part of this day the
weather inclined to be squally, with light rain;
middle part fine clear weather. On observing
the sun at noon, I found we had crossed the
line, the latitude being 1° 33′ S.; longitude
90° 25′ E. The prince Bryan Boroo was ill of
the measles, three other South Sea islanders
confined by illness, and one of them so unwell
that his recovery was despaired of.

Nothing remarkable having occurred since
the 5th instant, I pass over the interval without any observation; and the reader will understand the same practice to have been followed,
henceforth, when he finds many days passed by

without any remark; the ordinary state of the winds, weather, clouds, &c. having little or no interest for the general reader, being neither amusing nor instructive.

9th.—At one o'clock this morning Tariou, a native of Whylootakey, the first of his countrymen who ever ventured to quit his native island, departed this life. I was extremely sorry for his loss, which deprived me of the pleasure of restoring him safe to his friends and country. He had been rather sickly for a short time at Calcutta, but recovered, and joined the ship in good health. The first seven days of his illness the surgeon visited him but once, of which I had occasion to take notice; and after this he remained some days without nourishing food. I sent the chief officer to the Doctor, to point out the necessity of allowing him and the other sick some sago or arrow-root, which he complied with. At half past seven A.M. we committed his remains to the deep, sewed up in his hammock with two twelve-pound shot attached to it; one of the Otaheitans on board, a christian of the Protestant persuasion, performing the funeral service extempore over the body. Another of the islanders was on the Doctor's list ill of the measles. Latitude at noon was 6° 8′ S., longitude 95° 17′ E.: the thermometer in the shade 84°.

12th.—Light airs and calms, with hot sultry weather, throughout the day. Five Europeans, six Indians, and one lascar ill of various complaints, and unable to perform their duty on board.

Finding the surgeon paying no attention to the food of the sick, and that ten of them were drawing salt provisions, ordered the same to be discontinued till further orders, substituting sago, arrow-root, &c. Latitude at noon 8° 16′ S. longitude 98° 42′ E.

This morning a young bird of the booby species rested on the rigging. It was immediately made prisoner, and a drawing of it taken by the draughtsman.

14th.—Moderate breezes from the westward throughout the day, with passing showers of light rain early in the morning and late at night.

Found the officers of the ship much inclined to quarrel among themselves. In breeding their quarrels I was sorry, but not surprised, to find that Doctor Tytler had taken an active part. I admonished the young men, and pointed out to them the necessity of observing decorum and unanimity, on account of the respectability of the service, and for the satisfaction of their honourable employers, which considerations I trusted would prevent similar occurrences in future.

We were visited this day by several aquatic birds; one gannet perched on the rigging, and was captured by a sailor. Latitude at noon 9° 51′ S.; longitude 100° 32′ E. Thermometer on deck 83°.

15th.—Unsteady weather throughout the day. Having entered a part of the ocean little frequented by navigators, gave the officers of the watch strict charge to keep a good look-out a-head, and to go forward occasionally to remind the men of their duty. Latitude observed 11° 22′ S.; longitude 101° 42′ E. Thermometer on deck 84°.

16th.—Light breezes and calms: passed under the sun in the forenoon. At 6. P.M. Huno, a native of the Marquis Islands, who joined me in the *St. Patrick* at Otaheite in December 1825, died after an illness of eight days. Huno had joined this vessel in good health; I therefore sent the first officer to the surgeon (who considers no disease to be contagious) to ascertain the nature of the complaint of which this man died. His reply was that he did not understand his complaint, being ignorant of the Marquis dialect. Latitude observed at noon 12° 38′ S.; longitude 102° 36′ E. Thermometer 84°.

17th.—Light airs and calms, with rain and unsettled weather throughout the day. Our having yesterday passed the 12° of south latitude, which is said to be the southern limit of the north-west monsoon, and being about to enter into the south-east trades, I supposed to be the cause of the unsettled state of the weather. Close in with the coast of New Holland, on former voyages, I have found the westerly winds extend as far as the 15° of south latitude at this season of the year.

Got the between-decks properly cleaned out and fumigated, with the view of eradicating the disease which seemed to be spreading in the ship.

17th.—This afternoon the chief officer, and a sailor named Dale, were taken ill. Latitude at noon 13° 11′ S.; longitude 102° 51′ E.; thermometer 82°.

18th.—Strong breezes from the westward with a high head sea; the vessel pitching very much, and shipping seas so as to render the cooking difficult. Latitude at noon 13° 40′ S.; longitude 103° 42′ E.; thermometer 82°.

20th.—The wind this day settled to the E.S.E. which proved to be the true trade.

21st.—Fine strong trades throughout the day. At two o'clock we sat down to dinner as usual; but the surgeon was immediately called away to render assistance to a lascar who had fallen from the upper deck into the fore-hold. He did not appear to be in the least hurt. On

inquiring the cause of this accident, I was
informed that the man had been smoking an
intoxicating and poisonous plant called gunja,
well known in the East; I therefore gave directions to have the lascars' chests examined, and
whatever gunja was found to be brought to me.
Shortly after the officer returned with one bag
and a parcel of this deleterious plant, which was
immediately thrown overboard, to prevent further accidents from its intoxicating effects.
Latitude 19° 12′ S.; longitude 103° 31′ 30″ E.;
thermometer 80°.

21*st.*—Being much annoyed for some time
by the offensive odour intruding from Doctor
Tytler's cabin into mine, which was separated
from it by a thin Venetian only, I discovered
that the scent was occasioned by the Doctor,
his son, a tailor, a dhoby (or washerman), and
one khansaman (or butler), in all five persons,
with their personal baggage, &c. sleeping in the
same apartment, which was only nine feet nine
inches long by eight feet four inches wide, in a
tropical climate, with the thermometer standing
at upwards of 80°. To prevent the contagion
which might arise from this heterogeneous litter,
I determined to put an end to their sleeping
thus in future, and in the evening issued orders
to that effect.

26*th.*—Throughout the day a perfect calm,

with cloudy weather. Got no observation for
the latitude, and no sight for the chronometers,
for three days past. At half-past three this
morning, Wahoey, the Marquis man, died of
a decline, with which he had been long affected.
He was the seventh that had died of the natives
who accompanied me to Calcutta from the
islands. Committed his body to the deep at half-
past seven, sewed up in his hammock, with some
18lb. shot to sink him. Shortly after a large
shark came close to the ship, and was caught
with a bait; but in hauling it on board escaped. It immediately returned to the bait;
I gave directions, however, not to attempt to
take it, being apprehensive that the body of our
unfortunate shipmate had been devoured by
the voracious monster. The thermometer stood
at 76°.

Received a complaint from the second officer, that Doctor Tytler had thrown a Bible at
his head, and endeavoured to irritate and insult
him by various sarcasms : such as, that he swore
all the week and read prayers on Sunday ;
that his dress in performing divine service was
not sufficiently clerical, and the like. The officer hinted to me that he must decline reading
prayers in future if subjected to such scurrilous
remarks.

27*th.*—At half-past one this day, the second

officer came and informed me that there was "a
mutiny fore and aft the ship," to use his own
words. He stated, that on the 24th of January
last Doctor Tytler had endeavoured to persuade
him that I was mad, and ought to be confined
to my cabin; that I was acting contrary to my
instructions, and had all the actions of a madman. He requested him to watch me; adding
that he might observe me sometimes eating the
carpenter's chips, which was a sure symptom
of a certain species of insanity. He also informed me that on the 28th of January last
the chief officer shewed him a letter on service which he had received from Doctor Tytler,
who stated that, as medical officer in charge
of the expedition, he would recommend my
being confined to my cabin, being deranged,
and requiring to lose a large quantity of blood.
The second officer said that he had represented to the other officers his intention to inform me of this mutinous act of the Doctor's,
and that he often told them he considered the
Doctor's life in his hands, as the letter was
clearly sent with no other view than to cause
me to be laid violent hands on, and placed at the
Doctor's mercy.

I then called the chief officer into the cabin,
and inquired into this affair. He admitted having received a letter from Doctor Tytler, con-

taining the words mentioned by the second
officer, and that the reason he did not inform me
of it was that he was unwilling to cause further
troubles on board. He added, that Doctor
Tytler asked him next day if he had received
the letter, which he acknowledged he had.

I then called the draughtsman of the ship,
who said he also had seen the letter, and taken a
copy of it, which he destroyed about three days
ago. He admitted, however, that its contents
were as represented by the second officer; and
stated that, soon after seeing it, he had a conversation with Dr. Tytler, when the latter declared that I was mad.

From all this corroborating evidence, and
collateral circumstances, proving the existence
of a settled plan to deprive me of the command
of the ship, and throw me into confinement on
the pretence of insanity (after which I might
have been disposed of according to the Doctor's
will and pleasure), conceiving my person to be
in danger, I immediately resolved to adopt
decisive measures. My first step was to place
Dr. Tytler under arrest. I walked up to him
on the quarter-deck, and clapping my hand
upon his shoulder, said aloud, " I arrest you
in his Britannic Majesty's name." I considered
this to be the proper mode of proceeding, and
that going through the regular form openly

would render it more solemn and impressive. This I state thus particularly, because, strange as it may seem, the simple circumstance of placing my hand upon his shoulder was laid hold of by quibbling lawyers as a ground for subjecting me to an expense of above five hundred pounds, under the fictitious plea that it constituted an assault and breach of the peace!

'This will be a caution to all commanders in future, that the maintenance of subordination and of their just authority, the preservation of the ship, and the prevention of bloodshed, with the attainment of the objects of the voyage, however important, may be held as nothing by the quibbling sophistry of the law, in comparison with the monstrous informality of touching a mutineer's shoulder, in pronouncing the words, " I arrest you in his Britannic Majesty's name!"

After the Doctor's arrest, not knowing to what degree the spirit of insubordination might have extended, having observed him often in private conversation with the sailors, who were many of them from the same part of the kingdom as himself, and uncertain therefore how far an artful intriguer might have succeeded in ingratiating himself with these rude and simple men, having also lost confidence in some of my officers, from knowing that they had for many weeks concealed from me these underhand

mutinous proceedings, I first placed a sentry at
my cabin-door to prevent the danger of immediate attack; and as there were some arms, the
property of the Government, in the Doctor's
cabin, I directed the chief officer to secure
them, so as to preclude the Doctor and his
adherents from making any resistance.

Shortly after I sent the chief officer a letter
on Government service, to be read to the
Doctor, of which a copy is subjoined:

To the Chief Officer H C. Ship Research.

Sir:—I will thank you to call upon Doctor Tytler, and
inform him that, notwithstanding his mutinous conduct (in
trying to get me arrested on board the ship I now command,
and his wish to bleed me to death, or to ruin my constitution
by his pretensions), that it is not my wish to close confine
him to his cabin. He may therefore walk the deck as usual;
but, on no pretence or account whatever, is he to converse
with any individual belonging to the ship.

After reading this letter to him in presence of another officer, you will please to return it to me immediately.

At Sea,   I am, &c.
27th Feb. 1827.   (Signed) P. DILLON.

P.S. You will, at the same time, inform Doctor Tytler,
that he no longer can be allowed to take a seat at my table,
but will be supplied from it with such food as he may require
at each meal.   (Signed) P. DILLON.

The following memoranda were added to the
letter by the chief and second officer:

I, the undersigned, do hereby certify that I read the contents of this letter to Doctor Tytler as directed, and that

his reply was, he would rather stop in his cabin; by so doing he would give no offence.

Feb. 27, 1827, 5 P.M.   Signed by the Chief Officer.

I, the undersigned, do hereby certify that this letter was read in my presence to Doctor Tytler by the first officer. The Doctor replied, that he would much rather continue in his cabin, if he was not allowed to communicate with his brother officers, until he was handed over to justice at Van Diemen's Land.

Signed by the Second Officer.

Feb. 27, 1827, 5 P.M.

In the evening I distributed six or seven pairs of pistols amongst some old and trusty shipmates, with directions to be ready to use them when called on.

2d March.—Light breezes from the eastward. Shortly after daylight we were visited by a pair of tropic birds, which bore us company throughout the day. Latitude at noon 28° 16′ S., longitude 98° 36′ E. Thermometer in the shade, 72°. Caught a fish of the Boneta species, which weighed ten pounds and a-half.

14th.—At an early hour this morning we were visited by a whale of the black species, which came so close to the ship that the two small orifices or breathing-holes in the head could be plainly seen: the animal appeared to be about thirty feet long. We were also favoured with a visit from a few albatrosses and other aquatic birds.

On inquiry this morning, I found there was one man ill of a bowel complaint, who had been unwell from the time we left Calcutta; that another had lost the use of his limbs the night before last, and a third was incapable of doing his duty from an attack of the rheumatism. I therefore wrote to the chief officer a letter on service, to be read to the surgeon in presence of the second officer, to the following effect, *viz.*

" That he should inform the surgeon that a few of the crew were indisposed and required medical assistance, which assistance I requested, as a point of duty, he would render without delay.

" That as the surgeon, I was informed, was disposed to remain in his cabin during the continuance of the cold weather, sooner than disturb him from it, I would cause the sick with an officer to wait on him there : that is, if he would rather prescribe for them there than on deck, or in their quarters."

On this letter being read to the Doctor he agreed to attend to his duty, which he had discontinued doing ever since he had been placed for two hours under close arrest.

28th.—Throughout these twenty-four hours strong gales from W. by N. to W. by S. with a high sea, the vessel rolling gunwale in and shipping seas in various parts. At intervals

there were several of the most furious squalls
I have ever met with by sea or land. At an
early hour this morning we were obliged to
close reef the top-sails. Our quarter boats were
raised from their slings into the mizen rigging
by the violence of the squalls, where we lashed
them for the present. At noon the sun shewed our latitude 43° 21′ S. The longitude was
133° 35′ E. Run by the log 180 miles on an
E.¼S. course. Thermometer on deck 53°.

With a view to ease the vessel of her top
weight I got the mizen top-mast struck, and the
top-gallant yards sent down on deck : we then
struck the top-gallant masts. In performing
this duty, the main-top-gallant mast broke short
off at the sheave-hole in the mast head. Towards night the gale appeared to abate, the
squalls being neither so strong or frequent as in
the early part of the day.

31st.—Winds from W.S.W. to W.N.W. the
first and middle part of this day : at dusk it
shifted to N.N.W. Our latitude 43° 22′ S. at
noon ; the longitude, by mean of two chronometers, 144° 1′ 30″ E. The thermometer on deck
55°. Run 150 miles on an E. by N. course.

The sea appeared of a light colour, as if we
were at no great distance from land. The
chronometers at noon shewed the distance
of the S.W. Cape of Van Diemen's Land to

be ninety-one miles and a-half on an E.$\frac{1}{4}$S. course.

At a quarter before 11 P.M. the watch called out " land a-head." I immediately went forward, and could plainly see the south-west Cape of Van Diemen's Land bearing from E.N.E to E. by S., at a distance of seven or eight leagues.

About midnight hauled to the southward under easy sail to wait for daylight. At this period the wind blew almost a hurricane.

1st April.—The day commenced with very strong gales from the north-westward, accompanied with tremendous squalls of hail and rain : expected to see the fore-yard broke to atoms every moment. Finding it exceedingly dangerous to approach the coast in such violent unsettled weather, I determined to scud away to the S.E. and heave-to. The seas ran mountains high : one of them stove the gig boat on the poop.

At 8 P.M. hove-to under the main top-sail close-reefed, and was glad to find the ship kept-to remarkably well. The weather continued throughout the night as above. It was extremely cold, and the poor lascars rendered unserviceable by the severity of the weather.

2d.—Strong gales throughout the first and middle part of the day, with hail, rain, and sunshine, the sea breaking over the ship in various parts. The seamen were employed repairing the damage sustained in the rigging last night and this morning.

At 4 o'clock this afternoon the violence of the gale appeared to abate. At midnight the weather became settled, and I bore away under easy sail to the N.W. by N.

3d.—Moderate breezes throughout the day with fine weather. Winds from south-west in the morning : towards noon shifted to the northward, where it settled with fine weather. Latitude 44° 7' S., longitude 148° 45' E. Thermometer on deck 53°.

4th.—The first and middle part of the day the wind blew a moderate breeze from the northward : latter part inclined to calm. At half-past 6 A.M. the shores of Van Diemen's Land were in sight from the South Cape to Cape Pillar. At noon the following head-lands were in sight : the Eddystone, bearing W.; Tasman's Head, N. and by W. one-half W.; Fluted Cape, at the entrance of Adventure Bay, N.; Cape Pillar, N.N.E. At 3 P.M. got soundings in fifty-two fathoms sandy bottom, off the entrance of D'Entrecasteaux's Channel. At midnight Tasman's Head bore W. and by N. two leagues : the wind so light that the ship had not steerage way.

5th.—First part of the day, light airs and calms, with fair weather ; latter part moderate breezes from the southward, with rain. At daylight Penguin Island, at the entrance of Adventure Bay, bore W.N.W. ; distance off two leagues. Cape Frederick Henry, W.N.W., Cape Pillar, E. half S. At 2 P.M. a moderate breeze sprung up from the southward. Took advantage of this chance, set all sail, and stood in for the river Derwent. At 6 P.M. entered the river, and at 9 P.M. came to anchor in fifteen fathoms water two miles from Hobart Town.

CHAPTER IV.

OCCURRENCES AT VAN DIEMEN'S LAND.

6th.—At daylight went on shore to report my
arrival. Doctor Tytler requested permission
to land, which I could not comply with,
as the New South Wales port regulations forbid the landing of individuals in their ports
prior to permission being obtained from the
governor.

At half past ten I was introduced by the
Collector of Customs to the Lieutenant-governor of Van Diemen's Land. I made him acquainted with the objects of the expedition,
which appeared to afford him great pleasure,
and he applauded the Bengal Government much
for their philanthropy. I then informed him
that I required supplies of provisions, and was
authorized by the Government to draw on the
authorities at Van Diemen's Land for such sums
as might be requisite to defray the ship's disbursements. In reply, he told me that he
would do every thing in his power to expedite
the ship's departure from Van Diemen's Land,
and directed me to transmit him the powers
with which I was furnished, saying he would

send for the commissary, and arrange the matter without delay. He directed me to call next day at ten o'clock, when I informed him there were two passengers on board, the one a French gentleman, consul from France for Cochin-China; the other a Captain in the Bengal army. He directed me to bring them on shore with me to his office next day, and I then took my leave.

Shortly after quitting the government-house, the Collector of Customs followed me into the street, and delivered the following message: " Captain Dillon, the Lieutenant-governor sends his compliments to you, and directs me to inform you that he has received a letter from Dr. Tytler, and that he will feel obliged if you will allow the Doctor to land." My reply was, " certainly." I then went on board the ship in company with the Collector, and sent a message to the Doctor, giving him permission to go on shore, but intimating that I expected he would return in the evening; on which the Doctor left the ship. In consequence of the promises made me, I immediately bespoke supplies of provisions, &c., and made arrangements to sail on the 11th.

7th.—This morning I went on shore according to appointment, accompanied by M Chaigneau and Captain Speck of the Bengal

army. We arrived at the back-door of the Lieutenant-governor's residence, which was on the
road side, at ten o'clock. An orderly demanded
our business, and I informed him that we came
according to an appointment made yesterday.
The orderly then entered the house, and shortly
after returning informed me that the Lieutenant-
governor was engaged, but would see us in a
few minutes. The morning was excessively
cold, and we were attired in our light Indian
clothes : the thermometer standing in the open
air at 39°. My companions, as well as myself,
were thus detained in the open street, where we
suffered much from the cold, until half past
twelve o'clock, when we were ushered into the
Lieut.-governor's office. He informed me that
he had seen the commissary, and he found it
was not convenient to assist me. I strongly
remonstrated, and assured him that I had bespoke my supplies in consequence of the promises he had made me the previous day, and that
those with whom I had made my arrangements
would not allow me to retract. I further stated,
that if those promises had not been made, I
should have sailed to Port Jackson in quest
of the aid which I was denied in this port.
To this remonstrance he replied, " Very well,
Captain Dillon, go into the market, and try
to negociate your bills with the merchants, and

if you cannot succeed, I will assist you without delay."

He then adverted to the objects of the voyage,
and seemed to discredit all I had acquainted
him with the day before, observing, that it was
very extraordinary I did not ascertain all the
requisite information relative to la Pérouse's
shipwreck, while on board the *St. Patrick.*

I could not account for the very great change
in his conduct during the short space of
twenty-four hours, until I discovered that Doctor Tytler had seen him in the interval, and
represented every thing connected with the
expedition in such a way as to mislead a man
like him. I had two interviews with him this
day, at the latter of which he informed me that
he had seen Doctor Tytler, who complained
greatly of me ; but that he did not wish to
interfere in the matter, and therefore referred
the Doctor to the police magistrates.

Finding that Doctor Tytler did not return
to the ship last night or this morning, according
to my orders, and that there were several sick
on board, I directed Dr. Scott, the colonial surgeon, to attend daily till they recovered.

Understanding that Doctor Tytler had been
at the police office, I went there accompanied
by two gentlemen to ascertain his business,
when the magistrate, who was an old friend and

intimate acquaintance of mine, told me that the
Doctor had preferred charges of assault against
me, and sought the protection of the law; he
was therefore bound to call on me to find sureties to keep the peace until Monday the 9th
instant, at which time the business would undergo a full investigation.

It was my intention, before I touched at Van
Diemen's Land, to prosecute Doctor Tytler for
the letter he had written to the chief officer on
the 28th of January last, which in my opinion
(as well as in that of others who had read or
heard its contents, and been informed of the
circumstances connected with it), was penned
with the intention of inducing the officers and
crew to mutiny and arrest me, under pretence
of insanity; I was determined, however, to pass
over for the present all the attacks and insults
offered to me by the Doctor, rather than cause
a moment's delay to the expedition, and to prefer my charges against him in Calcutta at the
termination of the voyage. Of this forbearance
Doctor Tytler took advantage, and made the
first complaint, regardless of the consequences
to his employers. Intent alone on his own ma-
lignant views, he raised an inquiry which he
was aware might probably occupy some months
in litigation, by which the Hon. East India
Company's ship *Research* would be detained in

the port of Van Diemen's Land, at the heavy
and unnecessary expense to the Company of ten
thousand rupees per month, independent of the
risk thus incurred of not reaching the Mannicolos in the proper season.

9th.   This morning subpœnas were served on
board the ship at the instance of Doctor Tytler,
on some of the officers and crew, who attended
with me at the police office at ten o'clock accordingly.   The first witness examined was
Captain Speck, who deposed the truth.   The
next was the chief officer of the *Research.* With
respect to this person's evidence, as, by having
so long concealed the machinations going on
against me, he had become almost as deeply
committed as the Doctor himself, it was to be
expected that he would speak more with the
leaning of an accomplice, than with the truth
and impartiality of an honest disinterested witness.   His story was, of course, supported by
the Doctor's dependent, Helmick, who though
nearly *black* in complexion, said he became
quite *pale* with fear at my loading a blunder-
buss ; and he was followed by Munro, my
clerk, who had come in along with him from
the ale-house, both more than half seas over,
where they seemed to have been primed for the
occasion.   On this drunken and partial testimony of accomplices, I was called on to enter

into sureties to appear before the next sittings
of the Supreme Court, to answer a charge of
assault, by having laid my hand on the Doctor's
shoulder, when I arrested him on the quarter-
deck.

Captain Speck not being able to procure
lodgings on shore, resided on board the ship
with me; but the Doctor having deserted from
the *Research*, took up his lodgings at a tavern in
Hobart Town. It happened that Captain Speck
gave a dinner to a few of his acquaintances at
the same house, and in consequence of Dr.
Tytler living there, invited him out of courtesy
to be of the party. I, of course, declined being
present.

10*th*.—I was informed this morning by a
gentleman on shore, that on passing the tavern
the preceding evening, he beheld Doctor Tytler
without coat, jacket, or hat, and with his shirt
sleeves tucked up making a great noise, as if he
had just left a boxing-match. I inquired into
the cause of this, and learnt that the Doctor
had become much intoxicated after dinner,
when he began to vociferate, "that he was now
where the British flag flourished *unrestricted*:
that he had always been oppressed under the
Company's government, and could not obtain
impartial justice among them; that now he was
under the British flag, he would serve the Com-

pany no more, and was disgraced by wearing their uniform : on saying which he pulled off his uniform coat and flung it upon the floor, which was the reason of his sitting without coat or jacket during the remainder of the night. I also understood that he insulted the whole company ; but next morning, being made sensible of his error, sent an apology to each of them by Captain Speck.

In the course of the day I went round to the principal merchants, and offered to dispose of bills on the Bengal Government for cash, to meet the ship's disbursements, which were now likely to become considerable, as she would be detained for several weeks at the instance of Doctor Tytler. The merchants told me that the trade between Calcutta and Van Diemen's Land had become so limited that they had no remittances to make.

11*th.*—Landed this morning, and waited on the Lieutenant-governor. I informed him that I could not succeed in getting my bills nego-ciated. He replied, with reluctance, that he would order the commissary to advance me 4,000 Spanish dollars, at the rate of 4*s.* 4*d.* each (amounting to £866. 13*s.* 4*d.*); but that he expected I would give him a set of bills upon the Secretary of the Hon. East-India Company in Leadenhall Street, for the amount.

I told him that I had no authority to draw on
England, and shewed him my letters of instruction, authorizing me to draw on the Bengal
Government. He read my letters, and replied
that he would not advance the cash on the faith
of the authorities in India; and that it was only
with a view of obliging the Home government
that he was willing to advance the money under
any circumstances.

I soon guessed the source whence he derived
the information under which he acted, and
accordingly begged of him to pay no attention
to the misrepresentations of a man, who had
been a most troublesome person to society at
large for the last fourteen years. Finding him
however remain inflexible, I had no alternative
but to draw on the Chief Secretary to the Hon.
East-India Company in London, and did so
accordingly.

I then proceeded into town, where I met a
gentleman, who informed me that Dr. Tytler
boasted that when the trial had come to issue
he would get me put into confinement, and that
the chief officer should take the command of the
ship and proceed on the expedition. This the
Doctor also mentioned to M. Chaigneau, who
strongly reprobated such a plan of proceeding,
urging that he was greatly interested in the
success of the voyage of discovery.

I immediately called on two gentlemen who were in the commission of the peace, and had been intimate acquaintances of mine for several years, and mentioned to them what I had just heard. They informed me that, through the assistance of a certain Methodist preacher, the Doctor, who was much addicted to evangelical and theological discussion, had ingratiated himself into the favour of the Governor, and that he was regarded at head-quarters as quite a saint. They also told me that the Judge of the Supreme Court was suspected of regulating his decisions agreeably to the Governor's fancy.

12th.—I found, on going on board, that the chief officer allowed the crew to insult the petty officers with impunity in consequence of their being my old servants and followers. My clerk, also, was drunk daily, who could not have obtained the means of becoming so had the chief officer done his duty.

The chief officer had never served on board of an armed ship till he was appointed to the *Research*, and was as ignorant of the management of guns, small arms, quarters, &c. as he was of practical seamanship. The most common merchant man in the port was kept in neater order than mine, which was facetiously dignified with the appellation of the " Lascar man-o'-war." I had reason to suspect that officer had in view the prospects held out by Doctor Tytler, of his becoming commander of the ship in the event of my confinement, and that, actuated by those hopes, he neglected to enforce that subordination among the crew which was necessary, hoping by that means to remove any obstacle which their refusal to sail under his command might throw in his way: for the men, naturally averse to control, would joyfully prefer him for their captain who was least strict.

21st.—From the 7th inst. to this date I was amused by the promises of the Lieut. governor respecting the money I had applied for, and which he had promised to advance *without delay.* This morning, however, I acquainted him with my intention of sailing for Port Jackson the day following, should I not procure the cash before then. He declared that the delay was not occasioned by him, and that he would instantly send for the Commissary, and inquire into the cause of his tardiness in complying with my request.

At noon I met the Commissary, who directed me to draw out my bills, saying that he would thereupon pay me over the 4,000 dollars. I immediately therefore caused the bills to be prepared, with letters of advice, and returned to the commissariat department, the head of

which being absent, I was requested by the
person in charge to leave my bills, which he
would shew to the Commissary upon his return;
adding, that if I would call in about an hour he
would have the money ready for delivery. I
accordingly called at the appointed time; but,
lo! the office was shut, business had ceased for
that day, nor was it to be resumed till the following Tuesday. The first thought that sug-
gested itself was that I had been played a trick.
" Yes," thought I, " in securing my bills for
£866. 13s. 4d. they have possessed themselves of
a tolerably sufficient guarantee that I shall not
sail to-morrow morning. If this is not a *ruse de
guerre*, it is at least a good stroke of commissary
generalship."

I instantly repaired to the Government-house,
intending to complain of this breach of faith on
the part of the Commissary-general; but what
was my surprise when I found that the Governor had left town, and was not expected to
return till Monday. I was subsequently informed that the Commissary had also treated
himself to a rural excursion, on which he had
set out at the very time I was, according to his
own appointment, to have received the money
that was to accelerate the despatch of the
Research.

It would be difficult to convey a just idea of

the disgust I felt at this shuffling conduct, which compelled me to remain in the port, or to hazard the loss of the set of bills, by a trick played me with the view, no doubt, of detaining me for the issue of Dr. Tytler's complaints.

24*th*.—This morning at ten o'clock the trial came on, at the instance of Dr. Tytler, against me, before a court-*martial* (I may well call it), consisting of the Chief Justice (who upon this occasion I am to suppose acted as judge-advocate), and six military officers of the 40th regiment. The prosecution was conducted by the acting attorney-general, who was Doctor Tytler's advocate. He opened the proceedings with a long and eloquent speech, in the course of which he availed himself of every opportunity to disparage me in the eyes of the court, and to traduce me in the most abusive style. Among other appeals to the members of the court with a view to prejudice them against me, he forcibly reminded them that the plaintiff was one of their own profession (a military man!), and how much they were bound in honour to mark their just sense of the insult offered to that profession in the person of Dr. Tytler.

As a full account of the trial would occupy too much of the reader's time and patience in this place, and is fitter for an appendix, the following brief sketch of it must suffice. The case rested in a great measure on the evidence of the prosecutor himself, and, as might be expected, he was supported, as far as he could be, by those in the vessel, who knew that having been privy to his machinations, by his defeat and eventual conviction they themselves would be compromised.

The Doctor talked as if he had been one of the greatest men in India; represented himself as being the person who got up the expedition by his influence and talents, and as the only man on whom the Government relied. In short, like the philosopher in Rasselas, who thought that the winds, and seasons, and the motion of the spheres, depended on his nod, the Doctor gave himself out as a man of mighty importance, whose labours for the good of mankind and the enlightenment of posterity were obstructed by a tyrannical captain, who, he said, had, without any cause, subjected him to the most cruel and ignominious treatment.

Thus he ended as he began. He introduced himself to me as the victim of persecution; he still pictured himself as a martyr. I was now converted into his persecutor; and his former oppressors, as he then called them, in India, were turned into friends and benefactors, who would fit out distant expeditions at his word, to afford him an opportunity of closing his career gloriously.

To illustrate this I need only quote the following portion of his evidence.

In the course of a cross-examination the following was elicited :—

Q. I ask you, Dr. Tytler, whether or not the Government had, in point of fact, the whole matter of this discovery in contemplation before this (the Asiatic Society's) meeting ?

A. It is morally impossible for me to know the secrets of Government. I understood it was with the greatest difficulty on the part of Government that they fitted out the expedition, on account of my explanation of the cypher on the sword-guard, of the letters M.F.F.; these were represented to Lord Combermere, who agreed to it.

Q. Then it was through you that this expedition was fitted out—on your representation ?

A. I was expressly told so. The secretary of the Medical Board told me so, and he knows more of the secrets of Government than me.

He further stated as follows :—

The disagreements I mentioned before between the Government and myself were entirely settled at this time, and I was on the point of joining my regiment. I had been appointed a month before. I think it was in consideration of the misunderstanding, that this expedition was to give me an opportunity of shining, and closing all our differences. (A loud laugh in the court.) These words were made use of to me by Mr. Swinton.

Were it not that I do not wish to occupy too

much of my journal, I could point out at least fifty more falsehoods in Dr. Tytler's evidence. What I have, however, quoted verbatim from the proceedings, taken in short-hand by an expert stenographist, and notarially attested as correct, will establish Dr. Tytler's claim to a dispassionate and impartial regard to truth ; or, to speak without irony, it will fully prove how little was the regard he paid to it when likely to militate against the principal object of his prosecution : namely, to have me imprisoned and himself constituted leader of the expedition, the chief officer being the sailing commander !

In the above-quoted passage he pretends that the Government of British India was so sorry for having had a difference (or rather a thousand differences) with the great Doctor Tytler, that to make it up with him they fitted out an expedition to the South Seas, at an expense of 150,000 rupees, to give him an opportunity of exploring the tract of the Queen of Sheba, the golden coasts of Ophir, and the course of the aerolite, which he says (in 1823) travelled through the air from the island of Java to Allahabad, where the Doctor then resided, to give him warning of his approaching voyage to the part of the world whence it came—and thus end his life with the practical confirmation of

these and other such visionary dreams, in which
he had wasted so many years, thereby insulting
the understanding of the public.

On the statements of this man, whom every
sensible person in India had for many years
regarded as a crack-brained enthusiast (which
seems to be now lamentably confirmed by his
complete derangement of intellect), the sage
military court of Van Diemen's Land came to
the sapient conclusion that I was blameable
for laying my hand on his shoulder and placing him for two hours under close arrest, or
for threatening him with irons and corporal
punishment, if he did not desist from his attempts to excite mutiny and bloodshed in the
ship.

I cannot enter here into the gross contradic-
tions and prevarications which occurred between
him and the chief officer about his (the Doctor's)
letter to my officers, instigating them to confine
me as a lunatic. It appears that when he found
it failed to produce the desired effect (either
from the cowardice of the conspirators or the
sense of duty prevailing among the rest) he was
glad to get his letter back again, and to destroy this important document, which, if it
could have been produced, would have exposed him and his accomplices to be tried, and
perhaps executed as mutineers.

I have been thus prolix in my comments upon this, to me memorable trial (since it cost me £521), not so much from a regard to private feeling, as with a view to demonstrate the necessity, in future, of closely inquiring into the characters of persons applying for employment in the public service.

28th.—This day the prosecution and my defence having closed, the Judge summed up the case to the members of the court to the following effect :—

He premised that they were not to try the merits of this case by their notions of mutiny or martial law; that, in point of fact, the ship in question was precisely similar to a merchant vessel trading from London to these colonies, and that the defendant had no more authority than the master of such a ship would have over his officers and crew. He observed, that the only points for the consideration of the court were, first, had an assault been committed ? and then, had a justification been made out to their satisfaction ? A justification might be made out in two ways: either by the Doctor writing a letter to the officers, representing the captain to be mad when he knew at the same time that he was not mad, and by that means dispossessing the captain of the command; or by his representing what he believed to be true, but what was not so in fact; and that the defendant, at the time he put Doctor Tytler under arrest, believed the Doctor had made an untrue statement for the purpose of taking the command from him. The Judge expressed his opinion that, in either of these cases, the justification had been made out, and the defendant would be entitled to a verdict; but upon the latter point the members of the court ought to be satisfied that the Captain called his officers together, and consulted them upon the subject, and took all proper means of informing himself upon the nature and contents of the communication made to the officers.

In either case, the court was desirous that the gentlemen should specially find the facts upon which their verdict should be founded.

The members of the court retired for about an hour and a half, and returned the following verdict: — " Guilty upon the fourth count.* " The Court-Martial are of opinion that Doctor " Tytler should have exercised more discretion " in introducing observations which he knew " were irritating to the feelings of Captain " Dillon."

Captain Dillon was then ordered to attend on Tuesday to receive judgment.

* The fourth count was for arresting Dr. Tytler, and putting my hand on his shoulder in so doing, which was construed into an assault.

If this was not qualifying a verdict, it would be difficult to say how it could be qualified.

The counsel for the defendant said that his client was in attendance to receive the judgment of the court. To which the Judge objected in these words :—" I could not think of passing judgment in this case without looking over the evidence again. If the defendant is prepared with bail, I will take it at once. I will give judgment on Tuesday next."

The Judge then addressed himself to me in the following words :—" The custom here is, when a defendant is found guilty, to commit him to prison until judgment is passed. I, however, do not wish to put you to that inconvenience, if you are prepared with bail for your attendance here on Tuesday next at ten o'clock."

I inquired, " What bail is necessary ?" The Judge's answer was, " Two sureties in £40 each, and yourself in £80;" which sureties were immediately entered into.

The Lieutenant-governor was at this time absent in the country, and not expected to return till Monday evening. Had the Judge substituted the following words : " I should like to consult the Governor before I pass judgment upon you," for those which formed his excuse for the postponement of judgment till the following Tuesday, he would have deserved more credit for sincerity.

The following account of two cases tried at Hobart Town, Van Diemen's Land, the one at the suit of the Attorney-General against Doctor Crowder, and the other, Doctor Crowder against Captain Carns, both for assaults of a most glaring nature, will afford a correct idea of the general and equable manner in which justice is administered there.

The ship *Cumberland*, from England, commanded and owned by Captain Carns, arrived off Hobart Town in the early part of 1825. On the passage out a dispute arose between Doctor Crowder and Counsellor Stevens, the result of which was that Physic horsewhipped Law most severely; who did himself justice by instituting an action against the assailant, and recovered fifty pounds for the damage done to his person. A few days after that on which the assault was committed on board the *Cumberland*, the captain, who was a Leviathan skipper, observed the poor Doctor on the poop, and without any previous warning, seized him by the back of the neck in his huge fist, and dashed him upon the quarter-deck, breaking two of his ribs by the fall. For this wanton assault, Dr. Crowder, finding himself worsted in a legal prosecution by Mr. A. Stevens, sought reparation by the same means, and obtained a verdict: but what were the damages? Why, we must not apply the rule of proportion to solve this query, or we should never even approximate it: the damages were *forty shillings!* Yes, forty shillings for two broken ribs, wantonly, and I may almost say, savagely broken. Twenty shillings a joint were awarded by the judge; which would lead us to suppose he considers broken or fractured limbs less in the scale of personal grievance than a horse-whipping, however well merited, since for the latter he adjudges a compensation twenty-five times greater.

29*th.*—At noon this day I was told that the the ship *Hope,* of London, on a voyage from Port Jackson to this place, got on shore last night at the harbour-mouth, and was in great distress. I immediately repaired on board the *Research* and despatched the second officer with a boat's crew to assist in trying to get her off. I found my ship, as usual, filthy in the extreme, and pointed this out to the chief officer: who replied that of late I had found great fault with him, and he requested I would engage another person in his stead. I was not sorry to hear him say so, but supposed he was not in earnest. I immediately afterwards went on shore.

30*th.*—Shortly after breakfast I met Dr. Scott,

the colonial surgeon, who had been on board the *Research* to visit the sick. He informed me that my chief officer talked of leaving the ship at Hobart Town, and was about coming on shore to request permission to that effect. Shortly afterwards the chief officer called on me for this purpose, stating that he felt uncomfortable on board the *Research*, and therefore hoped he might be permitted to leave her. To this I did not object, but requested he would return till the second officer should come back from the wreck, or until I had engaged with another to take his situation.

This afternoon the Lieutenant-governor returned to town, and the Judge, whose motions I watched very narrowly, immediately repaired to his residence, where my fate was, as I suppose, sealed.

1*st May*.—I paid my morning visit to the ship as usual, and observing something very offensive on the cables, I hinted at this repeated inattention to the chief officer; who replied, " Capt. Dillon, I wish to quit the ship : get another officer." I immediately went on board of the free-trader *Albion*, mentioned to Capt. Ralph, her commander, how unpleasantly I was situated for the want of a proper officer, and begged of him to spare me one of his. He replied, that his chief officer was detained at Sydney as a witness on a law-suit; that he had returned in the ship *Hope* to rejoin the *Albion,* but had not come up yet, in consequence of the wreck of that vessel at the mouth of the harbour; however, that when he arrived, he would spare him to me.

Shortly afterward I saw the gentleman alluded to on the public wharf, and mentioned to him the conversation that had passed between Capt. Ralph and myself, offering to engage him on the same terms and allowances which my present officer enjoyed. To this he agreed; and as I was going to the court, I promised to deliver up charge to him, as chief officer of the *Research,* on my return in the afternoon. At ten o'clock the court-house was opened. The Judge-Advocate of the court-martial took his seat, and inquired in a petulant tone if *Peter Dillon* was there? I stood up. The learned judge then shortly adverted to the facts of the case, and stated, " that he considered it necessary to mark my conduct, and by that means prevent such behaviour in future by commanders of ships, either to officers or passengers; and although it was true that no violence had been used, and that the prosecutor had been in close confinement only two hours, yet the facts of the case, in his opinion, manifested bad feeling, and were attended with circumstances of ag-

gravation.   The sentence of the court was, that
I should be imprisoned two months in the gaol
of Hobart Town, pay a fine of £50, and enter
into sureties, in the sum of £400, to keep the
peace for twelve calendar months."

Here then is another admirable sample of the
impartial disposition of the Van Diemen's Land
executive.   The Tasmanian judge seems to
proportion the rigour of his sentences in an
inverse ratio to the amount of injury done : so
the Indian Government, being the most innocent, must be punished most severely.*   He
scorns the vulgar practice of ordinary lawyers
and judges, in forming their decisions according
to the atrocity of the actual breach of the
law : he flies into the regions of feeling, con-
sults the *animus* which dictated the action, and
awards accordingly.   So he says himself : at
least, his review of the circumstances of the case
implies as much.   But, alas ! he is not always
consistent, as witness the case of Doctor
Crowder *versus* Capt. Carns, in which he awarded only the nominal damages of forty shillings
(barely sufficient to carry costs), for two broken
ribs caused by the unwarranted assault of the
defendant.   Did he, in this matter, consult feel-

* By my confinement, the expedition, with all the expenses
attending it going on, must be detained two months : that is, I
am fined £50, and the public treasury of Bengal at least £2,000 !

ing? and if he did, whose feeling did he consult? the feeling that actuated the defendant
to assault an inoffensive man, or his own feelings upon the subject? I will not pursue this
parallel further.

The result of all this is only another instance
of the fallibility of judges and rulers, and must
convey a just idea of the mode in which justice
is administered in these remote regions. The
military men who formed the jury, and the
lawyers who were their advisers, could hardly
be expected perhaps to form a just opinion of
the kind of discipline which is necessary at sea,
where the captain stands alone like an absolute
monarch, with nothing to support his power
but strict subordination and obedience.

In short, the good people of Van Diemen's
Land seem to have been imposed on by the wild
rhapsodies entitled " Tytler's Illustrations of
Ancient Geography and History," which were
apparently regarded there as the *ne plus ultra* of
human ingenuity. They seem to have believed,
on his authority, that he was at least one of the
sons of the prophets, and I his persecutor;
that, as he pretends, Sumatra was the Ophir of
the Scriptures, and Java the isle of Sheba : and
had he continued the voyage with me, he would
no doubt have treated the world with a learned
treatise, proving that the island of Mannicolo

was the Laputa of Gulliver, which, yielding to
the universal force of gravitation, had at last
ceased to float over its dependent isles, and
sousing like a water-fowl into the Pacific Ocean,
had taken root, swallowing in the vortex thus
created the ships under the command of la
Pérouse. Surely no punishment could be too
severe for the person who cut short the pro
phetic career of so great a man in the eyes of
his wise disciples!

The sub-sheriff invited me to accompany him
to my newly assigned lodgings, and on my way
thither I was met by the high-sheriff. This
gentleman, who is the son of a wealthy English
banker, felt much for my situation, behaved
with the greatest kindness towards me, and introduced me to the governor of the prison, who
relinquished one-half of his apartments to me
in the kindest manner, and treated me with
every mark of respect, in which he was joined
by his amiable lady. He is the son of an English gentleman, and emigrated to Van Diemen's
Land about three years ago, with the intention
of becoming what is here locally termed a set-
tler. With this view he took possession of his
estate in the interior; but was soon afterwards
plundered of all his property by the gangs of
runaway convicts who infest the woods, and

are commonly distinguished by the name of
" Bush-rangers."

Thus reduced, and his lady being afraid to
remain any longer among such scenes, he retired from his estate to Hobart Town, where
he received the appointment he now holds.

Notwithstanding the bombastic shew of justice exhibited by the learned and very pliable
chief justice, I was fully aware of the intended catastrophe of this judicial farce, having
been well advised of its drift for some days
before, and therefore felt perfectly at ease in
my novel situation, knowing that it was not
their intention to carry into effect more than
one-eighth of that part of the sentence which
related to my detention in prison. But, being
aware of its main object, I took special care to
defeat their projects.

Before my imprisonment it was hinted to me,
through the means of a gentleman in office,
that this would form a part of my sentence, and
that matters were to be so arranged as to make
it appear that my enlargement should be principally owing to Dr. Tytler's interposition on
my behalf, which it was presumed would pave
the way to a complete and permanent recon-
ciliation between us. That if this were not the
case, I should necessarily be detained till the

full expiration of the term, and that in the mean time the chief officer would take the command, and proceed on the voyage.

Unfortunately my imprisonment had prevented me from putting the new officer in charge, though I had engaged him.

2*d.*—I was visited by the most respectable persons in the town; particularly by Mr. Edward Lord, brother to Sir John Owen Lord, member of parliament for Pembrokeshire. Mr. Lord succeeded to the government of this colony on the decease of Governor Collins, and administered affairs for a considerable time much to the satisfaction of the colonists.

The Judge and the Lieutenant-governor were highly incensed at the numerous testimonies of respect shewn me upon this occasion by so large a portion of the aristocracy, whom they wished to treat me as unworthy of their notice. Mr. Lord, with Messrs. Bethune and Kemp, two of the principal merchants in the town, procured a petition to the Governor to be drawn up, praying for a remission of my sentence as far as regarded my imprisonment, for the sake of the expedition in which I was engaged, and it was signed by the most respectable and wealthy persons in the colony, who took a deep interest in my fate in consequence of the cabals by which I was oppressed.

Mr. Lord, who was an old acquaintance, shewed himself also my firm friend in this affair, notwithstanding the danger to which he thus exposed himself of forfeiting the patronage of the local administration, and all the indulgences and immunities usually bestowed on those who sympathize in the Governor's feelings on points in which he takes any interest.

3d. — This morning I transmitted to the Lieutenant-governor the petition which had been drawn up yesterday by the gentlemen of Hobart Town, and accompanied it with a letter from myself, stating that the objects of the expedition must fail if I was detained in prison two months, as the monsoons would change before I could then reach the Mannicolos, and thus frustrate all my plans. I further stated, that I was willing to pay the fine of £50, and to enter into sureties to return to Van Diemen's Land at the termination of the voyage, and undergo the remainder of my imprisonment, offering to bind myself in any amount he might think necessary.

4th.—In order to frustrate the Doctor's designs, I removed my servant, Martin Bushart, from the ship to a friend's house, and sent Mr. Ross, the other interpreter, to Port Jackson; so that if the ship's command were wrested from me, there remained no interpreters on

board, nor a person who knew the latitude or
longitude of Mannicolo.   Martin Bushart declared that he would never abandon me, and
that should he be forced on board under any
other commander, they might beware of the
consequences the moment he landed at Mannicolo or Tucopia.

This evening I was visited by the Counsel
for Doctor Tytler, who addressed me in the
following words: " Captain Dillon, you have
sent a letter to the Governor respecting your
release, but I can assure you that you will not
be released unless you make matters up with
Doctor Tytler, and give your officers as bonds-
men in the sum of £400, that you will keep the
peace towards the Doctor during the remainder
of the voyage."

I replied, " Sir, do you suppose I am going
to sea with my hands manacled?   Did you ever
hear of the captain of a ship going to sea under
such restrictions?   The law, if I can call it
such in Van Diemen's Land, has already made
a sufficient provision for Doctor Tytler's protection: what more is necessary? Doctor Tytler
can rejoin the ship and continue his duty. I will
not molest him, unless his conduct merits it."

The Counsellor now wished to bring the
matter to a crisis: I informed him that he
must consult my legal advisers, and sent for

them immediately. He told me that if I did not shake hands with the Doctor, the Governor would send the ship to sea under the chief officer's command. I replied that this would be piracy; and that to provide against it, I had some days past sent all the papers belonging to the ship to Sydney; therefore if she went to sea, it must be without papers or interpreters. This latter difficulty, he observed, would be surmounted by the police compelling Bushart to go on board. " Perhaps so," said I; " you may deprive me of my servant, as you have of my liberty. If Bushart is forced on board by the police here, let those who detain him there beware of the consequences when the *police at Mannicolo* become acquainted with the circumstance. Their decisions at Tucopia and Mannicolo in matters similar to these are very summary, and severe retaliation is the principle on which their ideas of justice are based: be cautious, therefore, how you act in this respect." He then began to soothe me, and requested me not to be angry, for that he was but jesting. To this I answered, " How can I be otherwise than angry, when I reflect on the injustice done me? Though you, sir, were unmercifully horsewhipped by Doctor Crowder, you recovered only £50 damages. I have neither used horsewhip, stick, or fist, yet here I am imprisoned."

At this moment my legal advisers came into the prison yard, and the counsellor, not much admiring the recent turn I had given to the conversation, withdrew with them.

5th.—At an early hour this morning I understood from a friend that the counsellor had called last night at the house of Captain Speck, in company with Doctor Tytler, where they met Monsieur Chaigneau and the chief officer, from whom the Doctor obtained a certificate, to the effect that, from what had passed on board between Doctor Tytler and me, it would not be proper that we should sail again together. He also informed me that the chief officer was directed to attend at the Government-house to-day in order to be installed into the command of the ship.

This person called upon me about half-past nine o'clock, and informed me that he had been directed last night to wait on the Governor this morning, who wished to see him on some point relative to the command of the *Research*. He added, that he was then going to the Government-house, and would call upon me on his return. About noon he again made his appearance, at which time I was engaged with my legal adviser; in whose presence he told me he had not seen the Governor, but was spoken to on the subject by his secretary, who asked him if he

would undertake the command of the *Research*
and complete the voyage. The officer, who
well knew that he would not be countenanced
in such a measure by Monsieur Chaigneau, the
French agent, the other officers, the South-Sea
islanders, and others on board, declined accepting of the command, and was requested to sig-
nify his answer in writing. I advised him not to
give a written answer until a written proposal
should be made to confer on him the command.

7th.—I was visited this morning by the Rev.
Philip Connolly, Roman Catholic chaplain, and
his friend the high-sheriff, who told me that
they had drawn up a petition to the Lieutenant-
governor, which would be signed in the course
of the day by all the civil and military officers,
praying him, for the sake of humanity, and the
success of the expedition on which I was engaged, to release me.

In the evening I received the petition, signed
by a number of highly respectable individuals,
among whom were the names of four members
of the court-martial. Dr. Tytler's own counsel
also subscribed it; but a similarity of disposition
inclining him to sympathize with the Doctor, he
added some remarks with which I felt so disgusted, that I declined allowing his name to appear as a petitioner in my behalf.

Leonard Helmick, whom the Doctor had endeavoured to get on shore before the trial had
come on, was absent from the ship since the
24th ultimo, nor could I obtain, by my frequent
applications to the magistrates, any effectual
assistance to get him apprehended and recon-
ducted on board.

8th.—At a late hour this evening I was called
on by a friend, from whom I understood that
the secretary to the Lieutenant-governor was
much displeased on hearing that the military
officers had signed the petition for my liberation, and that he lost no time in repairing to
the military barracks, where he severely lectured the officers alluded to for their contumacy.
He told them that they were soldiers, and
ought not to interfere in such matters, and that
he felt confident the Governor would be highly
displeased upon learning the fact, and would
not fail to mark his sense of their conduct.

This speech made such an impression on the
mind of the foreman of the court-martial that he
arose in haste, and without delay proceeded to
the house of the honest sheriff, whom he disturbed
from his dinner, and begged of him for God's sake
to shew him the petition for a few moments in
order that he might erase his name from it,
being apprehensive that its appearance there
would mar a suit he was then making for a fur-

lough to proceed to Europe to enable him to settle some private affairs.

9th.—While at tea this evening with my worthy host and hostess, M. Chaigneau and the chief officer called on me. Shortly after (about 5 P.M.) I received a letter from the Lieutenant-governor,* stating that the sheriff had been written to, directing him to discharge me from custody on my payment of the fine and entering into the prescribed sureties to keep the peace.

On receipt of this letter I sent to my solicitor, who hastened with it to the judge, and urging that, as the preliminaries to my enlargement might be arranged in half-an-hour, I should be released that evening. This irregular method of doing business, however, was not to be countenanced by so upright and strict a member of the bench, who informed my attorney that there were regular office hours for transacting business ; that at the proper time to-morrow I could be brought up by writ of *habeas corpus*, and having in open court complied with the conditions of my release, I should be discharged. This judicial manœuvre inclined me to think I had been once more duped.

---

* It was sent me by the hands of Mr. Savary, the banker from Bristol, who shortly before arrived in the colony, to which he had been transported, and where he is a very useful member of society.

The explanation to this religious regard for legal formulæ may be gathered from the following particulars :—It was rumoured in town, that as soon as I should have regained my liberty, it was my intention to force Doctor Tytler on board the *Research*, and compel him to complete his engagement as surgeon for the voyage. To avoid this, Dr. Tytler had engaged a passage to Port Jackson in the *Albion*, Capt. Ralph, who was to sail the next morning, and had I been released that evening, he was fully impressed with the idea that I would compel him to return to the service from which he had absconded, and therefore induced his friend to detain me till the last moment, in order to afford him the means of escape.

10*th*.—At 10 o'clock this morning I was called on by Mr. Edward Lord and Mr. Bethune, who offered to become sureties in the bond which I was about to enter into, and shortly afterwards my solicitor repaired to the judge's house, with the information that I was prepared to comply with the legal forms which were deemed by him indispensable preliminaries to my enlargement.

The judge upon this looked out of the back window of his apartment, and observing a ship under weigh proceeding out of the harbour, inquired of the solicitor what ship was sailing out of the port ?   The latter replied, " the *Al-bion* :" then, resumed the other, " I suppose Dr. Tytler is gone ?"—" Yes, your worship," was the reply.   The judge then continued : " I will not put Capt. Dillon to the inconvenience of going through all the forms required by law ; let the sureties be entered into in presence of a magistrate, and the fine be paid : that is all that will be necessary to obtain his liberation."

Of course all this was performed without delay, and I left the prison with Mr. Lord under one arm and Mr. Bethune under the other, and thus escorted, met the Lieutenant-governor in the street.   If the countenance be the index of the mind, there was sufficient pourtrayed in his at that moment to warrant a surmise that these gentlemen would be remembered on a future day, for the testimony of esteem thus paid to one who, they knew, enjoyed so small a portion of his Excellency's good graces.

Not wishing the ship to be detained longer, I sent my agent to the colonial secretary to request the dollars for which my set of bills had been drawn, and delivered to the commissary, nearly a fortnight ago.   The first question put by him in reply to my agent's demand was, " Is Dr. Tytler gone ?"   This being answered in the affirmative, he replied, " We will ad-

vance Capt. Dillon the amount, but must first
have a bottomry bond on the ship." As night
was approaching, we were obliged to leave
matters *in statu quo.*

I was furnished with powers to draw upon
the authorities at Van Diemen's Land, but not
to bottomry the Hon. East-India Company's
ship under my command. Had such a condition been proposed to me on the 7th April,
when first I applied for the money, I should
have sailed to Port Jackson, where my agents
would have advanced me the sum required.
I could not do so now : the amount of debt
contracted for the ship's supply during the period she had been detained by Dr. Tytler must
be discharged before I could depart.

11*th.*—This morning I wrote to the Lieutenant-governor, requesting he would direct
payment to be made for the bills which the
Deputy-Commissary held from me ; and that
although I was not authorized to give a bottomry bond on the Hon. Company's ship *Research*, still my exigencies were such, that if he
persisted in the demand I would do it.

12*th.*—At noon I received a letter from the
Lieutenant-governor, stating that he would now
order the money to be paid on a bottomry bond
on the ship *Research* being given ; and with this
letter I waited upon the secretary, who said he

could do nothing in the matter until he had
seen the Attorney-general.

The Secretary's office was soon after shut, not
to be re-opened till Monday ; and thus were
two days more lost, and the ship unnecessarily
detained at an enormous expense. This was, no
doubt, a manœuvre, to give the Doctor time to
get clear off, and enable him to relate his story
the first at head-quarters.

14*th.*—I called on the secretary this morning
at office hours, who sent for the Attorney-general, and after a three hours' farce, the subject
having been discussed in all its various shapes
(the *Albion* sailing with all her speed in the
mean time), it was finally determined that the
cash should be advanced without the bond ; and
at one o'clock I received a bank cheque for the
amount, which I handed over to the ship's agent.

The person whom I had engaged on the 1st
instant, waited on me to-day, for the purpose
being placed on board.   I accordingly wrote to
my chief officer, stating that, in reply to his application of the 30th ult. and 1st instant, requesting me to engage another officer in his
place, I had complied with his solicitation, and
engaged one who was prepared go on board to
take charge, requesting him, at the same time,
to deliver over to him the various stores, &c.,
and take his receipt for the same.

15th.—I was much surprised this day by the receipt of a letter from him, informing me that it was not his wish to quit the ship ; and saying, that at the time he gave me notice of his desire to leave, he expected the command of the *Hetty* schooner.

17th.—Received information this morning that the person who was my clerk had been in the habit of stealing the ship's rum, and selling it to the crew at the rate of two rupees per bottle.   I sent on board for a man named Proctor, who I understood was one of those to whom he had surreptitiously disposed of the rum, and who informed me that he had bought spirits from Munroe, and that others on board had done so likewise.   Hereupon I was resolved to prosecute him for felony.

This day I also received intelligence that the chief officer had induced the European part of the crew, through the agency of Henry Sutton, a seaman on board, to write to the Lieutenant-governor, stating that they wished to be discharged from the ship, since their officers were about to be displaced, and others substituted of whose character they knew nothing.   The letter was written by Munroe, at the request of Sutton ; but some of the crew refusing to sign it, a dangerous fellow named Graham, and another, threatened to cut their throats if they did not comply.

18*th.*—Several letters passed between my chief officer and me on the subject of his delivering up charge to the person whom I had engaged at his particular request, signified to me upon the 30th of the last and 1st of the present month; but finding him not inclined to move without putting me to some trouble, I convened a meeting of captains of ships, some of whom had been naval officers, whom I appointed to meet to-morrow, in order to take their opinion as to how I ought to act upon the present occasion. My chief officer was apprized of my intention by letter, and requested to attend the meeting at the store of Captain Bell, on the wharf, at 10 o'clock next morning.

19*th.*—This morning I started, in company with my attorney, for the purpose of going on board the ship to inspect some bills of exchange drawn in favour of my agents in Calcutta by a person here on my account, which bills had been kept back for more than two years. On reaching the boat, I was called away upon some business that I could not neglect, and my attorney proceeded without me. Having, however, remained on board for some time, and finding that I did not come off, he proceeded on shore

again where I met him.   He informed me that
he had held some conversation with my chief
officer on the subject of his quitting the ship,
who said that if I addressed him another letter
on the same subject, he would immediately
deliver over charge to the person newly appointed., This, of course, I did without delay.

I had my clerk in attendance, for the purpose
of bringing him before the police for feloniously
purloining the ship's rum.   From this act of
justice my attorney dissuaded me for the present,
urging that I should be bound over to prosecute
him,ɪ and thus incur an additional delay.   I
therefore sent him on board, with directions to the
draughtsman ɪto inform the newly appointed
chief officer on no account whatever to allow
him to quit the ship.

I then repaired to the meeting of captains
convened for to-day, whom I found assembled at
the appointed place.   The gentlemen who met
together on this occasion were Lieutenant Han-
by of the Royal Navy, commander of the *Hetty* schooner ; Captain Walsh, superintendent of
marine, Hobart Town, formerly a captain in the
country service ; Captain Bell, late commander
of the Hon. Company's chartered ship *Minerva*,
now principal of the mercantile house of " Bell
and Co. ;" and Captain Wilson, formerly commander in the English trade to South America,

and now a merchant. On my arrival I found
that my chief officer had not thought proper to
attend, and I proceeded to take the sense of
the meeting ; when it was unanimously agreed,
that he having acted very improperly, should
not be suffered to continue any longer on duty
as chief officer of the *Research*. Shortly after
this I received a letter from him stating that it
was his intention to proceed in the *Guide* brig
towards Bengal.

At 2 P.M. I received a letter from on board,
without signature, the purport of which was
that the ship's company wished to see me on
board. I informed the bearer that I never allowed seamen to command me either to go on
board or to go on shore : that it was my place
to order, and not to be ordered. Though I had
business on board, I declined going, having
heard that my late officer had been distributing
rum amongst the seamen, who were all drunk.

About 4 P.M. Mr. Deane, my new officer,
came on shore to acquaint me that my clerk had
escaped from the ship unknown to him. On inquiry I found that he had gone in the boat with
my late officer's baggage ; and that the draughtsman had gone on board of the *Guide* to make
inquiry concerning him, where he learnt that
my clerk had been with the baggage, and was
now on shore. To the last part of this in-

formation I paid little credit, suspecting that my late officer took him to Sydney with the intention of conveying him to India, where a part might have been allotted him in the drama got up by the Doctor for their mutual exculpation. Thus I was deprived of my clerk's services, together with a sum of money he stood indebted to me. However, that no means might be left untried for his apprehension, I despatched a police officer in quest of him to the several punch and dancing-houses in town, who, as I had expected, returned unsuccessful.

This afternoon I paid all my bills and shipped my stores, with the intention of proceeding to sea at daylight in the morning.

CHAPTER V.

OCCURRENCES FROM VAN DIEMEN'S LAND TO
PORT JACKSON.

20th.—I WENT on board with the pilot about 8
A.M., and shortly afterwards ordered the anchor
to be weighed.   In a few minutes the chief officer entered the cuddy, telling me that the crew
would not heave up the anchor, but that they
wanted to speak to me.   My reply was, that I
had nothing to say to them : that if they wished
to communicate any thing to me they should
commit it to paper.   In the course of about
half an hour I received a note without signature, and merely subscribed in these words :
" Your obedient servant, at the request of the
ship's company."

The tenour of the note was, that as the officers
who had been placed over them in India had
been removed, and others substituted of whose
characters they were ignorant, it was their wish
to be discharged.   Now the port regulations
here forbid the discharge of seamen, but finding
my men in an actual state of mutiny, I addressed
them in the following words : " My men, I have
no authority to discharge you in this port : but
such of you as persist in a refusal to do your

duty, are at liberty to leave the ship, bearing in mind that by so doing you forfeit all claim to whatever arrears of pay may be due to you, as well as every article belonging to you on board, which revert to the India Government." When I ceased speaking, seven of the most resolute of these fellows stepped into a shore-boat; but two of them immediately returned through the port-holes, the other five putting on shore.

We now hove up the anchor and sailed down the river, the Europeans being all nearly drunk, their faces dreadfully mangled, with black eyes, broken noses, and scratched jaws, occasioned by the spirits that my late officer had distributed among them previously to quitting the ship, with the intention perhaps of stimulating them to assault the officer who superseded him. Having post-office packets to deliver at Port Jackson, and being now in want of a naturalist and second officer, to supply the place of those who had deserted the expedition or been dismissed, I determined to proceed thither to procure them.

At 1 P.M. we cleared the Derwent, which I believe to be one of the most corrupt spots on the face of the globe. On beholding this scene of iniquity and oppression sinking in the distance, I could not refrain from exclaiming, "Van Diemen's Land I bid you adieu! Land of corrup-

tion and injustice, farewell! Adieu to the place
where the crackbrained antiquarian and noisy po-
lemic of India, the redoubtable and learned naturalist, botanist, historiographer, geographer, and
doctor of all arts and sciences (if we believe
his own account of his literary acquirements),
Robert Tytler, so easily succeeded in impres-
sing a belief of his worth and excellencies on
the minds of a governor, secretary, preacher,
acting attorney-general and judge, who looked
up to this visionary pedant as a second adm'ra-
ble Crichton."

I cannot but lament that I had not at first
sailed to Port Jackson : there I should have met
with no obstruction in refitting ; there I should
have enjoyed the right of trial by jury, and my
case would have been adjudged by honest and
upright men : whom no whining cant nor fear
of offending a military governor, could bias.
Had my case been tried there the decision would
have been quite the reverse of what it was.
Dr. Tytler's assumed pretensions would not have
imposed on any one.   He would have been compelled to concert his plans unaided by the ministers of government, unassisted by the adminis-
trators of that law which rigidly punishes the
crimes of mutiny and desertion.   The surgeon,
naturalist, botanist, mineralogist, and recorder
of proceedings to the supreme government, as

he called himself, must have continued his functions with his mutinous spirit somewhat chastened, and rendered more amenable to his superior; I should have been saved the enormous amount of law expenses to which I have been subjected; the Hon. Company would have been saved some thousands of pounds; and in all human probability, the expedition would have been rendered more satisfactory.

21st.—The winds for the greatest part of these twenty-four hours were from S.W. to N.W. Crowded all sail for Port Jackson. Latitude at noon 43° 8′ S.; longitude 149° 32′ E.: thermometer in the open air 54°. We were accompanied by several aquatic birds, none of which were seen by us on the passage to Hobart Town. At noon put up for public sale the few tattered garments left behind by the mutineers who deserted yesterday, and placed the amount to the ship's credit as being forfeited.

26th.—Throughout these twenty-four hours we experienced fine weather and smooth water. At 11 A.M. the coast of New South Wales appeared in view to the westward of Cape Howe. Ran 109 miles on a W. by N. course.

27th.—Light and variable breezes. Tacked ship at 10 A.M. Coast of New South Wales in sight. Performed divine service as usual on Sunday.

At noon Bass' Head in sight, bearing W. by N. per compass, distance off seventy-one miles. Latitude by observation 37°38′ S. : thermometer on deck 64°.

28*th*.—Our progress to the northward very slow, occasioned by the light variable winds, our whole run for the last twenty-four hours not exceeding forty-seven miles. At noon the latitude observed was 37° 9′ S., at which time Cape Dromedary, on the coast of New South Wales, was in sight, bearing N.N.W. ½ W. per compass, distant fifty-four miles; thermometer on deck 66°.

29*th*. Light airs and cloudy, with mizzling rain at intervals. Mount Dromedary in sight the major part of this day. At noon it bore W. by compass twelve leagues. Thermometer on deck 66°.

30*th*.—The weather throughout the day was much the same as yesterday. At 10 A.M. the clouds cleared off the coast, at which time Cape George bore W. by N. ½ N. three leagues; the wind from the south-eastward. Stood to the northward along the coast with all sails set. Thermometer on deck 61°.

31*st*.—Light variable winds and calms the first part of the day, all sail set standing to the northward along the coast. At 8 A.M. Hat Hill, Port Aikin, Botany Bay, and the light-house on Port Jackson, south head, all in sight. A perfect calm from 8 to 11 A.M. There was a small schooner in sight under sail in Botany Bay.

At noon light variable airs from the southward. Botany Bay entrance bore by the compass W¼S. Latitude by observation 34° S.; thermometer on deck in the shade 67°.

31st.—At 3 P.M. made signal for a pilot and fired a gun, and at 5 P.M., after repeating the gun frequently, one came on board, who took charge of the ship, and stood in for the harbour. At 6½ P.M. anchored in five and and a half fathoms water: the North-Head bearing N.E. by E., and the Light-house S.E. ¾ S. This situation placed us in mid-channel between the south-head reef and middle harbour. Divided the crew into three watches, with an officer at the head of each.

Shortly after anchoring sent a boat to town with the Calcutta post-office packet and several letters for the Bengal Government, requesting the colonial secretary to forward them with the least possible delay. Found that my late surgeon, whom I meant to apprehend as a deserter, had sailed for India, having only remained at this port one day, when he fortunately found a vessel wherein to effect his escape before my arrival.

June 1st.—Throughout the day light sea and

land breezes, with fine weather: mechanics and people employed as necessary. At noon received a visit from the master-attendant. At 6 P.M. put ashore for the purpose of procuring a naturalist; but in this I failed, as well as my agent, and the clerk whom I sent up with the despatches.

2d.—Land and sea breezes during these twenty-four hours. People employed cleansing the ship in various parts. Procured some sheep, poultry, vegetables, &c. in the course of this day.

3d.—Winds and weather as for days past. People employed as necessary. At 11 A.M. proceeded on board, not being able to procure a naturalist, although I offered most liberal terms. I engaged here a new second officer, a steward, and three English seamen.

In the course of the afternoon the ship *Eliza-beth* sailed for the Isle of France, in company with the *Albion* for Batavia. I understood that they were to adopt the eastern route, through St. George's Channel.

Several boats having visited the vessel during our stay here, in some of which spirituous liquors had been conveyed on board, a part of the crew became intoxicated and riotous. Fearing from this circumstance that some convicts were secreted on board, I called all hands aft, and explained to them the consequences should any be discovered after the ship had put to sea.

The gunner having requested permission to remain at Port Jackson with his wife and family, I granted him leave, appointing his mate to the vacant post, conditionally, on his being careful, and shewing himself competent in all respects to perform the duty that thus devolved upon him.

In this colony, where so many strange occurrences take place, I was however surprised to find that Mr. Scott, formerly, I am told a merchant in the Mediterranean, latterly secretary to the commissioner of inquiry sent from England, in which capacity I had seen him here in 1820, was now converted into a clergyman of the established church. This versatile genius, having laid aside the day-book and ledger for the Bible and prayer-book, by divine grace and ecclesiastical favour, now took precedence of his former master, and was even become the spiritual head of the reverend and venerable Samuel Marsden, who has here for many years laboured so zealously in the cause of Christianity as to be justly considered the apostle of the South Seas. As an individual, knowing the virtues of this truly pious and venerable man, I could not help feeling much for the cruel and unjust persecutions he has lately suffered.

CHAPTER VI.

OCCURRENCES FROM PORT JACKSON TO NEW ZEALAND.

4th June 1827.—First part of the day light airs and calms : latter part, winds strong from the northward. At 9 A.M. weighed and stood to sea. At 11 A.M. the pilot left us. Latitude obs. at noon 34° 50′ S. when the point of South-head bore W. 4 miles. Thermometer in the shade 70°.

Not knowing whether fresh water could be procured at Tucopia, and dreading the disposition of the Mannicolese, where, if I should succeed in finding anchorage, and require water, it would be exposing my men to too great hazard to land them among hundreds of savages armed with poisoned arrows, I determined to take in water at the nearest known watering-place to Mannicolo, and thus, by having a sufficient supply of this indispensable article of consumption, I could set the natives at defiance, until an opportunity offered of establishing a friendly intercourse with them, as I understood them to be very hostile to Europeans since the wreck of the two French vessels upon their coast. I therefore determined to sail for the Friendly Islands, to which place I expected a short passage, it being the middle of winter in these southern latitudes, at which time the wind mostly prevails from the west. Having arrived there, I could water and resume the voyage without delay.

13th. — Nothing worthy of notice having occurred for the last nine days, I pass them over as uninteresting.

I have crossed this part of the Pacific Ocean at least twenty times, and have uniformly had short passages till now.

For the first two days after quitting Port Jackson, the winds prevailed from the westward; from that period the wind blew from S.E. to N.E. At 1 o'clock this morning it blew a violent gale, accompanied by heavy falls of rain. The main-topsail was split, and we were obliged to heave-to for the remainder of the day.

14th.—At 8 A.M. the gale abated: the wind shifted from N.E. to N.N.W., when we swayed up the top-gallant mast and yards, which were housed during the gale. Set all sail, and stood to the eastward. Latitude at noon 34° 22' S.; Longitude 164° 40' 30" E.

17th —We have had for the last three days the winds mostly from the eastward Latitude at noon 34° 24' S.; longitude 167° 23' E.

Being on a voyage fraught with danger, not only from the seas, but from surprise while at

anchor in the ports, on shores which are inhabited by barbarians relentless and treacherous, or by cannibals, who besides their naturally savage disposition, are further impelled to
seek our destruction by their horrible propensity
to devour us,—I deemed it more imperatively
necessary that the officer on watch should at all
times and in all places be on the alert.

To prevent the recurrence of a most disgraceful instance of criminal neglect which took place
this morning, I caused the following remark to
be placed on the log-board, for the information
of the officers keeping watch :—

" Received information that one of the officers has been in the habit of sleeping on deck
in his watch : found it to be the case. Looked
over the offence this time, although such conduct is in direct violation of the articles of
agreement, and contrary to the rules and regulations of the service. It endangers the life of
every individual on board, as also the property
of the Hon. East-India Company. I am determined, should such an occurrence take place
again, to disrate the officer and send him off the
quarter-deck. An officer who sleeps on his
watch. exposes himself to the sarcasms of the
common sailors, and can never command with
authority, having placed himself in the power
of his inferiors."

Latitude by observation to-day, 34° 24′ S
Longitude by lunar observation, 167° 29′ 30″ E.

23d.—Having met with so much bad weather
and foul winds on this passage, I gave up the
idea of proceeding to the Friendly Islands, and
thought of proceeding to Tanna, one of the
New Hebrides, to complete my water and re-
stow the ship, which duty had not been performed since leaving Calcutta ; and there but
very indifferently, through the unseamanlike
conduct and want of skill in the former chief
officer. On the 20th instant, the second officer had informed me that he found seventeen
water-casks empty in the hold, besides those
which had been emptied for the ship's use.

Before determining to bear away, I deemed
it prudent to ascertain the exact complement of
water on board, and to my utter astonishment
found only twenty-seven casks, being little more
than one cask to every three individuals in the
ship.

From this circumstance it would appear that
my late chief officer did not cause more than
half of the casks to be filled at the Derwent,
although he wrote to me stating that all the
water-casks in the ship were filled by a person
on shore, with the exception of three, which
he stated would be immediately filled by the
crew. I had therefore now no alternative but

to proceed for New Zealand, and there complete my water, notwithstanding such a proceeding was likely to cause some delay.

At 5½ P.M. the boatswain caught a very large
shark of the brown species, an occurrence highly gratifying to " his excellency " Morgan
McMarragh, inasmuch as it promised a feast of
no ordinary delicacy.   He declared that the
mogow (their name of the shark) was most de-
licious food, and proceeded to exemplify his
taste by scoring off a piece for his supper. But,
notwithstanding his argument was thus ably
supported by example, the sailors did not seem
to pay much attention to either, and were
about to toss the remaining part of the monster overboard, when, vexed to the heart to see
so much excellent fish thrown away, he commenced an earnest expostulation with them on
the subject, advising them to preserve it for the
ladies at the Bay of Islands (at which place
they would soon arrive), who sing, he said,
most melodiously, sweeter by far than the
nautch girls of Calcutta : giving them reason
to hope that they might, on their arrival in the
bay, expect numerous visits from those Eastern
Catalanis.

25th.—Fresh breezes, and cloudy throughout
the day : winds from N.N.E.   Shortly after
daylight observed that the sea assumed a light

colour, an indication that we were not far from the coast of New Zealand. Our latitude by observation at noon was 34° 53′ S., longitude 172° 2′ E. Thermometer in the shade 63°. At half past one P.M. land in sight bearing N.N.E. per compass, distance ten leagues, which proved to be the Three Kings, off the north coast of New Zealand.

The wind blowing directly from the shore, we could not approach it. Carried as much sail during the night as the ship could conveniently bear, beating to windward.

26th.—First and middle part of the day strong breezes from the north. At 1 P.M. hard squall with rain: at 2 P.M. it fell nearly calm with variable airs. At 5 P.M. a light breeze sprung up from the south-west, accompanied with fine clear weather. At noon the latitude observation was 34° 31′ S.; thermometer in the shade on deck 64°. At 6 A.M. the Three Kings hove in sight, and at 8 they bore N.E. by N.½N. six leagues. We had all sail set working to windward, as it blew directly from the shore. At 4 P.M. the centre of the Three Kings bore N.E. by N. six or seven leagues. We had all sail set steering to the northward, with a view of passing on that side of them, not wishing to be caught in this un-

settled weather between the islands and Cape
Maria Van Diemen.

27th.—The first part of the day, light variable airs from the south-west; the latter part
perfect calm. At daylight this morning we had
the Three Kings in sight, bearing E. by S., distance about ten leagues. Latitude by observation at noon 34° 7′ S.; thermometer on deck
63° in the shade. At sunset the centre of the
Kings bore E.½S. per compass, eight or nine
leagues.

28th.—Unsteady breezes throughout these
twenty-four hours, from N.E. to N. by W. with
occasional showers of rain. Carried as much
sail as possible, working the ship to windward.
At noon the Kings bore E.½N. per compass ten
leagues. The thermometer on deck at the same
time stood at 61°.

29th.—The first and middle part of these
twenty-four hours strong breezes and cloudy,
thick weather with rain; winds from N. to N.W.
Latter part light breezes with clear weather;
winds from W.N.W. to W.

Being on the starboard tack standing to the
westward till 4 A.M., tacked about and stood
to the eastward. At 10 A.M. the Kings were in
sight. At noon the centre of them bore E. by
S. distance nine miles. The wind being free,
stood to the eastward under a heavy press of

sail, and happily succeeded in passing them at
3 P.M., this being the fifth day the ship was
in sight of them.   This was rather an extraordinary occurrence at this season of the year, as
the wind generally blows strong from the westward, enabling ships from Sydney to make a
passage to the Kings in eight or ten days at
most; but, unfortunately for our expedition,
the ship had been now twenty-seven days on the
passage.

CHAPTER VI.

OCCURRENCES AT NEW ZEALAND.

1*st July* 1827. – Though the first part of this day had been squally, in the middle and latter part we had fine pleasant weather. At daylight stood in for the Bay of Islands, and at 9 A.M. anchored in five and a half fathoms of water in Corararicka Bay. The ship was surrounded before letting go the anchor by several canoes, containing a number of natives. Being Sunday, we were all attired in our best. I spoke to them in the native language, but they did not recognize me for a long time. At length one of the young ladies called out most lustily, notwithstanding her delicate sex, " *Rangatheera no Patareeckee*," it is the captain of the *St. Patrick ;* alluding to the ship which I commanded here last year. This recognition was re-echoed in every New Zealand throat, and nothing for some time was audible but the word " Peter," the name by which 1 am known by the South Sea Islanders.

A man who appeared to be of some consequence in one of the canoes, requested to be admitted on board, but this I refused ; alleging as my reason that he had nothing to barter.

He replied that he had.   I repeated that I
could see nothing: but he, pointing to the
stern of his canoe, in which sat a pretty female
about twelve years old, insisted with a signifi-
cant glance that he had something better than
a " *buocka*" (hog).   I thanked him for his
kind intentions, but replied, that the ship was
tabooed (*i e.* sacred, or not to be approached)
until another anchor was let go, and the sails
handed.   Our conversation then assumed a
political cast, in the course of which he informed
me that he was the nephew of Boo Marray, a
great and powerful chief, and the proprietor
of this harbour, who, he said, my friends at the
river Thames had killed about twelve months
ago.   He also said that Boo Marray's son had
been killed with about two hundred warriors,
and that there was an expedition then fitting
out against the Thames tribes, consisting of all
the allied chiefs of the north, who were fully
determined to exterminate the whole of the
Boroos and McMarraghs.   He then inquired
where the two young men were that belonged
to the Thames country, whom I took from
thence in the *St. Patrick*.   Being informed that
they were with me he then said, " You must
deliver them up, that we may kill and eat them
directly."   He was clothed in a war mat, with a
mantle of dog-skins thrown loosely over his

shoulders; his countenance at this moment assumed an aspect of the most savage ferocity,
his eyes starting from their sockets with the
intenseness of desire to seize on the innocent
relatives of a people with whom he happened
to be at war. It is hardly necessary to say, I
replied to his cannibal request by telling him
that the young men were under the protection
of the British flag and guns, and should not be
molested while on board: that they were *tabooed*.
When on shore they might be treated conformably with the laws of New Zealand ; but the intimation of his intentions regarding them, would
make me careful as to where they should land.

I ordered up my friends, Brian Boroo and
Morgan McMarragh, who went to the side of
the vessel and commenced a conversation with
their would-be devourer. The chief spoke to
them with as much nonchalance as if he had
never expressed a wish to pick their ribs or sup
on their roasted chine: a business that, if I
might judge from the preparations his canoe
exhibited, he seemed to have entertained some
idea of, prior to putting off to the ship. He
spoke in terms of the highest respect and praise
of Brian's father, saying that two of Boo Marray's sons were taken in battle, with other men
of consequence belonging to his tribe, and en-
slaved. That Brian's father shortly afterwards

ordered them to be released, and furnished them with a canoe, in which they returned to their native district, and were now two days' march in the interior, but would pay him a visit the moment they heard that he had arrived.

The ship being moored, this gentleman was allowed to come on board. Brian Boroo and he took each other by the hand, and gently inclined their heads until their noses touched. Their conversation then turned upon the heroic exploits of Brian's countrymen in the late wars.

Several young ladies condescended to come on board, and the decks were shortly crowded with females, some of whom made a very genteel appearance, being dressed in English gowns, shirts, and petticoats: others were in their native costume. Without solicitation, they proceeded voluntarily to amuse us with songs, dances, war whoops, and comic performances, in which they succeeded inimitably.

Many of them were so kind as to remain all night on board, and indeed did not depart during the ship's stay. This, however, I would not have permitted, were it not that I knew they expected it as a matter of course. It being the practice with whalers touching here, to receive and treat them very kindly, and a deviation from such custom on my part, might tend to engender suspicion and distrust in their minds, which was a feeling I particularly wished to avoid.

This mode of acting toward savages is in my opinion founded on the soundest policy. All savage nations with whom I have had intercourse for the last nineteen years, when meditating any thing against the lives of those whom they regard as enemies, as the first step secure their wives, children, and the aged, and place them beyond the reach of those they intend to attack. When neither women nor children are to be seen, it may with certainty be concluded that an attack is in contemplation : whereas their allowing them to remain on board a ship, is a sure guarantee of their peaceful intentions. They become, as it were, hostages for the lives of the seamen who are employed on shore to procure wood and water ; for should a party on the land have formed any design on the lives of the boat's crew, others interested in the safety of the females would oppose the execution of it, and would naturally reason thus : " if you molest those people, my sister, my niece, or my daughter, who are now on board, will be murdered."

I have been at islands where nothing could induce the natives to come on board till they beheld a couple of women and children moving about. Their fears then vanished, and gave

place to the most implicit confidence; and not
only would the men venture into the ship, but
they would bring their females also to visit the
strangers.   Confidence being thus established,
I always managed to have a sufficient number
of women on board on a friendly visit, while
my men were employed on shore wooding,
watering, and searching for sandal-wood.

The opening or entrance of the Bay of
Islands is formed between Point Pocock on
the north-west and Cape Brett on the east.
The distance between the Point and Cape
Brett is about four leagues in breadth.   The
shore may be approached within a cable's length
on either side of this large bay.   There is only
one danger to be avoided, which is the Whale
Rock of Captain Cook, laid down on my chart
of this bay

Within half a mile of the islands which front
the coast from Cape Brett, near Thapecka
Point, which forms the eastern boundary of
the harbour of Corararicka, the hills on each
side of the bay present to view a covering of
green fern and innumerable trees of various
sizes and species.

2d.—Light breezes, with fine weather; wind
from the westward. Thermom. in the shade 61°.

My people were employed in hoisting out the
long-boat, and getting down the lower yards,

in order to replace them with new ones, they having been much injured by the late stormy weather.

Shortly after daylight several canoes put off to the ship, laden with hogs, potatoes, &c., a part of which I purchased in exchange for muskets and gunpowder.

About 10 A.M. I went ashore, accompanied by Monsieur Chaigneau and Mr. Griffiths the surgeon. We landed at the watering place, where we found the stream very scanty, owing to the long drought. The natives received us kindly, and conducted us along a path which they said led to an Englishman's house.

We shortly reached a very neat hut, surrounded with a palisading of about nine feet high. On entering it, we found the inhabitants consisted of an English cooper and his wife, a native of New Zealand. The man informed us that he had been cooper's mate to a whaler, and had been left on the island in consequence of ill health; that he had not thoroughly recovered yet from his illness, and never expected that he should. He is sometimes employed by the shipping that touch here in repairing their water-casks, making buckets, and performing any other work that they may occasionally require in the way of his trade, for which he receives gunpowder, flints, musket-balls, cut-

lery, ironmongery, &c., and barters those articles
with the natives for hogs, fish, poultry, wild
ducks, pigeons, and potatoes, whereby he ekes
out a very comfortable subsistence for himself
and wife.

He is under the protection of a mighty chief,
named King George, who was up the river
at the timber district, procuring spars for his
son-in-law, the captain of an English whaler,
shortly expected to arrive from the fishery,
whither he had also taken his wife.

The cooper told us that he understood a
company had been formed in England for the
purpose of establishing a factory here, and to
procure spars, flax, and the other productions
of New Zealand. That for this purpose a ship
and cutter belonging to the company arrived
from England, under the command of their
agent, Captain Herd, with mechanics of the
descriptions most likely to promote the end in
view. They consisted of ship-carpenters, saw-
yers, blacksmiths, and flax-dressers, and they
had on board with them machines for sawing
and flax-dressing.

Captain Herd, however, disliked the appearance of the New Zealanders * so much that he
abandoned the expedition, and proceeded to

---

* And certainly, from his own account, he was perfectly jus-
tified in so doing.

Port Jackson, and on his arrival at Sydney such of the mechanics as desired it were discharged. Four of them returned to New Zealand, took up their lodgings with the cooper, and were now employed on the other side of the bay, by the missionaries established here, in repairing a small schooner that plies to New South Wales, and brings supplies for the missionary establishment.

We passed a little further along the beach, and came to another small cabin, inhabited by a blacksmith that belonged to Captain Herd's expedition, and settled here when it first touched at the islands. He is married to a New Zealand woman.

Further on we came to a third dwelling, occupied by four Europeans, employed in sawing plank. Johnston, the proprietor of it, was discharged from a whaler about three years ago, and forming the resolution to settle here, united himself with a native woman of the country, who had two fine children by him. He disposes of his planks to the ships which touch here, receiving in return tea, sugar, biscuit, flour, and such articles as the cooper accepts for his work.

This man informed me that he lived under the protection of Moyhanger, the chief who accompanied Mr. John Savage to England in 1805 or 1806, and was the first New Zealander that ever appeared in Europe or at the British court.   Moyhanger is a chief of considerable importance, brother to queen Terrooloo, the mother of the great and powerful king George.

We extended our walk across an isthmus that conducted us to a beautiful bay, about a mile and a half distant from the ship.   Here we found the village and fort of the late Boo Marray, in which was a house, built of plank, of English construction, or rather resembling the houses of New South Wales, with glass windows. It consisted of two apartments; the one a bed and the other a dining room.   The house was furnished with some chairs, a table, bedstead and bedding, a looking-glass and dressing-case, with various other necessaries.   This house, I understand, belongs to the captain of an English whaler called the *Emily*, son-in-law to the late Boo Marray, and at the time of my visit the gentleman and his wife were absent at the fishery on the equator.

The personage who conducted us from the watering place was Thee Thory, chief of Wyemattee, holding a rank similar to that of a marquis in Europe, and brother in-law to the great chief Shanghi.   He was, without exception, one of the finest made men I ever met with.   He informed me that Shanghi had lately made war upon the Wangeroa tribe, one half of whom he slew, and drove the other half from that part of the country.

Wangeroa is about sixteen miles from the Bay of Islands, and is the place where the dreadful catastrophe of the *Boyd* took place. It was here that the crew and passengers of that ill-fated ship were cruelly massacred and devoured, in the year 1809.

In 1823, or early in 1824, this savage tribe attacked the *Mercury*, an English whaler brig, and plundered her of every thing portable on board. The captain and crew sought safety in the boats, abandoning the ship to the fury of the savages, leaving only the chief mate and steward on board. Being taken by surprise, they could not bring the latter off with them, but proceeded with the boats to the Bay of Islands, and joined some whalers whom they found at anchor there. The two men would have been massacred but for the interference of one of the missionaries established at Wangeroa, who reached the vessel just in time to save the lives of his hapless countrymen. Having succeeded in persuading the natives to quit the brig, and the wind at the same time springing up from the shore, the mate, assisted by the missionary and steward, made sail and stood out to sea.

At the time the islanders boarded her the *Mercury* touched the ground, which rendered her very leaky, and those on board were therefore compelled to abandon her, taking to the whale-boat in order to preserve themselves from going down. Shortly afterwards the vessel was thrown on shore near the North Cape, and became a total wreck.

We learnt from the Europeans who resided on shore that the object which the four carpenters before-mentioned had in view in returning to New Zealand, was to proceed to Hookianga, a harbour on the west side of this island, distant from hence about thirty-five miles, and there build a vessel on their own account. Messrs. Cooper and Levery, and Messrs. Raine and Ramsay, two respectable firms at Port Jackson, have each I understand, an establishment at Hookianga for procuring pork, flax, spars, planks, &c., and are very well treated by the natives, who have permitted them within the last twelve months to build two or three small schooners.

In the afternoon I returned to the ship, in company with my conductor, the Marquis of Wyemattee, who seemed highly pleased with her warlike appearance; but particularly viewed with eager eyes the musket-rack : indeed so intense was his attention to these fire-arms, that it was not an easy matter to divert it to any other object. He expressed a very anxious wish to go to Bengal, and inquired from Prince Brian Boroo (whom he tenderly embraced) if he was likely to meet with as good a reception at Bengal as his kinsman Shanghi had experienced in England, who was kindly received by his royal brother, King George the Fourth of Great Britain, who bestowed on him a coat of scale armour, impervious to musket-balls, spears, or arrows, and an elegant double-barrelled gun, with a vast variety of other presents.

Prince Brian endeavoured, though without effect, to dissuade him from encountering the Indian climate, which he represented as very unhealthy; saying it was intolerably warm, and so much infested with musquitoes as to prevent sleep. That the only person he (the prince) met in Bengal to give him muskets, food, lodging, or clothing, was his friend Peter, and that, all things considered, he had much better remain in his own country. However, the idea of all the fine things that his kinsman had received in Europe so wrought upon the marquis's imagination, that his resolution to see Bengal could not be conquered by Brian's rhetoric, and he avowed his intention of acquainting Shanghi, his brother-in-law, of the affair, who knew and had sailed with me when he (the marquis) was quite a lad.

Thee Thory made me a present of seven hogs, and forty or fifty baskets of potatoes, each weighing about seventeen pounds; in return for which I presented him with an old musket and some gunpowder, as the most desirable gift I could confer, which was evinced by the thankfulness of his countenance on receiving them. He then bad me adieu, and set out for his brother-in-law's residence at Wangeroa.

At night I gave the officers the strictest charge to keep a good look-out, and not to suffer their vigilance to be lulled by the friendly appearance of the natives: for though they gave the whalers a friendly reception, our conduct was not to be guided by theirs, since our circumstances were so widely different. The small arms, ammunition, cutlasses, &c. which we had on board, were powerful stimulants to a fierce and warlike people, and might act as an additional inducement to them to surprise us, as they did the *Boyd* and the *Mercury*. It was incumbent on us, for the general safety, to keep the most vigilant watch during the night.

3d.—My first visit to this bay was in the *Mercury*, in November 1809. My next was in command of the *Active* brig, of Calcutta, in June 1814, sent here by the Reverend Samuel Marsden, to convey Messrs. Kendall and Hall, missionaries, to try the disposition of the natives, and ascertain if it were possible to establish a mission among them with any degree of safety.

My third visit was in August 1823, while commanding the *Calder*, of Calcutta. My fourth was
also in the *Calder*, in February 1825 ; my fifth
in the ship *St. Patrick*, in April 1826 ; and the
present made my sixth visit to New Zealand.

The following chiefs went passengers from
here to Port Jackson with me in the *Active*
in 1814 :—Dueetarra, Korrakorra, Tui, king
Shanghi, Depero, son to Shanghi, and The-
nānā.

Before I reached this port in the *St. Patrick*
last year, I had been in the river Thames, where
I lay at anchor during the months of January,
February, and March, purchasing and taking in
a cargo of spars for the East-India market.

4th.—I was visited this morning by queen
Terrooloo, her brother Moyhanger, and her son
king George, who were on their return from
the spar district to their respective residences
at Korraricka.

Shortly after king George came on deck he
inquired for Brian Boroo, who after some persuasion on my part came up from below. King
George approached him and embraced him
tenderly, as did his mother and Moyhanger,
and in a long and eloquent speech to Brian
Boroo and Morgan M'Marragh, desired them,
on their arrival at the Thames, to inform
their friends that himself and the chiefs of the

north had not forgot the death of Boo Marray :
that it was his determination to set out for the
Thames as soon as the potato crops were housed
(which would be in January next), to seek
revenge for the loss of Boo Marray, and several
other friends, slain in battle about twelve months
ago. He at the same time admitted that the
battle in which Boo Marray was killed took
place in the middle of the day, that there was
no treacherous night-work in it, and that it
was all fair fighting. He then presented Brian
Boroo with a few baskets of potatos, and assured him that he had the greatest regard for
his father, and was exceedingly sorry that the
laws of New Zealand compelled him to seek
blood for blood, and go to war with Brian's
friends.

Moyhanger is a man with a small shrewd
eye : his countenance indicates all that cunning, characteristic of one brought up in a state
of nature. On seeing the lascars, he knew they
were from a country he once visited. He en-
quired of me if I had seen his friend " Missi
Savage." I knew he meant Dr. John Savage,
now a full surgeon in the Hon. East India Company's service at Calcutta. I replied, " I saw
Dr. Savage a few months ago, who asked me
whether Moyhanger was alive or not. I told
him I believed you were alive ; that you were

now known by the name of king Charley ; and
that I had seen you when I was here in the
St. Patrick."

He wept bitterly, and said, " Missi Savage
was a very good man : he took me to England
and brought me to King George's house. I was
a fool at that time ; I did not know what was
good. When King George asked me what I
liked, I told him some *tokees* (iron tools) and
nails. Had I asked for muskets, he would have
given me a hundred. We did not know the use
of them in New Zealand at that time, and set
no value on them : but were I to go to England
now, and King George the *meidey* (meaning
King George the son) were to ask me what I
liked in England, I would say ' boo, boo' (that
is, ' musket, musket ')."

I requested him to inform me how he got to
England. He gave his narrative nearly in the
following words:

" Missi Savage came here in a whaler from
Port Jackson : I went with him. We were four
months going from here to St. Helena, where
we lay at anchor some weeks, until a number of
large ships from the lascars' country (India-
men) came in. We left the whaler, and went
on board of one of them. We all sailed together
from St. Helena for England. I saw the coast
of France before I got to London, to which

country, I understood, Marion belonged, who was killed in Parao Bay a long time ago.

" After I arrived in London, a friend of Dr. Savage (Earl Fitzwilliam) took me to King George's house : I was dressed in my New Zealand mats. We entered a large room, and shortly after King George and Queen Charlotte came in. I was much disappointed : I expected to see a great warrior ; but he was an old man that could neither throw a spear nor fire a musket. Queen Charlotte was very old too : she was bent with age. They behaved very kind, and asked me what I liked best in England to take home with me. I told them *tokees*. Queen Charlotte put her hand under her mat into a little bag that was there, and took out of it some red money (meaning guineas) and gave it to me. Queen Charlotte asked me to give the war-dance of New Zealand. When I did so she appeared frightened : but King George laughed, saying, ha ! ha ! ha !

" I then went out with my friends, and got the full of my hand of white money (shillings) for one of the red ones. I thought the people in England very foolish to give so many white monies of the same size for the red one of Queen Charlotte.

" Shortly after this I got a wife with some of Queen Charlotte's red money ; her name was

Nancy. She was very fond of me, and proved pregnant. She used to ask me if the child when born would go to New Zealand, and if it would have such marks on its face as mine.

" I was then ordered on board the *Porpoise* man of war, and went with her to St. Helena, the Cape of Good Hope, and Madras, where I saw Governor Barlow, who looked very much like you : I believe he is your father. He is great man." (In this I did not undeceive him.)

From what I could now make out, I supposed him to have gone up the Persian Gulph. He described some country he visited that I could not properly understand.* However, he soon after stated himself to have sailed from Madras for England, and on his arrival there to have been put on board a whaler commanded by Capt. Skelton. In her he proceeded to Van Diemen's Land, and from thence to New Zealand, without touching at Port Jackson.

He, with his sister the queen, and his nephew king George, begged and intreated of me to take him with me to Bengal to see his friend Mr. Savage ; and being ten or twelve men

---

* Since my arrival in England I have been informed that Moyhanger did not make the voyage to India, as he here represented, no doubt to serve some purpose or gratify some fancy of his own.—*April* 1829.

short of my complement, I agreed to it. He said he could not pull the ropes, but that he would make a good soldier and fight, either on board the ship or in the boats. I told him to be prepared, and that I would take him on board when I was about to sail.

As Moyhanger mentioned the name of Marion, I deemed it prudent to inquire into the circumstances that led to that gentleman's massacre in this bay. From what I learnt, Capt. Marion being on a voyage of discovery in 1772, touched at the Bay of Islands, where the ships anchored in a bay, now called ' Man o' War's Bay,' situated at the back of Parao Island, which is one of those islands fronting the coast from Cape Brett to near Tapecka Point. Queen Toorooloo said she recollected perfectly well the massacre. That there was an European female on board of Marion's ship, whose name was Micky ; and that she had a child with her, but whether male or female I could not make out. Micky had been on shore at Parao washing some linen ; and a party of the Wangeroa tribe being there on a fishing party, stole some of it. A scuffle also ensued between the seamen and natives about some fish that were taken in a net. Micky was alarmed, and made the best of her way off to the ship in one of the boats. In the mean time Captain Marion, unacquainted with what had taken place, landed, and was killed.

The account of what had happened shortly reached the ships, and two hundred men went on shore armed with muskets; but the natives, confident in their numbers, and unacquainted with the deadly effect of fire-arms, faced them boldly. The patoo-patoo and spear stood no chance against musket-balls, and the Wangeroa people, who fell in dozens, could not conceive how it happened, not being able to discover the instrument by which they were wounded. At length they flew to the main land, and sought safety in a fortified place, supposing they had been engaged with spirits, who blew fire and smoke at them out of their mouths through the muskets. The musket they called "boo," which word in New Zealand signifies "to blow." They were pursued by the Frenchmen to the main land, where vast numbers were killed.

The person who murdered Captain Marion was named Cooley (or the dog): he was a native of Wangeroa; and it is rather extraordinary that the Wangeroa tribes were the first and last to molest and injure Europeans.

There are several songs composed by native bards on the battle and death of Marion, in which the name of Micky and her child are frequently mentioned. I have heard those

songs sung on various occasions, but did not
understand the meaning of them till now.

When the natives learnt that Monsieur
Chaigneau, the French gentleman attached to
the expedition, was a countryman of Marion's,
they called him by the name of Marion, and
continued to do so during our stay here.

Towards evening king George left the ship
with his mother and uncle, having each of them
teased me out of a musket.

5th.—This morning at daylight I went on
deck, pointed out to the carpenter and the other
mechanics their respective jobs for the day, and
returned to my cabin.   Shortly after the chief
officer informed me that the carpenter refused
to work, pretending to be sick; which I considered rather extraordinary, having but a few
minutes before seen him, when he did not complain of illness. I proceeded therefore on deck,
and was informed that the carpenter had retired
to bed; on which I sent for him, and directed
him to go to work: he refused, and told me
plainly he would go on shore. To deter and
affright him from this step I had recourse to the
following expedient   I asked him if he had
seen any preserved human heads offered for sale
by the natives since our arrival? He replied,
" Yes."—" Then, sir," said I, " if you attempt
to desert from the ship, I will pay the natives

to preserve your head and bring it here as a curiosity." This threat had the desired effect.

Seeing the four carpenters belonging to Capt. Herd's expedition settled on shore, with as many wives as they thought proper to keep, and under no control, my carpenter had formed the wish to join them as already stated.

I sent the surgeon to see if there was any thing the matter with the man, who reported that he was intoxicated, and ought not to be exempted from work. I therefore sent for him again; but, as he hesitated in coming up from his birth, I desired him to be informed, that if he did not immediately return to his duty I would punish him. He then approached me in a menacing posture, with a sharp-pointed chisel in his hand, and as I expected he was going to stab me, I seized on the first weapon I could make use of to defend myself. This happened to be the leg of a chair: with it I succeeded in keeping him off, and ultimately forced him to ascend the main rigging and proceed into the top, where he resumed his duty.*

The officer then complained to me that the

* This gross insubordination arose from the example set to my crew by the Van Diemen's Land convict judge, who had given them to understand that I had no more authority or control over my men than the master of a merchant vessel trading between London and Botany Bay. However, I soon convinced them to the contrary.

officers of the night-watches had great trouble
in getting their respective watches on deck last
night, and that several of the crew were then in
a state of intoxication. I was not surprised at
this, such occurrences having frequently taken
place on board during the time of the former
chief officer, but I was at a loss to ascertain how
they procured the liquor. The only rational
conjecture I could form was that they had been
plundering the hold, or my cabin stores, as I
had already lost nearly eighteen dozen of wine.

Two of the men who refused to work were
this day punished with a few stripes of a rattan
and rope's-end.

The European part of my crew were without
exception the most abandoned set I ever met
with; they were all deserters from other ships,
not one of them going by his proper name.
They had been suffered to act as they pleased
by my late chief officer, and were indulged in
their sloth and filth, of which neglect the ship
displayed evident marks. If an officer now requested them to do their duty, he was treated
with the grossest insolence; as they fancied
that they ought to be permitted to act in the
same manner as formerly, and that the lascars
should clean the ship, leaving these mutinous
unprincipled rascals nothing more to do than
steer the vessel, eat, drink, and sleep.

6th.—Yesterday and to-day, which were the only days of fine weather that we have had since our arrival here, I had the people employed in stowing and cleaning the hold fore and aft. The weather being much unsettled, impeded our progress, as we had to hand all our dry provisions on deck before we could get at our water-casks, which were stowed in the ground tier; and when an occasional shower of rain came, or any appearance of it, we had to put our provisions off deck immediately to preserve them, and get them up again when the weather would permit.

The ship having been much injured, both in her spars and bolts, during the late gales, I employed a carpenter from the shore, with a blacksmith, to assist those on board.

At $2\frac{1}{2}$ A.M. the moon shone with peculiar brilliancy. All was hushed in the most solemn silence on deck : not a foot in motion throughout the ship, although there ought at that time to have been fifteen men on the alert, that being the complement of which each watch consisted. Supposing all was not right, I went on the quarter-deck, when to my astonishment, I beheld the second officer sound asleep upon a small cask, loudly snoring as he sat. I did not disturb him, wishing to ascertain how long he would continue in that situation.

There was not one man of the watch to be seen, and the vessel seemed deserted by all, save the sleeper and myself. I reflected on the risks to which the lives and property of all on board were exposed by this shameful disregard of my most positive injunctions, and my mind dwelt with pain on the instance before me of a dereliction from all the principles of duty.

While I was thus employed, one of the men having at length perceived me, with cool deliberation walked from the poop to the quarterdeck, and feigning to look out of the port near to which the officer was still sitting asleep, he had the audacity to stand upon his foot, although I was steadfastly looking at him all the time. Observing his intention, which was to awaken him, I reproved his unmannerly behaviour, and asked him how he dared take the liberty to disturb the gentleman while sleeping so comfortably? The man replied, that he had only come from the poop in order to look through the port at a canoe which he supposed to be coming up to the ship. This was but a petty subterfuge, for on board of a ship we always get upon the most elevated situation to look out for approaching danger; but this man, on the contrary, had descended to the quarterdeck from the poop, to look through a port that was nearly blocked up by a twelve-pounder.

The officer being now awake, I addressed him nearly in the following words: " Sir, are you devoid of all sense of manly and honourable feeling, thus to expose this ship, the property of the Hon. East-India Company, with all the lives on board, to the savage inhabitants of New Zealand! Can you so soon forget the remark I placed on the log-board on the 17th June last, for your guidance as well as that of the other officers in the ship? do you forget whose conduct gave rise to that remark? To what purpose did I address you and the other officers on Monday evening last, when I so strictly charged you to be vigilant, particularly at night? Did I not endeavour most forcibly to impress on your mind, that no confidence is to be placed in savages, who at best only await favourable opportunities for destroying us? Consider the melancholy catastrophes of the *Boyd* and *Mercury :* do you wish to have the dreadful scene reacted on board the *Research ?* What do you mean by this conduct? If I were in a port where I could procure another officer to fill your situation, I would instantly dismiss you. Such conduct is disgraceful to the character of a British officer and seaman ; and if again repeated I shall disrate you, and send you off the quarter-deck." He listened attentively, and promised to behave better in future.

8th.—Fine pleasant weather throughout the day. At 7 A.M. an English South-seaman, called the *Emily* of London, arrived here from the fishery with a full cargo of sperm oil. She had put in to refit, and proceed thence to London direct. On board of her was Boo Marray's daughter, whom I had often seen before. She wept bitterly on seeing me, as I was a particular friend of her father, who she said was now no more.

It is the custom in New Zealand, when friends or relations meet after long absence, for both parties to touch noses and shed tears. With this ceremony I have frequently complied out of courtesy; for my failure in this respect would have been considered a breach of friendship, and I should have been regarded as little better than a barbarian, according to the rules of New Zealand politeness. Unfortunately, however, my hard heart could not upon all occasions readily produce a tear, not being made of such melting stuff as those of the New Zealanders; but the application of a pocket handkerchief to my eyes for some time, accompanied with an occasional howl in the native language, answered all the purposes of real grief. This ceremony is dispensed with from strange Europeans; but with me it was indispensable, I being a " *Thongata moury;*" that is, a New Zealander, or countryman, as they were pleased to term me.

After the excess of our sorrow at the recollection of Boo Marray had subsided, the captain's lady seemed very much pleased on learning that Brian Boroo was on board the *Research* and in good health. She said that he had been an old sweetheart of her's, and intreated of me to protect him from the fury of her brothers and tribe. Both she and her husband dined with me to-day, and she handled her knife, fork, and spoon, and otherwise conformed to our rules of table etiquette, in a style that would do credit to many persons laying claim to a greater share of refinement.

The commander of the *Emily* informed me that he procured his cargo of oil on or about the equator, between the longitudes of 175° E. and 175° west. His water falling short, he touched at Simpson's Island, in latitude 0° 25′ N. and longitude 175° 32′ E., to procure a supply. With this view he sent two of his boats on shore with their respective crews, where one remained for the purpose of digging a well in the sandy beach, while the other put back to the ship for the casks.

On the return of this last boat the natives rushed out from the woods, armed with lances and daggers, the sides and points of which were

set with sharks' teeth, and attacked the Europeans so suddenly that they were thrown into some
confusion.   In one of the boats were two muskets, one of which was rendered unserviceable
by the water, but with the other one of Brian
Boroo's subjects did a good deal of execution.
The party were compelled to abandon one boat
to the fury of the natives, and retreat in the
other, after one European and one New Zealander had been slain in the affray, whose bodies
fell into the hands of the savages.   A second
attempt to land was not made.

9th.—Moderate breezes and fine weather.
Our people employed rafting off water-casks.
The run of water on shore is very small at this
season, the rains not having properly set in yet.
The whole force of the stream was not greater
than if it ran through a pistol-barrel.   I kept
the people on shore during the nights as well as
the days to fill the casks.

I was visited this morning by a lascar, and
an Otaheitan named Jemmy, whom I had seen
on board the ship *City of Edinbro'* in this port
in November 1809.   They left that ship, and
have since resided among the New Zealanders.
The *City of Edinbro'* belonged to the Cape of
Good Hope, and was owned by Messrs. Shortt
and Berry, of Cape Town, both of whom now
reside in New South Wales.   The lascar in-

formed me that he was treated very kindly by
the natives. His countrymen on board and myself made him several presents of ironmongery
and other things which might be useful to him
in his adopted country, and I also made Jemmy
some presents. He had a son with him, a lad
of about twelve years old.

Shortly afterwards Moyhanger came on board,
to know if I yet retained my intention of taking
him with me to Bengal, to see his friend Mr.
Savage? I told him that I would: when he said
that he had something to shew me, and drew
from under his cloak an old soldier's cap, asking
me if I could accommodate him with a red
jacket. Having satisfied him in this respect, he
observed that he should make a brave soldier,
and would no doubt look well in uniform.

In the course of our conversation he informed
me that his tribe had assisted Mr. Berry, of the
ship *City of Edinbro'*, to rescue the survivors
of the *Boyd* from the people of Wangeroa.
His mentioning this circumstance induced me to
inquire of him what he knew concerning the
unhappy fate of that ship, which he readily
agreed to relate to me.

Before giving Moyhanger's story I must relate some circumstances anterior to it, which I
am myself acquainted with, and which will serve
as a prelude to the tragedy.

The first European vessel that entered Wangeroa was the *Star*, an English South-seaman, commanded by Captain Wilkinson, who arrived there in the year 1805 or 1806. The head chief of Wangeroa at that period was named "Peepee" (or Cockle), who had a son. This chief requested Captain Wilkinson to take his son with him to Europe, where he might procure some *tokees* and fish-hooks for his father and tribe. The young man accordingly embarked with an attendant on the *Star*, and sailed with Captain Wilkinson to the seal fishery at the Antipodes Islands. While on board the young prince obtained the name of George, which he retained till his death, which happened in 1823. On the captain's return from the seal fishery he touched at Wangeroa, where George requested to be landed, and was accordingly restored to his friends, having been treated by the good captain with particular kindness during the voyage.

The next vessel which visited Wangeroa was the *Commerce* brig, which came here for spars in 1807.

After her, in 1808, the *Elizabeth*, belonging to Mr. Blackall, of Port Jackson, and commanded by Captain Stuard, bound for the Fejees, touched at Wangeroa on her voyage. It was in this vessel that Prince George a second time quitted his friends and native country, to

try what he could gain by adventure. He performed the voyage to the Fejees, and from
thence to Port Jackson, where he arrived in
November of the same year. Here he met his
old friend Captain Wilkinson, of the *Star*, and
did not require much persuasion to induce him
to embark with him upon a sealing expedition
to the South Seas.

It may be necessary to observe in this place,
that the rate of payment in whaling and sealing
ships entirely depends upon the success which
may attend the voyage, there being a certain
proportion of the skins or oil allotted to each
individual, according to the capacity in which
he engages, or his skill in the fishery. Hence
it is not improbable that the adventurers may,
on some voyages, make a very handsome " lay,"
as the South-seamen term it ; while it is equally
possible that they may have nothing for a long
and tedious voyage, the whole depending, as
before stated, on the success which they have.

The vessel in which George shipped was
employed till late in 1809 in a fruitless search
after seals, and the consequence was, that after
twelve months' labour and fatigue at sea, poor
George had nothing to receive : a circumstance
which, no doubt, preyed on his mind, being
incapable of reasoning on the fairness of the
system of pay in the sealing trade. It was suffi-

cient for him to know that he had worked enough for the white people to be entitled to some compensation, and not receiving any, he considered himself injured.

On his return to Port Jackson he shipped on the *Boyd*, without either *tokees* or nails, to return to his native country, almost as poor as he had quitted it. The *Boyd* was a ship of nearly 500 tons burden, and was commanded by Captain John Thomson: she belonged to the highly respectable firm of Boyd, Buckle, and Buchanan, of London. She was chartered by the British Government early in 1809 to convey convicts and stores to New South Wales, where having arrived, she was partly chartered by Mr. S. Lord of Sidney, to proceed to Wangeroa for spars, which were to be discharged at the Cape of Good Hope. Mr. Lord also put on board a large quantity of New South Wales mahogany, seal skins, oil, and coals, for the same market, in all amounting to £15,000 worth.

There was an East-India captain named Burnsides, who was a passenger in her, and who having by industry accumulated a fortune of £30,000, was on his return to end his days among his friends on the banks of the Liffey. This was an object poor Burnsides had always kept in view: it was the goal of his long and arduous exertions; a subject to which with much fondness he constantly reverted, during the period I had been intimately acquainted with him. But, alas! he was doomed to end his days far otherwise than among friends : he never again beheld the populous banks of the river Liffey, but was murdered on the savage shores of the Wangerao.

Having premised thus much, I shall now proceed with Moyhanger's narrative.

A few days after the *Boyd* had sailed from Port Jackson, the cook, by accident or neglect, threw overboard in a bucket of water a dozen of pewter spoons belonging to the captain's mess. Apprehensive of incurring a rope's-ending for his negligence, he formed the fatal resolve of exculpating himself by a lie, which, as it in the event proved, was the cause of the destruction of the ship, of the loss of seventy lives, British subjects, who were killed, roasted, and devoured, and of the demolition of property to the amount of nearly £40,000.

The cook, to screen himself from blame, informed the captain that George and his attendant had stolen them ; and the captain, without sufficient investigation into the affair, ordered the New Zealand chief before him, and directed the boatswain to punish him, who, being a powerful man performed this office with severity.

In vain did George urge that he was a chief, and ought not to be degraded by punishment : Captain Tompson only replied that he was a *cokey* (slave), thus adding insult to the injury. George still insisted that he was a chief, and that upon their arrival at New Zealand the captain *should see it !* His remonstrance, however, was of no avail, and he received a punishment the marks of which he bore on his back when he rejoined his friends.

Captain Thomson's behaviour in this affair cannot be too much censured. Savages are characterized by a peculiar susceptibility of indignity, while they are equally susceptible of gratitude. In fact, the extreme to which these opposite passions predominate in their breasts, forms one of the principal traits in the uncivilized mind. There cannot be the least doubt that from the moment George's appeals were disregarded, the *Boyd* and those on board were marked for destruction, as the only means of appeasing his thirst for revenge.

The ship arrived at Wangeroa, I believe, late in December the same year, and George with his attendant immediately landed, having apparently forgotten his recent chastisement, but inwardly vowing deep revenge. He hastened to his friends, and informed them that he had served the white men for two *raw-ma-*

*thies,** but had not received any thing in return ; that he came back nearly as poor as
when he first departed from among them ; and
that, to crown all his wrongs, the captain of
the *Boyd* had severely beaten him but a few
days before. He then uncovered his back and
exhibited the marks, yet livid from the effects
of the lash. This sight roused the feelings of
George's subjects to the highest pitch of indignation, and they vowed revenge on those who
had thus maltreated their chief. The shew
of friendship toward the devoted captain and
his people was however kept up to the last ;
and the next morning was appointed by Capt.
Thomson to proceed to the forest where the
spars grew, which was situated about nine or ten
miles up the river.

George now planned the massacre, which he
successfully and fatally carried into effect on
the following day. He directed those of his
countrymen who stopped behind in the village
to get on board the ship by dusk in the evening,
and that he with the party who accompanied
Captain Thomson and his men would murder
them, and clothing themselves in the European dresses, would under this disguise join
their countrymen on board before any tidings

* *Raw-mathy* signifies a year : literally a dead leaf, or the fall
of the leaf.

of the affair arrived, and when there they would complete the destruction of every white survivor.

The captain's arrangements in the morning unfortunately afforded too great a facility to the execution of this murderous project, having taken three boats with their crews up the river, and leaving very few hands to take care of the ship, or to defend her in case of an attack.

George before setting out reminded the villagers to obtain admittance to the ship before dusk, as arranged the evening before : this they faithfully performed.   In the mean time the Europeans proceeded up the river, accompanied by George and his tribe, until they arrived at the spar forests, where they debarked, and proceeded into the recesses of the wood in quest of trees fit for their purpose. The captain began to object against one that it was too crooked, another as being too large, and a third as too short, when George threw off his New Zealand cloak, and in very plain language told him that he should have no others, and continued, " Captain Thomson, see how you have served my back " (pointing at the same time to the marks of his punishment). The throwing off the cloak was the signal for a general massacre ; and George had scarcely finished the last words, when his brother dashed out the captain's brains ; and in a moment, before the least opposition could be offered, every European was laid dead on the spot.

The bodies being then stripped, were placed in the canoes, to be conveyed to the village and devoured, while George and a party of his men corresponding to the number of the murdered whites, attired themselves in the European clothes, and embarking in the boats, proceeded down the river to join the ship ; which they too successfully effected before any tidings had reached those on board respecting the bloody affair.

Here another dreadful scene of carnage ensued. The villagers, who, faithful to their chief's orders, had been some time in the ship, immediately began an indiscriminate slaughter of all those on board, in which they were instantly joined by George and his party, yet reeking with the blood of the hapless captain and his boat's crews! Terror and dismay seized all on board, and of the whole crew and passengers only four escaped! These were : Mrs. Marley, wife of a publican of that name at Port Jackson, with her child ; Miss Broughton, daughter of the acting deputy commissary-general at Port Jackson ; and the cabin-boy, whose name was George, and who had behaved with much kindness to the New Zealand chief during the voyage from New South Wales. Even these were forced to conceal themselves during the sanguinary scene, and were spared the next morning when discovered, the fury of the savages having by that time in a great measure subsided.

During the hurry of the slaughter six or seven seamen took refuge in the maintop, whither the murderers did not choose to pursue them ; and they also might have been spared, were it not for the following circumstance. Tippahee, a chief from the Bay of Islands, who had been to Port Jackson twice, and was friendly toward Europeans, happened to put into Wangeroa on a fishing party while the dreadful tragedy was acting. The sailors, immediately recognising him, besought him to save them by taking them on board of his canoes, to which he consented, desiring them to leap overboard and make the best of their way to him. In attempting this, however, some of them were overtaken and destroyed by the Wangeroans, while those who succeeded in gaining the canoes shared the same fate, Tippahee not being powerful enough to defend them from the fury of their enemies.

But the most horrible part of this scene was yet to be performed, a scene at which humanity must shudder—namely, the dissecting, baking, and devouring of our unfortunate countrymen ;

seventy human bodies were about to glut the horrible appetites of cannibals. As the description of the scene would only disgust the reader, I will spare his feelings, and drop the painful subject.

On the day after the massacre all the gunpowder was got on deck for partition among the natives, some of whom went on shore with their allotments; while others, less prudent, remained on board, brooding over and rejoicing at the complete success of their bloody operations, which put them in possession of so great a quantity of that which they prized above all other things. Among the latter was a chief who had possessed himself of a musket, and pleased with his acquisition, was carelessly snapping it, to ascertain, as may be supposed, the goodness of the lock; but happening to repeat the experiment over a quantity of loose gunpowder, it ignited, and communicating with some that was lying on the deck, exploded, destroying several of the natives then on board. By this means the ship took fire, and was quickly burnt to the water's edge.

Mr. Berry, then lying in the Bay of Islands, on board the *City of Edinbro'*, hearing of the melancholy occurrence, and understanding that four people had survived the massacre, in the most philanthropic manner succeeded in ran-

soming them from the savages, and restored
them all to their friends; except Mrs. Morley,
who died at Lima.

Various accounts of this horrid affair have
appeared, all more or less incorrect. The present may be depended upon as the most accurate yet published, having been obtained from
information communicated to me by a native,
who visited the scene of action a few days after
it had happened. The interpreter employed
for this purpose had been living there for four
or five years, and, from my own knowledge of
the language, could not, had he been so inclined,
impose on me.

12th.—At an early hour this morning we discharged the guns, which had been loaded for
some time, and were damp, in consequence of
the almost constant rains that prevailed since
our arrival here. The noise of the cannon produced great consternation on shore among the
natives at a distance from the ship, who supposed that we had commenced hostilities against
them, and were then actually employed in destroying their countrymen. They flocked from
all parts adjoining the bay to ascertain the cause
of our firing.

Among other spectators was a female orator
and priestess, of the highest rank and consideration among these people, called Vancathai.

This lady was regarded by her countrymen as more than mortal, and was supposed by them to have a powerful influence with the deity who presides over all departed souls in the other world. She was also supposed to have the power of *magotoo* (or bewitching her coun‑trymen to death) when she pleased. In all expeditions against the enemy, she was con‑sulted as to the probable result ; from her they learnt the most propitious day for sailing, and the day and hour most agreeable to the deity that his people should give battle. Of course this soothsayer possessed the most unlimited control over the minds of her blind votaries, and her auguries of the fate of a campaign not unfrequently tended to verify themselves, by inspiring diffidence or confidence, as it might be her inclination or interest to forward or defeat the objects of the enterprize.

This priestess is said to be friendly to Euro‑peans, and exhibits a pretty sure proof of her attachment by always choosing a husband from among them ; her votaries deeming her goddess‑ship too sacred for any intercourse of this nature to be permitted with her august person by ordina‑ry or unsanctified individuals of her own nation.

This lady boldly put off from shore, and entering the ship, demanded to see *Peter*. I immediately made my appearance, when she inquired the cause of the guns being discharged, which I explained to her entire satisfaction. Being a person of supreme dignity in the country, from her sacred character, as well as noble by birth, it was necessary that I should testify my veneration for so august a personage, in order to instil into the minds of the New Zealanders a just notion of the respect I entertained for their customs, religious as well as civil.

It may not be amiss perhaps to observe, that a strict regard to this line of conduct toward these islanders is the most effectual mode of conciliating their esteem : it serves this end more powerfully than bestowing the most costly presents. The one excites their cupidity, and ensures their friendship only in proportion to the amount of your gifts, and their expectation of more ; while the other insensibly gains their affections, and at a cheap and easy rate secures a place in their best regards. Indeed, it is much to be feared that to a deviation from this line of conduct may be traced many of those disasters which have befallen navigators.

I accordingly invited her highness into the cuddy, where she seated herself in an arm-chair, with a degree of majesty, and in a manner so unembarrassed, as plainly evinced that she was conscious of her own dignity.

This priestess presented a noble figure. She

appeared to be of a middle age; her complexion brunette, with sparkling black eyes; and her jet black hair, which was of a considerable length, gently flowed in ringlets over her shoulders, waving gracefully in the air as she walked· She was attired in the state robes of her country, and conveyed to the mind a forcible idea of savage royalty.

She had not been long seated before she remarked that the day was rather cold, and demanded if there was any rum on board, and if so, requested that some might be produced and given her. I told her that we had some, and ordered a decanter of brandy to be placed before her. After significantly eyeing it for some time, and not liking the colour, she observed, " this is not rum: I have never seen such as this before; let me have such rum as the whalers have on board."—With this request I immediately complied: she filled a tumbler nearly, and without hesitation quaffed it to the bottom. She then called for a segar, and having smoked a little, soon became very talkative.

The person who mostly attracted her notice was an elderly gentleman named Richardson, the surgeon's assistant. She inquired of me who he was. I made answer that he was our doctor and priest. With this information she seemed much pleased, saying that she herself was a

priestess and physician; and added, " Will not
my brother salute me according to the custom
of New Zealand?" that is, gently to incline
the head and touch noses. On the lady's request being communicated to Mr. Richardson,
he with much gallantry complied; but, unfortunately, on stooping his wig fell off, and exhibited a huge bald pate. It is more easy to
conceive than express her highness's alarm and
terror at this preternatural mode of salutation,
for she verily believed that he had taken of his
scalp by the aid of magic. She screamed most
dreadfully, having for the first time seen a real
proof of that skill in the black art, which she
pretended that she was possessed of. All her
female attendants joined in yelling most piteously on witnessing this phenomenon, and scamper-
ed with their mistress as speedily as they could
out of the cuddy, screaming out in the native
tongue, " a witch! a wizard! an enchanter!"

During the alarm Mr. Richardson recovered
his wig, and placed it on his head as before, to
the no small astonishment of some of them who
ventured to peep slily at him during the process.

After much trouble I succeeded in allaying
the fears of her highness and suite, who once
more ventured to sit down; not however without
casting many a terrified glance at our priest and
doctor, whom she did not require to salute her

a second time. She with much anxiety inquired if it was not by the aid of magic that he had disencumbered himself of his hair, and wished to know if he could with equal facility take off his head, which I did not altogether deny. This intelligence caused her to eye our doctor with a degree of profound reverence, and she requested I would inform her how many evil spirits he had influence over, and if he could also shake the hair and skin from the back part as from the front of his head. I replied, that with regard to the number of spirits over which he had control it was out of my power to inform her truly; but as regarded his hair, I assured her he could dismember himself from head to foot with the greatest facility.

During our conversation, one of the nymphs attending on the priestess, a girl of about fourteen years, slily approached Mr. Richardson, and mistaking a tuft of his natural hair for its moveable substitute, determined, by a good pull, to ascertain if the virtue lay in the hair or in its owner; but the hair holding fast, she was compelled to make a precipitate retreat, lest the magician should metamorphose her into a hog, those people believing in transmigration. This incident, no doubt, tended to confirm their belief in our priest's power, and caused a hearty laugh at the expense of the female casuist.

Before her departure, the priestess informed me that her husband had, about two months ago, left her to visit his parents in England, and requested that I would oblige her with one of my officers to supply his place; to which I jocularly answered that our Doctor was entirely at her service. But, whether it was that she dreaded his superior power, and therefore despaired of maintaining a proper influence over so mighty a magician, or that she fancied he was too old, I cannot say; but she would not hearken to my proposal of such a substitute, and pointed to a youth of about eighteen, the son of the governor of Valparaiso, whom I had taken on the voyage, his father having placed him under my charge while in South America. She said that she loved him greatly, and would thank me for him. I informed her that I could not comply with her request, he being a great chief's son, and could not be left in New Zealand. She then took her leave, saying she would come on board again the following morning.

Towards evening a boat returned, in which was Mr. Russell, who had been employed in making a survey of the bay.

13th.—We were engaged the greater part of this day in embarking our fire-wood, the weather being damp and dismal as usual.

About noon Vancathai, the priestess, again

visited us, accompanied by the late Boo Marray's two sons, who came to see Brian Boroo.
Some other chiefs also were in the train of the
priestess. They all embraced Brian Boroo tenderly, and lamented with tears the affair which
had severed the friendship of the two families,
and compelled them to seek blood for blood
from the friends of Boroo.

Boo Marray's sons related the account of
their father's death in nearly the following
words. They commenced by asking me if I
recollected, when laying at the Thames, loading
the *St. Patrick*, about fifteen months ago, that
I had applied to their father, who was then
going round to the Bay of Islands, to bring
with him two thousand men to cut spars for me,
as the Thames people were rather slow in performing the work. I replied, that I recollected
the circumstance perfectly well, and that I had
promised their father, if he succeeded in loading me in two months, a present of five muskets and two barrels of gunpowder.

They then resumed. Boo Marray, with upwards of two thousand men all armed, set out
for the Thames to cut the spars, but on their
arrival found I had sailed for this port. The
party then proceeded up the river in their canoes as far as it was navigable, from whence
they crossed to the Boroo country by land,

where they were hospitably received, and had gifts presented to them. Their father requested of the Boroo tribe to assist him in an invasion he then meditated upon the country of Wye-catto; but the Boroos declined, and begged of him to return peaceably to his own district; to which he agreed, and sailed down the river to the Barrier Islands, the place of general rendezvous for his forces. Here one of his chiefs, named Thowy, declared that he would not return home without killing some person, as he longed for a meal of human flesh. Thowy proceeded from thence to the main, where a party, anticipating his intention, lay in ambush, and cut him off with all his warriors.

Boo Marray waited several days for the chief's return, but finding he did not appear, concluded that some accident had happened, and went in search of him. On proceeding up a narrow creek in his canoe, the banks of which were very steep, a sudden fire of musketry was opened on him, accompanied by a thick shower of spears and stones from a party in ambuscade. Before Boo Marray's people could reach an eligible spot for landing they were nearly all killed: only himself, his eldest son, and a few others effected a landing. Boo Marray was shot through the thigh bone and fell upon one knee, when the enemy came in a body and attacked him. He shot two of them with his double-barrelled gun ; but before he could reload was despatched by them, and his head cut off.

Thus fell Boo Marray, by an unexpected assault from an enemy he could only discern from the deadly and sudden effects of their guns and spears. His enemies preserved his head, but devoured his body, as well as that of his eldest son, who died gallantly fighting by his father's side.

The two sons of Boo Marray, from whom I had this relation of the skirmish in which their father lost his life, escaping from the field of action, fled to the coast, where they were taken prisoners. One of them was desperately wounded in three places by a boat-axe, two wounds on the right arm, and one on the back. They were then sold as slaves or *kokeys* in the interior of the country, from which degraded situation Brian's father released them soon after, and supplied them with a canoe and provisions to enable them to return home, begging of them not to forget his kindness if his son should arrive in their harbour.

Brian admitted the probability of this story, but could by no means be induced to land amongst them.

While I was engaged on deck listening to the narrative of Boo Marray's sons, the draughtsman and officers were busily engaged in the gun-

room, concerting a plan to surprise and astonish
further the New Zealand priestess with the
transmigratory powers of the surgeon's assistant.
With this view they prevailed on him to submit
the bald part of his head to the draughtsman's
art, who in a short time metamorphosed it in such
a way, that had he been in ancient Greece or
Rome during the sway of Pagan superstition,
he might have obtained worshippers as the god
Janus, who had in pity to men condescended to
pay them a visit. His head presented the perfect appearance of an additional phiz, most
hideously pourtrayed on the bald part of the
cranium.

Vancathai, with her numerous female friends
and attendants, being seated in the cuddy,
begged as an especial favour that I would send
for the magician, and prevail on him to shake
off the hair and skin from his head as he had
done yesterday. She stated, as her reason for
this request, that those to whom she had mentioned the circumstance would not believe that
so wonderful a thing could be done by any
man, and that she had brought the most incre-
dulous with her to-day, that they might be eye-
witnesses of the miracle. Mr. Richardson with
much politeness consented to a repetition of it,
and approaching her highness, made a most
graceful bow, and in a moment cast off his arti-

ficial hair, when instead of an inoffensive bald pate, behold a horrible double face met the eyes of the astonished priestess and her companions.

Dreadful indeed was the confusion which immediately succeeded this display of even super-magical power. The cuddy was in a moment cleared of the visitants, and the magician left in peaceable possession of the apartment. Infidelity itself was now convinced of his magical powers, and there was not a native unbeliever in the ship.

Mr. Richardson now replaced his wig, and exerted himself to tranquillize those whom he had so much alarmed. Various were their conjectures respecting this supposed wonderful man, until I undeceived them in the evening; when their admiration of our ingenuity was only equalled by their groundless alarms at the effect of it. Mr. Richardson, however, had good cause to regret his willingness to entertain the swarthy strangers, for during our stay here they never ceased to tease and perplex him in a thousand different ways, especially by pulling off his hat and wig.

14th.—This morning I expected the ship would have been ready for sea, having completed the supply of fire-wood and water; but in this I was mistaken, for, through the negligence of the carpenter, four of the dead eyes in the lower rigging that had been broken by the straining of the ship during the tempestuous weather which we experienced in the passage from Port Jackson, were not yet repaired.

Wishing to make my further stay here as short as possible, I ordered a survey of the damage reported by the carpenter to be instituted by the officers, and the result made known to me; which was, that it would be dangerous to put to sea in our present state. A considerable time would necessarily be employed in completing the repairs, as hard wood was to be procured from the forests, and the iron straps to bind the blocks could not be completed by the smith for several days. I mentioned this impediment to a Mr. Anson, residing in the Bay of Islands: who in-formed me that in 1823 the ship *Brampton*, of London, missed stays in working out of the Bay during a gale of wind from the northward, and running on shore, became a total wreck; that he purchased a part of the wreck, and could supply me with as many oaken dead eyes, ready strapped with iron, as I might require. I joyfully closed with his offer, fearing that, to add to our difficulties, the blacksmith might not be able to raise sufficient heat with his small bellows to complete such heavy work: therefore to obviate further inconvenience in this respect, I not only furnished myself with as many as I needed for immediate use, but also with a few to spare.

16th.—Found it very tedious to get the old chain-plates removed, in consequence of the bolts having been driven and forelocked prior to the adoption of the new system of water-ways being put on the ship; and it being impracticable to drift or take the forelocks out of the bolts, I ordered the heads to be cut off, and new holes bored lower down the side.

19th.—The carpenter having completed the chain-plates, the fore-rigging was set up, and all made ready for sea. We were, however, prevented from sailing by a most violent storm which ushered in the day. It blew up the harbour with such violence, that at night we were obliged to wear out cable and bring both anchors ahead.

The officer formerly on board had paid so little attention to the ship's stowage, that when ready for sea she drew twelve or fourteen inches of water more forward than aft, which prevented her from sailing, steering, or staying so well as I wished. I attributed this to the dead weight of two bow guns weighing 30 cwt., four anchors of 12 cwt. each, two cabbooses, the one of iron the other of wood, bricks and mortar weighing at least 20 cwt., and all this independent of the usual dead weight in the fore part of the ship. The fore peak was also filled with kintledge, of which I had upwards of six tons on deck. Of the latter I was determined to rid myself, and was about to throw it overboard, not having a convenient place to stow it and it impeded the ship's way; but before I absolutely did so, whereby it could be of no use to any person, and the distance being great from any place where similar ballast could be obtained, I sent to the Missionaries on shore, acquainting them that I had a quantity of kintledge for sale, and would dispose of it upon reasonable terms; who agreed to take it from me at its prime cost in England. These terms were not very advantageous, but preferable to throwing it into the bay, which would occasion inequalities in the bottom, against which cables might rub and be injured, so I deemed it prudent to let them have it on their own terms.

22d.—Throughout yesterday the wind was variable, with constant rain. The crew were employed as necessary in the between-decks.

Succeeded this morning in unmooring the ship, after much trouble and fatigue. The weather being very unsettled, and wind variable, with a heavy sea setting into the harbour, I did not deem it prudent to sail this day.

23d.—The day commenced with moderate breezes and cloudy weather. At 8 A.M. we made the signal for sailing, and began to weigh the second anchor, which we found very difficult, it having got buried in the mud in the late stormy weather. A new eight-inch messenger broke twice before we could trip the anchor. We had but just succeeded in getting the anchor off the ground, when it commenced blowing a gale of wind on shore; we were therefore obliged to let it go again, or be stranded before sail could be set. In this state we remained during the day.

Martin Bushart had come along with me under the most solemn assurances of being relanded at Tucopia, after I had obtained a correct account (as far as possible) of the ships lost at Mannicolo. The cause of my not putting on shore while in the *St. Patrick* has already been explained in a former part of my journal. While I remained at Calcutta, his continual cry was to return to the island on which he had spent nearly thirteen years; nor would he sign the ship's articles there, alleging as his reason, that if he did so he should become one of the ship's company, and should any thing befal me during the voyage, the person who succeeded to the command might compel him to return to India, where he had no friends or prospects; and that as he was addicted to the use of spirituous liquors, which injured his constitution, he ought not to live in places where they could be procured.

I was thoroughly acquainted with the value of this man's services, and that the expedition could not be prosecuted with success without him, and therefore indulged him in many respects to conciliate his friendship, which I am confident I gained. Indeed, he displayed a striking proof of his attachment to my person at Van Diemen's Land; for when I was imprisoned there he quitted the ship to reside on shore, declaring that he would never more return to her without me, unless forcibly compelled.

Martin Bushart came to me this evening, saying, " Captain Dillon, you have proved a friend to me : we were together under sentence of death among the Feejee men, when fourteen of our companions were killed and eaten by them; I hope you do not forget that." I replied, " That fatal day has been impressed too indelibly on my memory to be so easily forgotten, Martin."—" Then, Sir," resumed he, " I have a favour to ask of you : I have attached myself to a New Zealand girl, who is now my wife according to the laws of her country, and she wishes to accompany me to Tucopia : I hope you will permit her." To this I had no objection, as I wished to take a

few females and children to Mannicolo, if it
could be effected by fair means, for the following reasons:

I have often conversed with savages, who
informed me that when first they beheld Europeans, they supposed them to have descended
from the clouds; nor could they imagine what
our business was in their country, unless to
carry off their provisions, wives, and children,
as slaves: this idea being grounded on the
universal practice in those islands of men carrying off the women and children of their enemies in their war expeditions; whilst, on the
contrary, when they pay a friendly visit to a
neighbouring island, or to a strange country,
their wives and children usually accompanied
them.

I have visited the most ferocious tribes in
the South Seas, and never failed of becoming
friendly with them.

Curiosity (that all-powerful passion in the
female breast, whether in the wilds of a savage
country, or in the elegant drawing-room of re-
fined and civilized Europe) never fails to induce the women on shore to approach the ship,
where, seeing some of their own sex on board,
they presently commence making friendly sig-
nals to them. The ladies on shore having thus
established a pantomimic acquaintance with

those on board, feel inclined to become more
intimate with the strangers, and approach the
sides of the ship, where, a few small presents
being made to them, and being otherwise kindly
treated, away they post to land with the glad
tidings, exhibiting the tokens of friendship.
More of them then put off in the expectation
of meeting with similar treatment, and a judicious distribution of beads, showy ribbons,
scissors, looking-glasses, &c., never fails to ensure a hospitable reception from them. Thus,
mutual confidence being established by means
of the women, it rests with the visitors to act'
with that prudence and caution which will not
fail of making it permanent.

Brian Boroo requested me to land him at
the river Thames, saying he would bring down
a plentiful supply of fresh provisions and vegetables, with some spars, of which we stood much
in need. I told him that it was my intention to
proceed there for those supplies, as there was
but little to be procured at this place; so many
ships having visited the bay of late, they had
cleared the adjacent country of all the spare
provisions. He then told me that there were
two young women on board who had relatives
living at the Thames, and desired much to see
them, and that if I would allow them to go
round in the ship, they would be extremely

thankful. To this I assented, as I considered
they would serve as hostages for the safety
of my people, while on shore cutting the
spars we required; and Brian made them acquainted with the result of his application on
their behalf, with which they seemed highly
pleased.

A native chief named Thenana, who had accompanied me in the *Active* from this island
in 1814, teased me sadly to be allowed to go
in the ship. I told him that he was too old,
and would die at Calcutta; but his reply was,
" I will go; I have plenty of muskets and
powder, and only want a barrel of musket-balls,
which having obtained, I will return by the first
ship to Port Jackson, from whence Mr. Marsden will send me home." This was a ready cal-
culation for an untutored savage : he traced in
idea his departure from hence, his arrival in
Bengal and the total fulfilment of his desires,
thence to Port Jackson, and back to his native
country, all in the space of five minutes, depending on Providence for the realization of
this fairy dream.

I told him that I would give him an answer
in the morning, as I should most likely dream
on the subject in the night : a course the most
likely to please him, as these people place implicit reliance on dreams, and I had resolved, too,

by that means to rid myself of his importunities.

24th.—At an early hour this morning the ship
was surrounded by several canoes, having on
board many chiefs of consequence, who had received notice of our intention to depart, and
had come with the double purpose of bidding
us farewell and receiving presents. The friends
of those natives who were to sail with us to the
Thames and to Mannicolo, came on board at an
early hour.   Each of them demanded something
from me as presents for their friends and relatives, urging that this was the general custom
with captains who took any of their people with
them to assist in whaling, sealing, or otherwise.
I observed that no benefit had been yet derived
from their services, and that most likely they
would run away from the ship after receiving an
advance.   They admitted that such tricks had
not unfrequently been played, and generally to
strange captains, whom they never expected to
see in their harbour any more ; but that they
could not think of treating me thus, for I was
their countryman, and came every year to see
them, and always behaved well to such of their
friends as accompanied me to foreign parts.
Upon this I made each person who was to accompany me a present.

Thenana, the old man to whom I was this

morning to give an answer, was very impor-
tunate to know if I had dreamt last night. I
informed him I had. He then was in pain to
learn the purport of my dream, which, after
I had adjusted my face to a most rueful length,
thereby affording some idea as to the result, I
delivered as follows:—" I dreamt last night
that we were at Calcutta, and that both you
and I died there. Now, should I die, which of
course I shall since I dreamt so, what will become of you? no person there knows you, and
it will be out of your power to return to New
Zealand."

He did not much admire my interpretation
of the dream, and applied to Vancathai, the
priestess, and resolver of such mysteries, for her
opinion on the subject. Vancathai, true to the
practice of her profession, observing that I did
not wish to take him, gave an appropriate explanation of the fatal consequences likely to
result from a contumacious neglect of divine
warning. Poor Thenana had therefore nothing
to do but submit to his hard fate, and thus I
quietly got rid of his solicitations; whereas had
I at first bluntly refused to take him, he would
have sought an opportunity to revenge himself,
even ten years afterwards.

We now began to heave up the anchor. The
priestess mounting the capstern, loudly implored

the gods of New Zealand to grant us a fair breeze and prosperous voyage, and that they would preserve us in all places and at all times from encountering the fatal oven!

At 9 A.M , the anchor being weighed and all sails set, with a light breeze approaching to a calm, the canoes went on shore. About an hour afterwards I heard a dreadful noise upon deck, and went out from my cabin to ascertain the cause. There I found Vancathai, the priestess, whom I supposed to have gone on shore, weeping bitterly. On inquiring into the cause, I learnt that for some time back an attachment had been formed between her and the boatswain, and that on this occasion, having gone down into his cabin to take a parting glass, she had remained on board till after the departure of her countrymen. Having been left below by the boatswain, who had to attend on deck, she helped herself to the liquor too freely, and quite overcome, fell asleep. The boatswain in the hurry of duty forgot her, and the first intimation of her being on board was the dreadful yelling she set up, when on awaking she found us under weigh, and at a distance of about three or four miles from the shore. She begged of me to get her on shore in the ship's boat, which I immediately ordered out for the purpose: for this she expressed herself extremely grate-

ful, and promised never again to drink
rum.

The names of the natives who joined us to
proceed to the Thames were Emooca and Perry-
cowy, two females; the others were Martin
Bushart's wife, Tetorey; the Marquis of Wyemattee; Moyhanger, alias King Charley; Robert Tytler, a New Zealand doctor; Phelim
O'Rourke, one of the Marquis's confidential
friends; and Murtoch O'Brien, son to King
Charley.

It is necessary to remark, that the New Zealanders are very fond of being called by European names, as they suppose it ensures them
a better reception on board ships. With this
view the above persons applied to be named
after Europeans, and the names I have given
them they will retain during life.

At noon the latitude observed was 35° S., when
Cape Brett bore E.S.E. four miles. We stood
along the shore toward the Thames, and at 8
P.M. the Poor Knights bore W.N.W. three or
four leagues.

While lying in the Bay of Islands, I was informed by the missionaries residing there that
Captain Dumont D'Urville, commander of the
French sloop of war *l'Astrolabe*, had been
there making a survey of the coast, and had
sailed about two months for the Thames and

Friendly Islands. I had received instructions
from the Bengal Government to meet with, if
possible, and communicate to him all the intelligence I could, respecting the expedition and
the fate of the Count de la Pérouse.

25.—We were driven considerably to leeward
during the night. At 8 A.M. the largest of the
Barrier Islands bore S.E.¾S.

As the wind was now, I considered that entering the Thames would be attended with much
loss of time, and communicated this my opinion
to Prince Brian Boroo, who implored me most
piteously to land him : that he was now in sight
of his country, and if he departed from it, might
perhaps never see it again. He stated that,
should he delay his return two or three years,
he would, in all probability, find his father, brothers, sisters, and friends, had been murdered
or carried off by the enemy ; and he therefore
wished to land and share their fate, whatever it
might be, as he had no desire whatever to survive them. He further observed, that his presence would encourage his friends, and the arms
which he had procured in India would be of the
greatest service in repelling the enemy. The
Marquis and Moyhanger also importuned me on
behalf of this fine young man, who is now nearly
civilized, and might by his conduct and advice

release his countrymen in some degree from that darkness in which they are plunged.

All the New Zealanders who joined the ship at the Bay of Islands were very sea-sick: so much so, that they would have made any sacrifice to be put on shore from the vessel. Nay, they were willing to be landed, although in an enemy's country, and trusted to Brian's mercy to spare their lives. I felt much for poor Brian and the others, and stood in for the river.

The season being now far advanced, I was particularly anxious to reach the Mannicolos before the north-west monsoon prevailed in those seas. At 9 o'clock I found it impossible to get close in with the land with the wind in its present quarter; in justice to my employers therefore I could not lose more time and was obliged to bear away. On observing the ship's stern point to his beloved land, poor Brian wept bitterly, as did also his friend Morgan McMurragh. I did all that was in my power to console them, stating that I was going to Tongataboo, the capital of the Friendly Islands, where there were several whalers fishing at this season of the year, and would sail from thence for the New Zealand fishery in summer, which was now fast approaching, and I promised that

I would prevail on the captain of the first whaler I fell in with to take them on board and return them to their native land. With these assurances they were pacified, as they knew how common a thing it is for above fourteen sail of whalers to be in the Bay of Islands during the months of December and January every year. During the winter they fish off the Friendly, Feejee, and Navigator's Islands, and return in summer to whale off New Zealand, where they complete their cargo, take in supplies of hogs, potatoes, fish, wood, and water, and refit their rigging and ships.

Each officer and seaman on board the whalers has his wife at the Bay of Islands, who on his return from the fishery joins him, and remains with him on board till the ship's departure. It often happens that these women accompany their husbands to the fishing station, as was the case with the daughter of Boo Marray, who was absent when I first anchored in the Bay.

I now determined to sail for Tongataboo, in the hope of meeting with Mons. D'Urville, and likewise to take in fresh supplies of poultry, hogs, &c.

In la Pérouse's last letter to the French minister of marine, which I here copy, he says that he intends touching at the Friendly Islands; I might therefore expect to obtain some information relative to him in the course of a visit to that quarter.

From M. de la Pérouse, dated Botany Bay, Feb. 7th 1788.

Sir:—I shall run up to the Friendly Islands, and obey all my instructions relative to the southern part of New Caledonia, the island of Santa Cruz de Mendana, the southern coast of La Terra des Arsacides of Surville, and the Louisiade of Bougainville, examining at the same time whether this last is, or is not, a part of New Guinea.

About the end of July 1788, I shall pass between New Guinea and New Holland, by another strait than that called Endeavour Strait, if any can be found.

During the month of September and part of October I shall visit the gulph of Carpentaria, and all the western coast of New Holland as far as Van Diemen's Land, but so that I may be able to get to the northward soon enough to arrive in the Isle of France about the beginning of December 1788.

At half past five this evening New Zealand was yet in sight. The New Zealanders mounted on the poop, and prayed to their deity to protect them, and grant that they might be enabled to revisit their native shores, of which they were now about to lose sight.

I shipped in the Bay of Islands a man named John Bumpsted, as a marine, who had been employed by the missionaries there as a farmer for three or four years. I also found an American of half-caste, who said his mother was an Indian squaw.

This poor fellow had lived with Johnston the

sawyer, who stated that he was an idiot, and his name John Downey; that he had arrived at New Zealand in an American whaler, where he was put on shore by the captain and officers as useless. He set out by land to find his way home to Boston in America, supposing himself to be then on the continent, and the New Zealanders to be American Indians of a different nation from that to which his mother belonged. He travelled for a full month through the forests of New Zealand, when he returned to the coast half-starved and naked, not being able to reach Boston, and the sawyer hospitably admitted him under his roof, where he had lived for the last five months.

Johnston complained of poverty, and begged of me to take the poor fellow on board, for that he should be obliged shortly to turn the wretched idiot out of doors, who would perish from the want of food.

I asked Johnston if the missionaries, who are supported in a luxurious style by charitable donations, would suffer this miserable being to starve. He replied, that they never allowed people from the ships to visit them; and that they represented all their countrymen (themselves of course excepted) as sinners and bad men, whenever the natives inquired the reason of their not behaving with sociability towards other classes of Christians besides their own missionary brethren.

I told Johnston that it was my intention to touch at Tongataboo, where provisions were plentiful, and the inhabitants humane, hospitable, and generous in the highest degree to all foreigners who reside on shore, and that I had no objection to take him there. The sawyer made my reply known to the unfortunate idiot, who gladly received the news, and embarked as a passenger for that place.

The natural productions of New Zealand, most in demand by the Europeans, are flax and spars. Since its discovery, hogs, potatoes, and all manner of garden vegetables and esculent roots, have been introduced, and now abound, forming an abundant and opportune supply for ships touching there during the whaling seasons. There are, however, two species of potatoes indigenous to the soil, which with the fern-root constitute the principal article of their food. The sea contiguous to the shores affords an abundant supply of excellent fish, which the natives catch and dry during the summer months, and lay up as a winter store. They have also a breed of dogs peculiar to the island, and much resembling the Pariah dog of India, which is considered as furnishing a most delicate dish. They manufacture a kind of cloth from the flax plant, with which, and their cloaks and mats, they defend themselves from the inclemencies of the winter. Their mats and cloaks are made in divers shapes and fashions, with ornamented borders of dark colour.

From the knowledge I have acquired of the New Zealand language, I succeeded in obtaining a very full account of their civil and religious customs, but want of time and space prevents me from giving any details in this place. I intend, however, to give a full description of them on a future day.

While lying at the Thames in the *St. Patrick* in 1826, the Bay of Islanders, under command of Shanghi, suddenly attacked a party of the Kayaparas, slew all the men, and made captive the women and children. With respect to their being cannibals no doubt can be entertained, for on that occasion an opportunity was afforded me of ascertaining the revolting fact.

After the battle between the Bay of Islanders and the Kayaparas I proceeded for the Bay of Islands, where King George had arrived before me in his canoe. He paid me a visit, and I promised to make him a present before I sailed. I was surprised by seeing my friend alongside early next morning demanding his present, and I replied that I was not going to sail yet. He answered, that as he was going to the west part of the island and would not return till I should have sailed. I was anxious to know his business, which he informed me was to carry presents of human flesh to his friends there, whom the Kayaparas had offended, and whose flesh was in the canoe. I demanded to see it, when he shewed me several calibashes filled with the shocking viand, baked in a South-sea oven to preserve it from putrefaction. I felt my blood curdle at the sight; so hastening to give George his present, I left him to proceed on his horrid mission.

CHAPTER VII.

OCCURRENCES FROM NEW ZEALAND TO TONGA, USUALLY
CALLED TONGATABOO, WITH REMARKS ON WHAT HAP-
PENED AT THAT PLACE.

3d August 1827.—ONE of those accidents
occurred to which a seafaring life is so liable,
and which often prove fatal. At an early hour
this morning I was awoke by the smell and
smoke of something burning. On getting up, I
found this arose from a small piece of canvas
which had caught fire in my cabin. I immediately threw over it the contents of the wash-
hand basin, and thus extinguished it. But,
being somewhat alarmed by the quantity of
smoke, I adopted the precaution of causing a
quantity of gunpowder (a half-barrel and three
empty casks) in the adjoining cabin to be removed. The accident arose from the guard
stationed to watch the lights having fallen
asleep, and the candlestick having been over-
turned by the motion of the vessel.

11*th*.—Nothing more worthy of note occurred
since our leaving New Zealand until the evening of the 9th, when a Marquesa man, named
Peter, attended muster armed with a club,

which was instantly taken from him. On inquiring into the cause of this conduct, I learnt
that for some days past the man had exhibited
symptoms of derangement; and therefore, in
order to prevent him from doing mischief, I
ordered him to be put in irons: I released
the poor maniac yesterday evening, on ascertaining that his aberration of intellect arose
from melancholy, and was not accompanied
with violence.

12th.—Light variable airs throughout. At
8 A.M. saw the island Eawa, or Middleburg,
bearing S.W. ½ S., distance eleven or twelve
leagues: all sail set standing for it. Latitude
at noon 21° 9′ S.; longitude 174° 2′ W. At 4
P.M. the extremes of Eawa bore from S.W.½W.
to W. by S.½S.

At 7 P.M. light variable airs from the eastward. Not wishing to approach the land before
daylight, I ordered the small sails to be handed,
and the ship to be hauled to the wind on the
starboard tack, and thus we spent the night
beating to windward.

In the forenoon of this day a shark of the
blue species was caught, and on being opened
was found to contain twenty-five young, all
alive, and each about the size of an ordinary
haddock. Neither the New Zealanders nor
any other of the South Sea Islanders would

taste of it, although the brown shark is much relished by them generally.

13*th.* - Light airs from the eastward. At 6 A.M. could distinctly perceive the north point of Eawa bearing W. by N.; made all sail and stood for it.

Some four or five years ago the natives of this island, to the number of about ten or twelve, were admitted on the decks of the *Supply* whaler, then standing off and on under easy sail, trading, and waiting for a boat to return from the shore. Suddenly they armed themselves with capstern bars, and clubs brought out of their canoes, under pretence of offering them in barter, attacked such of the crew as were on deck, killed the captain's brother (a Mr. Thornton), besides the carpenter of the ship and one seaman, and actually seized the captain and threw him overboard. Fortunately, however, he fell into a whale-boat that was hoisted on the ship's quarter, where he found a telescope, which, with admirable presence of mind, he presented at the natives that were pursuing him, who, supposing it to be a new description of firelock, immediately retreated, and thus the captain's life was preserved. By this time the crew, who were below at dinner, hearing the yells of the savages and the groans of their dying companions, became alarmed for their own safety, and seizing each a harpoon or lance, they sallied on deck, where, after having killed some of the murderers, they compelled the rest to seek safety by leaping overboard and swimming to their canoes.

Since that period these islanders have on several occasions enticed the crews of boats, sent there for various purposes from ships lying off and on, to land, when, having been seized on by hundreds of savages, who bound them individually to cocoa-nut trees, one of the prisoners has been despatched to obtain a ransom from the captain for the rest of his men, whom they would by no means release till their demands (in most instances four or five muskets and a couple of barrels of gunpowder) were acceded to, and the ransom actually in their possession.

Having occasion to visit these kidnapping gentry, to procure hogs, yams, &c. and to take in fresh water, I determined to benefit from the experience of others, and not be tricked by them. I therefore caused the guns to be loaded, and the marines daily exercised at their small arms, making them fire three rounds each.

The wind was so light that we approached the shore but slowly, and at noon the north point of the island bore W. and by N.$\frac{3}{4}$N. three leagues.

At 1 P.M. the island of Tongataboo was in

sight from the mast-head, bearing W.¾ S.   As
water was my object in touching here, if procurable, I resolved to anchor at Eawa.   At 7
P.M. got close to the north point of this island,
and stood along its west side to the southward;
fired some guns, and hoisted a light as a signal,
supposing that some of the natives might venture off, but they did not.

14th.—About 8 this morning two canoes,
paddled by three men each, came off to the
ship, loaded with yams, potatoes, sugar-cane,
cocoa-nuts, sea-shells, clubs, spears, &c. for
barter, and these were followed by several
others freighted similarly, and a brisk trade
was quickly commenced with them.

In the second canoe there was an American seaman, who had been left sick on the island about
two years before.   From this man I learnt that
it would be difficult to obtain water here, as
the spring which the inhabitants used was two
miles inland.   This unwelcome news determined me to put into Tongataboo; but the day
being far spent, I resolved to keep under easy
sail till daylight to-morrow, and then to stand
over for Tonga.

The chief of this island sent me a present of
a hog and some yams, with an invitation to call
and see him at his residence on shore; but not
feeling inclined to be bound to a cocoa-nut tree

for an indefinite period, or till an enormous
ransom was exacted for me, I declined the
honour of the invitation, accepting however of
his presents, and sending him in return a pistol,
bayonet, and some articles of cutlery.

At sunset the canoes quitted the ship for
the shore, having left four of their countrymen
on board. Finding I could converse in the
language of their neighbours on the Feejees,
they declared that they could not think of parting with me so soon ; they consequently remained on board all night, and entertained me
with various accounts of my old friends at the
Feejees since my departure from thence in
1813.

The American informed me that during his
residence on the island he had been treated
with the greatest kindness by the chief, who
had honoured him with his daughter for a wife.
He also stated that, understanding how to repair
iron-work, he was much esteemed by the natives, who found him abundance of employment, and paid him most handsomely in the
produce of the country for his labour in repairing their fire-arms, fish-hooks, &c. Notwithstanding the marked attention and honours,
however, which had been conferred upon him
by the prince, he was desirous of taking a passage with me. I inquired if his wife would not

be uneasy at his abandoning her; he replied that she would, but that he was very desirous to see his friends in America; however, that he would not act ungratefully to her. He then went on shore in one of his father-in-law's boats, for the purpose of bidding her farewell, and after the lapse of an hour or two he returned with his wife, a beautiful young Indian, aged about fourteen years, who appeared much affected at the American's intention of forsaking her. I endeavoured to console the lady, and presented her with a few necklaces of various-coloured glass beads, with which she was exceedingly well pleased, and departed in one of her father's canoes, after having taken an affectionate and tender farewell of her inconstant husband.

The American informed me, that about two months ago he had heard, for two or three successive days, the report of discharges of cannon at Tonga, and supposing that the island was besieged by a European force, his father-in-law and his subjects were much alarmed. Soon after a canoe arrived from Tonga, and brought intelligence that a ship with a white flag had anchored at the island, and that soon after a war had broken out between her crew and the islanders, which had caused the guns to be fired on the inhabitants. In these encounters three of the natives were killed and one of the

ship's crew, a few days after which the ship
had sailed.

From the above account I supposed the ship
in question to be the French sloop *Astrolabe*.

15*th*.—We had strong trade winds throughout
the day, with fair weather : towards night it
commenced raining, and the general appearance
of the evening indicated approaching bad weather.

At daylight stood in for Eawa ; but in consequence of a fresh breeze that blew, I did not
expect any canoes to come off to the ship.
However, notwithstanding the roughness of the
weather, and the surf beating high, we had
several alongside loaded as yesterday. Having
discharged them of their cargoes, I caused the
four natives who had slept on board last night
to return in them, having made each a small
present.

At $8\frac{1}{2}$ A.M. bore up with all sail set for Tonga,
and at $10\frac{1}{2}$ entered the channel between the
main island and the small ones which lay off it.
Soon after, shortening sail, I made a signal for
a pilot.

On passing the lagoon I fired a gun. There
were many of the islanders on the beach, and
several canoes paddling off toward the ship, in
one of which I observed a white man. I round-
ed the vessel to, in order to wait for him ; but

such was the violence of the wind and strength of the tide, both opposing his progress, that he could not overtake the *Research*. I then bore away under easy sail, and entered the channel between the fourth and fifth islands from the west point of the lagoon. Their names are Makhaha on the left, and Manooafai on the right hand.

Being at the mast-head myself, I observed the channel to be strewed with sunken dangers, such as coral banks, which certainly must have grown there since the harbour was surveyed by Captain Cook. It was with the greatest difficulty that I at length succeeded in evading these submarine reefs.

After getting out of this dangerous channel, I ran up with a fair wind and anchored in thirteen fathoms and a-half water, off the island Pangimodoo, which bore N.E., distance one mile. The anchor had not been gone more than a few minutes when we were visited by several canoes, each paddled by two, three, or four men. They were filled with the produce of the island, such as yams, sweet potatoes, cocoa-nuts, bananas, sugar-canes, and had also on board one cock and one duck. A brisk exchange was immediately commenced with them for cutlery and glass beads.

In one of these canoes was the white man

above-mentioned, whom I invited on deck, and found to be one of the crew of the *Port au Prince*, which had been cut off at the Harpie Islands, one of this group, in December 1806: his name was John Singleton. From him I learnt that the French discovery ship *Astrolabe*, Captain Dumont d'Urville, had been nearly wrecked in the channel from which I had just escaped, and had sailed from this port for the Feejees about three months ago. He also said that one of her crew had been murdered here, the circumstances attending which were as follow.

According to his account the *Astrolabe*, on entering the bay, had got aground upon the hidden dangers from which I had just escaped. She remained in this state for eight days, when she was floated off by a high tide and calm, having lost three anchors and two cables, together with her false keel; the ship however was reported to be not in the smallest degree leaky.

After the vessel had been on shore two days, the captain, despairing of getting her off, sent his cash, plate, and valuables to the Wesleyan Missionary station on this island, and shortly afterwards took to the boats, for the purpose of abandoning her. Fortunately, however, he was dissuaded from this premature step; he

rejoined the ship, and ultimately succeeded, by
means of an unusual high flow of tide, as just
stated, in rescuing her from her perilous situation. The Missionaries and English sailors
resident here bestow the highest encomiums on
Monsieur Jacquenot, the first lieutenant, for his
indefatigable and seamanlike exertions, and at-
tribute the salvation of the ship to him.

It is here necessary to observe, that the chiefs
of these islands pride themselves much on having Europeans resident among them; a feeling
that gave rise to the following unfortunate
affray :—The morning on which the ship was
about to sail, two of the crew, unperceived by
the sentinels, had leaped from the side into a
large canoe, where they were concealed by the
natives. The canoe immediately pulled for the
shore, and shortly after a boat, with eight or
ten men and an officer, put off for Pangimodoo
to procure sand; but the canoe reached the
shore first. The chief of this canoe having
acquainted those on shore that he had two
Europeans with him, the other chiefs became
jealous, and said, " We must have some white
men to live with us as well as you." The ship's
boat had by this time reached the land, and the
men on board being unarmed, were seized by
the natives and taken on shore.

Two armed boats were sent from the ship to

their assistance ; but before they could reach
the island the natives conveyed their captives
up the country, whither they were pursued ;
the islanders sallying from the woods, and re-
treating occasionally. Several houses were set
on fire by the assailants, and two of the islanders wounded, who died that night. The corporal of marines was one of the party that
landed : he left his companions, and pursued
the islanders up a foot-path through a wood,
where a native, who lay concealed, struck a
bayonet fitted on a stick through his head ; he
instantly expired, and was picked up by his
companions. A midshipman also was wounded
in the arm with a musket-ball. The party not
succeeding, then returned to the ship.

Captain Dumont d'Urville sent a message on
shore that he would get the ship close to the
nearest town and cannonade it if his men
were not instantly restored. The message was
answered by the islanders in the following terms :
" Inform the captain that, if he wishes to fight,
we are prepared to receive him : if he cannon-
ades us, we will get entrenched." On receipt
of this answer the anchor was weighed, and the
ship placed in a situation to bring her broad-
side to bear on the town.*

---

* It happened to be the sacred town of Ma Fanga, which, being
the supposed abode of their deities, and of the souls of their an-

At this town an incessant fire was kept up for two days without doing any mischief, when the natives became more bold, and sallied from the trenches. One of them, a chief, was soon after killed by an accidental shot, which hit an iron-wood tree, and rebounding from it, struck him. The people of consequence from all parts of the island now assembled; they censured those who had been the cause of the rupture, and succeeded in prevailing on the chiefs who seized the people in the boat to allow them to return before more mischief was done. In consequence, on the third day, those persons were re-embarked, without having received any injury.

It is much to the credit of the Tonga people, that they treated their prisoners in the most hospitable manner while in their power. The two deserters who were the cause of all this disturbance represented to the chief under whose protection they had landed, that if they were sent on board they must pay the forfeit of their lives; no inducement, therefore, could prevail on him to deliver them up, and the ship

cestors and deceased friends, has always from time immemorial been considered neutral ground, and as such respected in their most bloody wars. It is governed by the high-priest of the island, who guards the tombs of the deceased princes, presides at the annual sacrifices, and receives the first-fruits offered at the shrine of their deities.

sailed without them soon after for the Feejee Islands.

One of the Frenchmen left behind visited the ship this afternoon. I would not admit him on board, on account of his conduct to his former commander.

I was visited this evening by a native named Langhi, an old acquaintance of mine on former voyages. In November 1824, on a voyage from South America in search of sandal-wood, I put in here in command of my own ship, the *Calder* of Calcutta, burden 250 tons, mounting sixteen guns, when this man, and a native of the Fee-jees named Thaki, joined me as interpreters. We proceeded from hence to the Feejees, New Hebrides, New Zealand, and Port Jackson, where I left Langhi and Thaki at a friend's house, to await my return from South America, whither I was then bound. I sailed from Sydney on the 16th of March 1825 for Valparaiso, and on the May following the *Calder* had the misfor-tune to be wrecked. My next ship, the *St. Pa-trick*, was then in the harbour, and had just returned from New Zealand with a cargo of spars, having providentially weathered the fury of the gale. I sailed in her from Valparaiso in October 1825, bound to New Zealand and Cal cutta.

On my way I put in at Otaheite in November,

where I found Langhi and Thaki, who informed me that Port Jackson was too cold for them, and afforded neither cocoa-nuts nor yams; they therefore came to Otaheite with a Captain Henry, who resided there. That finding the Otaheitans had embraced the Christian faith, they did so too, and intended shortly to return to Tonga with some Otaheitan missionaries and schoolmasters, to instruct their countrymen. .That, pursuant to this resolution, Langhi, accompanied by one of his wives, an Otaheitan woman, and two missionary natives of the same island, set out for and arrived here shortly after I had left Otaheite, and with their assistance he succeeded in converting his chief, the great Thubow, and all his subjects in the district of Nogoluffa. He also stated that a boat drifted here from the island of Whytutakee with five men on board. I asked him to bring them to me as I had been several times at their island, which is situated in 18° 52' S. latitude, and longitude 159° 42' W.

An hour had scarcely elapsed when two of these poor people came on board, and desired to see me. They were admitted into the ship, and related their adventure as follows.

Pamono, a native of Otaheite, established at their island as a missionary and schoolmaster, requested ten of them to embark in a large boat, and go to an island in the vicinity of Whytuta-

kee, called Roratongu, with a letter to two of
his countrymen, who were established there as
missionaries and schoolmasters. They accordingly set out, but on their way had the misfortune
to be overtaken by a strong gale of wind in the
trades, which drove them past their port. They
drifted about at sea for five months, undergoing
all the pains and miseries that human nature
could support for the want of food.   Five
perished from starvation : the surviving five
were afterwards successful in snaring four sharks,
which with a few sea-birds that occasionally
alighted on their boat (and which were eagerly
grasped at and ravenously devoured raw) were
their only subsistence during the whole time
they spent on the waves. The clouds afforded
them a supply of rain-water barely sufficient to
preserve life.

After thus combatting with famine and danger for five months, they were at length providentially wrecked upon this island. Here the
natives most humanely assisted in rescuing them
from the surf, in which their boat had been
dashed to pieces, and when taken on shore they
were scarcely able to stand erect. They experienced the most hospitable treatment from
the benevolent inhabitants. During their two
months' stay they were quite restored to health
and strength, and were now anxiously awaiting

an opportunity to return to their beloved native island.

The boat in which the above adventures occurred has been a most unfortunate one. On my voyage across the Pacific from Chili, in October 1824, I touched at the island of Ulitea, one of the Society Islands, where I met with a Mr. Williams, of the London mission. He informed me that about six months before he had sent his boat up to Otaheita with letters to his brother missionaries, where she arrived safe, and sailed from thence a few days after, but had never since been heard of: he therefore supposed all was lost, and the boat wrecked. Having sailed, however, from Ulitea late in October and touched at the island of Wateeoo, five hundred miles to leeward of Otaheita, there I found the lost boat with her crew. She had been on that occasion drifting about at sea for three months, when fortune at last kindly threw her on the shores of Wateeoo. She appeared to be a heavy ill-built boat of about ten tons. I afterwards learnt that she had been towed from Wateeoo to Whytutakee by a Port Jackson schooner, where she was left for the unfortunate narrators of this adventure to make another unsuccessful trip in her.

This evening I divided the crew into three watches, attaching an officer and petty officer to each; the former to be stationed on the poop, and the latter on the forecastle, during their respective watches. With a view to keep their vigilance alive, I called their attention to the fate of the American ship *Duke of Portland*, which had been cut off at this place, and all on board murdered, with the exception of Eliza Morley, an English female, and three boys. I reminded them also of the melancholy fate of Captain Pimbleton and Mr. Boston; the one commander, and the other supercargo of the American ship *Union*. Likewise of the capture of the *Port au Prince* and massacre of her crew; the fate of two whalers at Vavow; and lastly, the affray between the natives and Mr. Dumont d'Urville, which happened only a few weeks before. With such awful warnings, I did not suppose even a lascar would venture to sleep during his watch.

16th.—Shortly after daylight several canoes came off loaded with the produce of the island, and a brisk exchange began. Received a visit from the Otaheitan missionaries stationed here, who spent the night on board. They consisted of three men, and two women, their wives.

About 3 P.M. Thubow, a mighty chief of this island, and believed by the natives to be nearly related to the gods, honoured me with a visit. He brought a present of hogs, yams, &c. Un-

derstanding that he had embraced the Christian
religion, I received him under a salute of three
guns, a distinction with which he was highly
flattered. He gave me to understand that he
wished to sleep on board all night, to which I
agreed. Immediately after tea he repaired to
the poop and joined his Christian brethren,
Langhi and the Otaheitan missionaries, in prayer.

At half-past 7 the quarter-deck was lighted
up with lanterns, and several of the crew
danced to the music of the drum and fife. The
New Zealanders, ten in number, performed the
war dance, with which the chief appeared much
amused.

I received a letter to-day from two gentlemen
belonging to the Wesleyan mission stationed at
a remote part of the island, wishing to be informed of the name of the ship that had anchored in the road the preceding day, which I
willingly communicated.

As it would not have been safe to send my
crew on shore to water, after what had recently
taken place between the islanders and the *Astrolabe*, I procured a sample of fresh water to be
brought to the ship, which I found to be excellent for present use, and, for aught I knew, good
for sea-store also.

17th.—First and middle part of this day clear
weather, with light trades and variable : hot

sultry weather; latter part close weather, with rain.

In exchange for cutlery, &c. we procured, in the course of to-day, about thirty hogs and three tons of yams. Little of the ship business was attended to, in consequence of the communication with the natives, who surrounded the ship by hundreds from daylight to dark, disposing of their commodities. To prevent surprise from them I kept twelve men constantly under arms, who paraded the decks with loaded muskets.

After breakfast, the chief Thubow presented me with one of the largest hogs I ever saw, and a hundred yams, which would each average seven pounds : in return, I gave him a musket, cartouche-box, bayonet and belts, with some cutlery. He shortly after took his leave of me, promising to return on the morrow. The Otaheitan missionaries also departed at the same time, after having received some presents of cloth, thread, &c.

18th.—Light airs from the northward, with hot sultry weather the first and middle part of the day : latter part heavy showers of rain.

We were visited by the islanders at an early hour, and a brisk traffic commenced. Having procured by 10 o'clock a sufficient quantity of yams, not having room for any more, I put a stop to that branch of the trade; and at noon, the long-boat being full of hogs, which was a sufficient supply, I also closed that, to the disappointment and dissatisfaction of the islanders, who were alongside with several tons of yams, and hogs in abundance. I may safely say that Tonga is the best island in the South Seas for ships to recruit their supplies at, provisions there are in such plenty.

I employed the chief of Mafanga, the shipwrecked Whytutakeeans, and the American who joined me on Tuesday last, to go on shore for water to Pangimotoo this afternoon. The boat returned at 2 P.M. with a raft of water, but so brackish as to be totally unfit for use. I inquired of the chief where he had procured the breaker of water submitted to me as a sample the other day; he replied, " on the main land." Accordingly, after dinner, I sent him there with the casks; and shortly afterwards the boat with the person in charge returned, stating that four men had been left with the casks on shore to sink a well in the sand from which the water was to be filled; and as the tide would serve at five o'clock in the morning, it would be necessary to send for the raft at that time.

The Marquesa man, whom I had occasion to mention before as having in a fit of intellectual aberration attended muster armed with a large

club, this morning, while standing sentry upon
the poop, fired his musket at the stern boat,
but fortunately the shot was harmless. His
madness, which was a kind of hypochondria,
led him to suppose that a part of the sail which
was quivering in the wind was an evil spirit,
at which he therefore took aim. To prevent
more serious mistakes I put him in irons.

19*th*.—Winds from the north first part of this
day, with heavy rain, thunder, and lightning.
At 2 A.M. the new starboard quarter-boat, that
was purchased at Van Diemen's Land, broke
her slings and fell from the quarter. This accident was caused by the second officer's neglect, who retired to sleep in the cuddy during
his watch on deck, and allowed the boat to become full of rain-water, and consequently so
heavy that the tackle could not support the
weight. I immediately ordered the larboard
quarter-boat down in search of her, which after
an absence of about an hour, succeeded in re-
covering her. She was towed alongside and
hoisted up, when it was found that she had sustained much injury by the fall, her guardboard
streak being staved, both gunwales broken, the
midship thawt and knees broken, with many
rents in the planks of the bottom and sides.

At 4 A.M. sent a boat on shore for the water
casks. At 7½ A.M., as it blew a strong gale from

the west, with the sea rolling in upon the beach,
I made a signal for the boat to return without
the casks ; but I had to repeat the signal with
three guns, two at the first recall, and another
in half an hour afterwards.

At 8 A.M., being apprehensive that the best
bower was foul, I let go the second anchor.
The wind shifted to W.S.W., where it remained
during the day, we then moored the ship.
Pongimotoo bore N.E. by E.$\frac{1}{2}$E. a short mile,
the west point of Tonga Island bearing W.
by N.

A chief who stopped on board last night, being weather-bound to-day, as no canoes came
off, begged to see our mode of dancing, in
which I gratified him. The European seamen
capered in reels and jigs to the sound of the
fife and drum, which were then varied by the
New Zealanders coming on the stage with their
warlike and animating dances. This curious
intermixture of different nations, manners, and
costumes, made an interesting spectacle,with
which he seemed highly delighted.

The lascars also performed their dance, according to the Asiatic custom, rapping their
toes and heels against the deck in symphony
with the squeaking of a wretched old fiddle,
without even its proper complement of strings.
Nevertheless the Tonga chief seemed to con-

sider this discord as verifying the line of Pope:

"All discord's harmony, not understood,"

and commended that as pleasing kind harmony which the Europeans could not comprehend.

I this day received information from one of the second officer's watch, that last night during the heavy rain, he had quitted his post on the poop and placed himself in my arm-chair which was in the cuddy, where he shortly fell fast asleep. It was during this time that the quarter-boat, which in Van Diemen's Land had cost £25, was suffered to fill with rain-water and fall from her slings. Finding, therefore, that no confidence could be placed in his promises, I resolved to visit him occasionally during his night-watch, hoping that my presence in that manner might serve as a check, and keep him more upon his guard; as I was very apprehensive that the islanders might some night pay us an unfriendly visit, in consequence of intelligence of our unguarded state being communicated to the shore by those who were permitted sometimes to sleep on board the vessel.

20th.—Winds from W.S.W. throughout the first and middle part of the day, with fine weather: latter part inclined to calm. Shortly after 3 A.M., on looking out of the cabin window, I observed a large canoe with some small ones approaching the ship, and ran upon the quarter-deck, where I found the second officer of the ship, who had charge of the watch, fast asleep in a chair. I awoke him and mentioned what I had seen : he rubbed his eyes, and said it was a canoe passing from the opposite shore to the island. I again warned him of the impropriety of sleeping during the hours of his watch, and observed that this was the third time of his being guilty of that unseaman-like offence, which might be attended with the most serious consequences. At New Zealand, at sea, and now for the third time, I had discovered him sleeping : and at many other times, which had not come to my knowledge, he had, no doubt, been guilty of the same offence.

Having finished my lecture I retired to my cabin, where I had not been more than half an hour before I was disturbed by a noise under the window. On looking out, to my utter astonishment I beheld a very large canoe with about seventy men in it, besides several others following her close up. Confounded at the sight, and it being dark, I seized the first arms I could find, which was a pistol, and flying to the poop with only my shirt on, on my way passed my second officer on the quarter-deck, again fast asleep. There was not a single man upon the poop, and under the impression that the natives were boarding us, on the impulse of the moment I fired into the canoe which was nearest the ship.

I was followed by Langhi, the native, who had slept on board the preceding night. On hearing the report of the pistol he ascended the poop, and called out to his countrymen to keep off; that if they did not, the ship's guns would be instantly discharged upon them. They immediately complied with his order, and begged of him to prevail on us not to fire. My pistol fortunately had done no injury.

I now ascertained that all the men on this officer's watch had been asleep as well as himself, and I immediately roused the ship's company. When all hands had appeared at quarters, I in their presence put the second officer off duty, it being unsafe any more to trust our lives and the safety of the ship to so unfaithful a guardian, who had not sufficient honour, principle, or resolution, to perform his duty.

We were surrounded, as usual, by crowds of canoes loaded with large hogs, yams, cocoa-nuts, &c., very few of which we purchased, being already sufficiently stocked. Several canoes, containing some Tonga ladies of the highest families in the island, also came on board to-day, in order to see the New Zealanders. I treated them all kindly, presenting them with glass beads, scissors, empty wine-bottles, &c., which they received with the most gracious conde-scension.

We got off two small rafts of water to-day, and sent the boat on shore at dusk for another raft. The chief of Mafanga, who went in her, left two of his sons and one daughter on board in my care, by which I had good hostages for the peaceable behaviour of the islanders while my men were ashore, this chief adding to his temporal ascendancy the more influential rank of high priest, with all its concomitant awe and veneration.

I received a letter from the suspended second officer, requesting permission to quit the ship, and demanding a discharge; to which I replied by a verbal message, that I had no objection to his going on shore, and that I would willingly give him a written certificate, stating in it my reasons for parting with him.

At $9\frac{1}{2}$ P.M. a boat approached the ship, in which was a Mr. Thomas, a Wesleyan mis-sionary settled at or near the west point of this island. From him I learnt that the mission there was rather precariously situated, in con-sequence of the hostility of the chief of that part to the tenets of Christianity.

The chief of Mafanga informed me that he would take the liberty of coming on board to-morrow, and that he would bring his wives and children to view the ship. This, he said, he was the more inclined to do, as he knew I was uniformly kind to the ladies—not a bad stroke of flattery, coming from an untutored savage. I inquired how many wives he had. He said eight. A pretty good share for a priest : and in this particular he seems to hold the same doctrines with the Koolin Brahmins of India.

21*st.*—Light winds from S.W. to S., with fine weather throughout the day. The people employed hoisting in and stowing the water, &c.

At an early hour the chief of Mafanga paid his promised visit, accompanied by a numerous retinue of Tonga ladies. I began to suspect that our ideas of the number eight did not correspond when, on counting his sacred highness' suite, I enumerated thirty one full grown females, with several children. I easily saw through this *ruse politique,* which was adopted, no doubt, with the view of obtaining a present for each, to support, or rather pay for the chief's compliment at parting yesterday. Each lady made me a small present of kava-root, some Tonga cloth, and shells ; which, as a matter of course, I returned by making a present in gross of thirty-one strings of glass beads, thirty-six pairs of scissors, and twelve empty bottles, which were thankfully received, and regarded by the best judges on the island as a most valuable gift.

Many canoes were alongside to-day, but their numbers were upon the decrease, owing to several of the natives having returned home without being able to dispose of their provisions.

I expected to complete our stock of water on the morrow, and to sail the day following.

22d.—Light southerly winds throughout, with fine weather. Completed our stock of water this afternoon : bought a good-sized spar for a long boat mast, in exchange for a musket.

As usual we were surrounded with canoes ; some laden with produce, others with ladies whom curiosity had enticed to view the ship. Among the number was Maffee Heppay, about whom so much is said in " Mariner's Account of the Tonga Islands." This lady was the wife of King Fenow, when that chief took the Port au Prince, at the Harpie Islands, in December 1806. She afterwards adopted Mr. Mariner as her son, and, as he states himself, behaved with the greatest kindness. This trait in her character induced me to invite her on board, and treat her with marked respect. As we were going to breakfast, she accompanied me to the gun-room, followed by a numerous train of female attendants. After breakfast I shewed her the first volume of Mr. Mariner's narrative, which contained a portrait of her adopted son habited in the costume of the Friendly Islands. She immediately recognized the likeness, and exclaiming " it is *Tokey*,"* she wept bitterly.

When this interesting scene was over, I made her a present of some chintz, blue gurrahs, glass beads, knives, scissors, hatchets, &c., which gave her a high opinion of my generosity. She said that I must be some relation to Mr. Mariner, or I would not treat her so kindly. She appears to be now about thirty-seven years old, and has a most graceful appearance, but is much afflicted by some disease on one of her hands.

I was particularly anxious to learn whether la Pérouse did or did not touch at this island, according to the intention expressed in his last letter, addressed to the French Minister of Marine, dated from Botany Bay, March 7th, 1788. To ascertain this fact, I got a good interpreter, an Englishman who had lived among the Friendly Islands for nearly twenty-one years, to question the chief of Mafanga, a man about sixty-five or seventy years old, and also another intelligent native not so old, but who had arrived at the years of maturity before D'Entrecasteaux anchored in this port.

* Tokey is the name by which Mr. Mariner is known in the Friendly Islands.

They stated that the first ships they or their forefathers had seen here were those under the command of Captain Cook; and that some years after two other large ships arrived, and anchored close to Pongimotoo, where some misunderstanding had arisen between them and the natives, which caused a chief named Gacoffoa (in English, "a high hill," on the Varow Islands) to be shot in or near his canoe. They likewise stated that, after Captain Cook's departure, and before the arrival of the two ships last-mentioned, two other large ships had arrived at the island of Namooca, or Rotterdam, but did not anchor: they stood off and on, having boats on shore trading.

When the trading officer landed, he formed a square, with lines of demarcation, in the midst of which he stood, guarded on either side by an armed sentinel. These lines were formed close to the boats, which were armed. This gentleman wore spectacles, and was called by the natives Lowage. Shortly after the trading commenced, Mr. Lowage bought a wooden pillow from an islander for a knife; but after the man had received it, he snatched up the wooden pillow and was in the act of running away, when Mr. Lowage drew a pistol from his belt and shot him dead upon the spot. He was a young chief named Coremoyanga. This alarmed the islanders, who ran into the woods, and Mr. Lowage and his party returned to their ships.

Next day several of the islanders ventured off, and trading recommenced. They received several presents from the Europeans, and all appeared to be amicably arranged. Two men of the island joined the ships, and went off with them. The following day those ships sailed to the westward, and nothing more has since been heard of them.

The two ships here alluded to must certainly have been those commanded by the Count de la Pérouse. The first ship of which we have any account that visited these islands was Tasman, the Dutch navigator, in A.D. 1642; the next was Captain Cook, in A.D. 1773; the third was Morillo, a Spanish navigator, in the *Princess* frigate, on a voyage from Manilla to St. Blas, in Mexico, A.D. 1781. He touched at only one of the Friendly Islands, named Varow. His narrative has been published; also that of Captains Bligh and Edwards in 1791, commanders of the *Bounty* sloop, *Pandora* frigate, and the *Providence* sloop.

The next ships we know of that touched here are those commanded by Admiral d'Entrecasteaux, on a voyage in search of la Pérouse. The natives plainly expressed that the two ships which visited Namooca arrived there after

Captain Cook's departure and before the arrival of D'Entrecasteaux. There are no accounts on record in the English, French, Dutch, or Spanish languages, of any two ships being in these seas at the time alluded to, except those of the Count de la Pérouse.

23d.—At 2 P.M. unmoored the ship, and got all ready to sail next morning. This morning I was visited by Maffee Heppay, the lady mentioned in yesterday's journal, who expressed much gratitude for my presents, and begged of me to write a letter to Mr. Mariner, informing him that I had seen her, and that she was unwell; that she entertained the highest regard for him, and hoped to see him before she died; adding, " I hope that he will visit his old friends at Tonga before long."

This afternoon, Bour, an Otaheitan soldier on board, asked permission to go on shore; which I readily granted, considering him a dangerous character.

The chief of Mafanga having completed my water, wood, sand, and yam baskets, I asked what recompense he required. He replied, " Two muskets, some gunpowder, one cooking-pot, and a few articles of cutlery, ironmongery, &c.;" which I willingly gave him, as his services were most important, since his friendly aid preserved my crew from the danger of being kid-

napped by his countrymen, and perhaps prevented the recurrence of a scene similar to that
which took place with the *Astrolabe*.

This morning a canoe came to the ship from
the island of Eawa, with a message from the
American's wife and father-in-law there, begging of him to return, as they were much afflicted by his absence. He communicated this to
me, and said that, on maturer deliberation, he
now wished to go back, and remain with his
kind friends among the islanders : he therefore
requested my permission to accompany the
canoe. I told him that I had no objection to
his doing so, and would pay him for his services
in procuring the water, &c. ; that his intention
of returning to his wife rather raised him in my
opinion, for hard must be the heart that could
resist the solicitations of so lovely a woman.
John Downy, the poor idiot from New Zealand,
made arrangements with his countryman to go
on shore and live with him, till an opportunity
should offer for their embarking in an American
ship for their own country.

I understood from John Singleton, the interpreter, that M. Dumont d'Urville had received
similar information relative to the ships which
touched at Namooca as communicated to me
by the natives ; and the same person likewise
informed me, that the *Dueythonga* (spiritual

chief) who reigned at the time of the *Port au Prince's* capture, had two pewter plates in his possession with French inscriptions on them, which had been procured from Lowage's ships; but that they being appropriated to the service of the gods, were held sacred, and at the death of the *Dueythonga* were buried with him. Singleton assured me that he had seen and handled these plates frequently.

This circumstance must therefore be regarded as strongly confirmatory of my hypothesis, that these ships were those commanded by la Pérouse. Hence it appears that I have traced his route exactly as laid down in his letter to the minister of Marine, dated from Botany Bay, 7th of March 1788, and that, conformably with his intentions therein expressed, he did visit the Friendly Islands. Nor is it to be wondered at that D'Entrecasteaux missed of this information, as he only visited Tonga (the capital), and was without interpreters. He might, therefore, not be able to make the requisite inquiries; and even if the natives had, unsolicited, communicated the fact, he might be unable to understand them. Fortunately for me I had not these difficulties to combat with : for besides being provided with able interpreters, I was myself acquainted with various dialects of the South-sea Islanders, some of which I understood as well as I did English.

24th—M. Chaigneau, the French agent, having interceded with me in behalf of the second officer, now suspended, and being aware that he had severely lectured him on the impropriety of his conduct, I hoped that the effect produced by a foreigner's reproof, and meditation, would leave a suitable impression on his mind : and being willing to pay a compliment to the French agent by attending to his solicitation, I promised to reinstate the offender. I therefore sent for him, and once more represented to him the heinousness of his behaviour, for which, on board of a ship in his Majesty's service, he would be liable to be shot ; adding that, notwithstanding his repeated transgressions, I was willing once more to try him, on the following conditions, *viz.* that he would in the presence of all the officers make a public apology to me for his conduct, and promise at the same time never again while on board the ship to sleep, or even to sit, during the hours of his watch at night : with which conditions he willingly complied, and I allowed him to return to his duty.

Light breezes from E.S.E., with cloudy weather throughout this day. The wind being so light, I could not venture to get the ship under weigh, so as to clear the reefs before night; I therefore employed the people about the rigging and otherwise as necessary.   Peter, the Marquesa man, who became a little deranged on the voyage, begged permission to remain here; which I agreed to, as in his state of mind it was dangerous to entrust him with arms.   In lieu of Peter and Bour, I shipped two of the wrecked Whytutakee men mentioned in a former part of my journal.

A female chieftain of considerable influence came to the ship's side to-day, and stated that several years ago an American ship anchored at the west part of this island, and was soon visited by the natives, among whom was her brother. That while on board one of them stole an axe, which so alarmed the rest lest they might be involved in his punishment, that they leaped overboard to swim on shore   On this a boat was lowered from the ship's side, and one of the natives (her brother) was seized, brought on board, and conveyed to America.   His friends had supposed for a long time that he was killed, till the serjeant of marines of the *Port au Prince* eased them of their concern, by inform-ing them he had quitted America, gone to Eng-land, enlisted as a soldier, and was now big-drummer in the Duke of York's band.   She

earnestly requested to know if this account of
her brother was true ; which I was sorry not to
be able to confirm, as I had not been in Europe
for twenty years. I promised, however, to
make inquiry.

Thubow inquired of me this morning at
breakfast where Mannicolo lay, for that, in all
the voyages of the Tonga people among the
islands, they had never heard of the Mannicolos.
I informed him that it was close to Tucopia, an
island of which he also professed ignorance,
demanding if it lay near Rothuma.   I told him
that it did, and that in going there I should
pass Rothuma.

He told me that a fleet of his canoes had, a
short time ago, returned from the Navigators'
Islands, bringing with them from thence two
Rothumans, who had by chance drifted thither.
These, he said, were now desirous to return to
their native island.   As I was to pass it I agreed
to take them, and one embarked this afternoon.
From him I learnt that, in company with some
more of his countrymen, he set out from Rothuma about eight years ago for an island to
the north-east of it, called Withuboo, to procure
shells.   Contrary winds had prevented them
from making their intended port, and after
having been three months at sea they made a
land, which proved to be the Hamoa or Navi-

gators' Islands, the natives of which treated them kindly. Some of his party still remained there.

This is a very satisfactory proof of my opinion of a north-west monsoon prevailing in these latitudes at a certain season of the year; for otherwise, how could so small a bark as a canoe make a passage from Rothuma, in latitude 12° 30′ S., and longitude 177° E., to the Navigators' Islands, in latitude 13° 27′ S., and longitude 171° 57′ W.

On my old friend, Tuckcafinawa, the high priest and chief of Mafanga, hearing mention made of Rothuma, inquired if I intended to call there: to which I replied in the affirmative. He then informed me that the priests of that island were tributary to his district, and that about three years ago he sent his eldest son with three large canoes to collect the tribute, from whence he had not since returned; that he was fearful he and his men had offended the gods and were cast away at sea, either going to or returning from Rothuma. He now wished, therefore, to send some people with me, to ascertain, if possible, their fate, and to collect the tribute now due to the deity by the chiefs and priests of that island. To this request I gladly acceded, for the double purpose of obliging the good old chief, who had been so essen-

tially serviceable to me, and also because, as I
had no interpreters of the Tonga language on
board, these would serve the purpose, should I
fall in with the two men who accompanied
Lowage's ships from Namooca. I supposed
that if these men escaped from the wreck at
Mannicolo, they would, in all probability, have
remained there, sooner than risk another voyage
with the strangers in the small vessel built by
them at Paiow, according to Martin Bushart's
account derived from the Tucopians.

In the evening he embarked his daughter, a
girl about fourteen years old, with her brother,
his second son, and a male servant, as being
the persons whom it was his desire to send to
Rothuma ; I would not have received so many,
if it were not that I might have occasion to
revisit Tonga before the voyage had terminated,
it being the only place where I could revictual
in the event of my not succeeding in discovering the wreck of la Pérouse at the Mannicolos
of the Tucopians. I would then have to visit
the Mallicolo of Captain Cook, to see what was
to be learnt there regarding the object of our
expedition. To reach the latter island, I should
be compelled to stand into the variable winds,
and of course, after such loss of time, have to
refresh at Tonga.

I considered that if I succeeded in prevailing

on the three persons put on board by the high
priest of Tonga, or upon any one of them, to
accompany me during the search, I might, by
treating him or them kindly, ingratiate myself
into the chief's favour, and secure to myself and
crew a kind reception and a repetition of his
offices.   I was further induced to take these
three people with me from the following circumstance.   At Tongataboo I met with an aged
Otaheitan woman, who had resided among the
Friendly Islands for the last fifteen years, and
who consequently was well acquainted with the
language ; and as I speak the Otaheitan language fluently, I supposed her services might
be very useful to me as an interpreter of the
Tonga language, for which I engaged her : but
she having succeeded in obtaining some presents
from me, deserted.

25th.—This day commenced with moderate
breezes and cloudy weather : wind from the
south-east.   Shortly after daylight weighed and
sailed out from Pongimoodo.   At 7½ A. M. anchored in nineteen fathoms water ; the sun being
obscured and cloudy, so as to prevent my seeing
any of the numerous coral patches with which
this bay is strewed.

At 9 A. M. I sent the chief officer, with Langhi
the Tonga pilot, to sound the bay out to the
passage through the reefs, and directed him par-

ticularly to see what course ought to be steered through that channel, as I was apprehensive if the wind should come any thing to the eastward of E.S.E., that I could not get through that way.

At 10 A.M. the weather became dark : shortly after we had a smart shower of rain. I considered myself fortunate in getting to an anchor in time. The bearings of the islands from our present anchorage were as follow : Pongimoodo, S.E. by S.; Makaha, S.E. by E.; Tafa E. ¼ N. one and a half miles.

About this time the good old chief of Mafanga came off in a large sailing canoe to the ship. He was at a loss to know our reason for anchoring so far out, and supposed that we had got on shore, or that some of our men had deserted us.

On the boat's return from the reef the officer made the following report, which I here insert, as it may be useful to other navigators departing from this port.

" We sailed from the ship N.W.½N. by compass, and N.W. until we reached the passage in the reef. The reef on the left hand side of the passage going out, extends from the large island of Otata from one and a half to two miles. Our soundings from the ship to the passage were from eighteen to ten and eight fathoms close to the reefs. The soundings across the passage from the left to the right hand reef were from eight to fifteen fathoms. The passage is a full English half mile wide, clear of all danger. The passage through the reef is N.N.W. per compass. We then made for the ship, steering S.E. and S.E. ½ S.; soundings variable, from eighteen to seven fathoms. Where we had nine, eight, and seven, it was on coral patches ; where we had from fifteen to eighteen, our soundings were mud and sand."

From the above account, this is certainly the best passage to go out by ; and to adopt it, ships ought to steer from the anchorage at Pongimoodo from N.W. to N.W. by N., and N. per compass, until the island of Tafa is brought to bear E.¼N., distance off one mile and a half: then steer for the passage from N.W. to N.W. and by N. If the trade wind should happen to be at N.E., a ship can lay out the channel N.N.W.

We had a few canoes off to-day with cocoa-nuts and fish. From the canoe that contained the fish, I bought six very fine for a boat-axe, which would each weigh five or six pounds. They were much resembling the schnappers of Port Jackson, which are very large, sometimes weighing from twelve to twenty pounds.

26th.—This day commenced with cloudy,

misty weather, for which reason I did not consider it safe to get under weigh till the sun
shone clear, when I might distinctly discern
the coral patches on my way to the reef.

The canoe of Langhi, the Tonga pilot, rigged
with a triangular sail, came off from one of the
islands to the ship. He proposed its sailing
before the ship to the reefs, and I willingly
accepted of his services.

At 8½ A.M. the clouds cleared off, and the
sun was unobscured; its rays were strongly
reflected on the different reefs and coral banks.
At 9 A.M. got under sail and steered out after
the pilot's canoe towards the reef: our course
per compass was from N.W. by N., to N.N.W.

At 10½ A.M. we got clear out to sea and hove-
to. The pilot's canoe then came alongside
with Langhi's friends on board; and at his request I gave him a musket, some gunpowder,
and a pair of razors, as his fee for pilotage, for
which he was very thankful.

On passing out through the reef the weather
was very clear, and I could plainly perceive to
the east or windward of my station two more
passages through it, both of a much larger extent than that in which I was. Each of these
passages I supposed to be more than a mile wide.
As soon as the pilot had left the ship I made
sail for the islands Hanga Tonga, and Hanga

Hapai, which were then in sight from the deck. At 4¼ P.M. those islands bore E. by N. per compass two miles; and at a quarter before 6 P.M. the island of Tiffooa was visible from the poop, bearing N. by E. eastwardly, eight or nine leagues. Steered N. by W. by compass, to pass to the westward of Tiffooas, also Latey.

My passengers and interpreters for Rothuma, *viz.* the Rothuma chief, the Tonga woman, and the Tonga men, were exceedingly sea-sick during this short passage. They gave me to understand that a sovereign specific against this ailment was the water of a roasted half-ripe cocoa-nut. Having some on board very fortunately, I lost no time in administering relief to them, and I set cooks to roast them so long as my patients would take the draught.

27th.—At 6 A.M. the island of Oghao, or Grand Mountain of Marilla, was in sight; and at 8 A.M. the peak of it began to disappear. We could plainly discern the top of the peak, although our distance from it at this time was fifty-two miles, bearing per compass S.S.E.½E. I am of opinion that in clear weather this island might be seen eighty miles at sea.

We kept a man at the mast-head on the look-out for the island of Latey, which we passed without seeing it. Latey is not very high, and the reflection of the sun being on that side, prevented us from having a distant view of it.

The trades were strong throughout this day, with fine weather. Latitude at noon, 18° 22′ S.; longitude 175° 24′ W. Thermometer in shade at noon, 74°.

END OF VOL. I.

London:

PRINTED BY J. L. COX, GREAT QUEEN STREET, Lincoln's-Inn Fields.

For EU product safety concerns, contact us at Calle de José Abascal, 56–1°, 28003 Madrid, Spain or eugpsr@cambridge.org.

www.ingramcontent.com/pod-product-compliance
Ingram Content Group UK Ltd.
Pitfield, Milton Keynes, MK11 3LW, UK
UKHW040617240426
470322UK00010B/180

* 9 7 8 1 1 0 8 0 8 3 3 3 1 *